Pastoral Care and Counseling
Redefining the Paradigms

"This remarkable resource succeeds in defining the current state of pastoral theology. It presents historical understandings available nowhere else, and names the issues and paradigms that are shaping the teaching of pastoral care in theological education. Written by scholars and addressed to reflective practitioners, it is not merely a supplement or update to the DICTIONARY. Rather these solidly grounded yet cutting edge essays are invitational and engaging to any one invested in the future possibilities of pastoral care and pastoral theology."

—Peggy Way

"The major contribution of this new volume is the attention it gives to how the practices of care have changed in the last fifteen years due to the inclusion of the voices of Euro-American, African American women and men, and international people."

—Edward P. Wimberly

"This is constructive thinking. It may enable us to see alternative paths in a world suffering under dysfunctional paradigms—like 'the clash of civilizations' and 'the triumph of Western Democracy.'"

—David W. Augsburger

"This is a must read for pastors, counselors, and anyone who offers or teaches pastoral care and counseling."

—Teresa E. Snorton

"The perspectives offered in this volume make the original DICTIONARY OF PASTORAL CARE AND COUNSELING a more valuable resource for the student and pastor. The bibliography alone is like havin⋯ ⋯⋯⋯⋯ ⋯⋯⋯⋯⋯ at your fingertips and demonstrates the wide-ranging r⋯ ⋯⋯⋯⋯ ⋯⋯⋯⋯⋯⋯ today."

Pastoral Care and Counseling
Redefining the Paradigms

Nancy J. Ramsay, Editor

ABINGDON PRESS
Nashville

PASTORAL CARE AND COUNSELING
REDEFINING THE PARADIGMS

Library of Congress Cataloging-in-Publication Data

Pastoral care and counseling : redefining the paradigms / Nancy J. Ramsay, editor.
   p. cm.
  Includes bibliographical references and index.
  ISBN 0-687-02224-x (pbk. : alk. paper)
  1. Pastoral counseling. 2. Pastoral care. I. Ramsay, Nancy J. (Nancy Jean), 1949-

BV4012.2.P276 2004
253—dc22

2004009554

04 05 06 07 08 09 10 11 12 13—10 9 8 7 6 5 4 3 2 1

MANUFACTURED IN THE UNITED STATES OF AMERICA

For
Liston Mills
1928–2001
and
Maxine Glaz
1940–2003

Colleagues whose intelligence, imagination, and energy
are woven through the present creativity and vitality
of pastoral theology, care, and counseling.
Their lives were a blessing to many;
their contributions continue to be so.

— CONTENTS —

List of Contributors   ix

Introduction   xi

Chapter 1:   A Time of Ferment and Redefinition   1
                Nancy J. Ramsay

Chapter 2:   Pastoral Theology as Public Theology: 45
                Revolutions in the "Fourth Area"
                Bonnie J. Miller-McLemore

Chapter 3:   Power and Difference in Pastoral Theology   65
                Christie Cozad Neuger

Chapter 4:   Globalization, Internationalization, and   87
                Indigenization of Pastoral Care and Counseling
                Emmanuel Y. Lartey

Chapter 5:   Ferment and Imagination in Training in   109
                Clinical Ministry
                Loren L. Townsend

Chapter 6:   Methods in Pastoral Theology, Care,   133
                and Counseling
                Joretta L. Marshall

Chapter 7:   Contemporary Pastoral Theology: 155
                A Wider Vision for the Practice of Love
                Nancy J. Ramsay

Bibliography   177

Emmanuel Y. Lartey
Professor of Pastoral Theology and Care
Columbia Theological Seminary
Decatur, Georgia

Joretta L. Marshall
Academic Dean and Professor of Pastoral Theology and Care
Eden Theological Seminary
Saint Louis, Missouri

Bonnie J. Miller-McLemore
Professor of Pastoral Theology and Counseling
The Divinity School and Graduate Department of Religion
Vanderbilt University
Nashville, Tennessee

Christie Cozad Neuger
Professor of Pastoral Care and Pastoral Theology
United Theological Seminary
Minneapolis, Minnesota

Nancy J. Ramsay
The Harrison Ray Anderson Professor of Pastoral Theology
Louisville Presbyterian Theological Seminary
Louisville, Kentucky

Loren L. Townsend
Professor of Pastoral Care and Counseling
Louisville Presbyterian Theological Seminary
Louisville, Kentucky

Pastoral Care and Counseling: Redefining the Paradigms serves as a supplement to the *Dictionary of Pastoral Care and Counseling* published in 1990. While much in the *Dictionary* continues to be useful, it is also the case that it was published just as significant intellectual and cultural changes were becoming apparent in the United States and globally. These contextual changes contributed to the emergence of two new paradigms in the fields of pastoral care, counseling, and pastoral theology that have eclipsed the dominance of the therapeutic paradigm.

This volume explores the impact of those changes through seven essays. The first provides an overview and describes the ferment and redefinition carried in the communal contextual and intercultural paradigms that increasingly provide a way of structuring the practice, research, and literature of the three fields. The second addresses pastoral theology as *public theology* exploring, for example, the shift in metaphor from "living human document" to the "living human web." The next essay reviews the significant attention that has been given to *issues of difference and the asymmetries of power* that accompany such differences as gender, race, and class. The *internationalization* of care, counseling, and pastoral theology addressed in the next essay describes the emerging theory and theology to support and inform practices of care now being generated by our colleagues around the world. Changes are also significant in *clinical training* contexts where racial, cultural, and religious pluralism as well as economic shifts created by managed care have prompted methodological and definitional changes. *Theological methods* that support care and counseling as well as the constructive insights of pastoral theology have changed dramatically in response to contextual and intellectual shifts, but also as the inclusion of European American women and women and men of other racial and cultural heritages brought new ideas and approaches. Finally, *pastoral theology* is significantly altered by the changing foci of the new paradigms, new participants as noted above, new theological approaches, interdisciplinary sources, and therapeutic models.

Each essay is shaped by five questions: How does this issue fit in the larger field? What do we mean by these terms? What developments brought us to this point? Where are we headed with this issue? What are the implications of this topic for formation and professional identity? The goal of the essays is to contribute resources for seminary classrooms and training programs, to promote research, and to inform the practice of care, counseling, and pastoral theology.

Pastoral Care and Counseling: Redefining the Paradigms reflects the experience and perspectives of the contributors. All six of us are Protestant Christians who are teaching in seminaries and divinity school programs. Most of us have been involved in the field as teachers and practitioners for at least twenty years. We are actively engaged in professional organizations such as the American Association of Pastoral Counselors, the Society for Pastoral Theology, The Association of Practical Theology, the International Council on Pastoral Care and Counselling, and the International Association of Practical Theology. Five of us are European Americans and one of us is African. While the essays were written individually, we began our work with shared discussion of the issues described here and collaborative reflection on each of the essays. We are glad now to invite you into our reflections on this very exciting time in the fields of pastoral care, counseling, and pastoral theology.

CHAPTER 1

A Time of Ferment and Redefinition

Nancy J. Ramsay

S ea change" is a phrase that characterizes the dramatic changes in pastoral care, counseling, and pastoral theology since the publication of the *Dictionary of Pastoral Care and Counseling* (1990). This essay offers an overview of these changes, as well as continuities across the fifteen to twenty years since the articles in the *Dictionary* were completed. These years have included significant redefinition and ferment that range across such issues as the scope of care; the authority for care; the identity, role, and account-abilities of those who care; the fact and significance of asymmetries of power in care; and the significance of difference for the practice and con-ceptual foundations of care. In the six chapters that follow, readers are able to learn of the dramatic changes as well as continuities in the field in more depth. In this overview I will summarize their particular research and draw out the implications of their shared reflections.

Most striking is the discovery that when read together the essays that fol-low disclose that two new paradigms have emerged that are gradually eclips-ing the Clinical Pastoral Paradigm that predominated in the *Dictionary*. The Communal Contextual and the Intercultural Paradigms reflect the significant intellectual, cultural, political, and religious dynamics that characterized the end of the twentieth century and continue early in the twenty-first century. The communal contextual paradigm draws on the ecological metaphor of a web to describe tensively held dual *foci*. The first is on ecclesial contexts that sustain and strengthen community practices of care. The second is on the widened horizons of the field that conceive of care as including public, structural, and political dimensions of individual and relational experience. The intercultural paradigm also draws on an ecological theme but responds more immediately to the fact and significance of cultural, racial, and religious pluralism as a context for practices of care whether responding to individual or larger systems. Historians have noted that pastoral care is especially responsive to its contextual dynamics. Certainly the intellectual, ethical, and political effects of postmodernity are especially evident in contemporary care and counseling, as well as pastoral theology. Obviously, the religious as well as racial and cultural pluralism in the United States has contributed to the emergence of these new paradigms as well. We will also explore the remarkable influx of European American women and women and men of other racial and cultural heritages since the publication of the *Dictionary*. These women and men have brought new interests, sources, and methods to the field.

Reflections on recent history are fraught with potential for misinterpretation. Certainly, some aspects of pastoral care and counseling in the twentieth century may prove to be aberrations in the much larger history of pastoral care and theology, while others may signal new lines of development that will be ongoing. For example, we have yet to see how the emergence of professionalization of care in the fields of pastoral counseling and chaplaincy will continue to develop. It is also the case that recent historical assessments seen through the therapeutic emphases of the clinical pastoral paradigm may well have obscured other social and ecclesial influences in the twentieth century that the communal contextual and intercultural paradigms are recovering.

No doubt any analysis of the internal debates and emerging literature of a field is deeply shaped by those who seek to name and interpret the issues. I come to this essay as a European American Christian clergywoman in the Reformed tradition, who has taught in this field over twenty years. I am also active in the American Association of Pastoral Counselors. I have deep commitments to assuring the theological integrity and constructive theological possibilities of pastoral care and counseling as well as their ecclesial foundations.

In the pages that follow I will offer definitions for key terms in the chapter and briefly review critical developments over the past twenty years. I will then review in summary fashion developments and emerging trajectories in six particular categories: public theology, difference and power, internationalization, clinical method, pastoral theological method, and pastoral theology. These six topics reflect the themes addressed by the chapters that follow in this volume. I will then briefly suggest the implications of the issues addressed in this chapter for the formation and professional identities of those who engage in the practices of care and counseling and pastoral theology.

Definitions

Clarity about definitions is important in reflecting on key themes in the field since 1990. The very fact that long-standing definitions found in the current *Dictionary* now require revision is a signal for how substantial and dynamic change has been and continues to be. The terms that will require clarity in this chapter include: pastoral care, pastoral counseling, pastoral theology, practical theology, and critical postmodernity.

Defining **pastoral care** in the *Dictionary* (1990), Rodney Hunter presumed a Judeo–Christian frame for a ministry of the church. Hunter describes care as "theologically informed ministry" (p. xii). Grounded in particular theological traditions, its goals are guided by the theological orientations of practitioners who are described as "representative religious persons"—not merely ordained persons—and communities of faith whose goals are nurture and support for persons and their relationships and "community relationships" (p. xii). Interestingly this reference to "community relationships" was not further specified and typically dropped out of subsequent elaborations of care that usually referenced "personal ministry." This passing reference to systemic contexts and institutional caring responses now represents a more significant dimension of contemporary definitions of care. Related to this broadened attention to context is John Patton's historical schema that observes ways pastoral care has been practiced from the perspectives of three paradigms: proclamation, clinical pastoral, and most recently, the communal contextual (Patton, 1993). These three function interdependently as they include attention to the faith perspectives offered, the persons offering and receiving care, the context in which the care is offered, and the community authorizing the care (Patton, 1993). Patton's schema calls attention to a shift in understanding care that reclaims it as a ministry of the church while also recognizing the importance of the context with its political, cultural, and embodied character.

Further, the term "pastoral" is now under scrutiny. In 2000, the Association of Clinical Pastoral Education, for example, revised its mission statement replacing *pastoral care* with *spiritual care* to describe its ministry. Theological care (Doehring, 2004) and soul care (Anderson, 2001) are other descriptors now proposed. These shifts represent accommodations to a demonstrably religiously plural context. Discerning the significance of replacing the adjective *pastoral* will take a number of years. For our purposes the term *pastoral care* will be retained, but in subsequent pages, the significance of this debate about the definition of care will be addressed. The definition that follows builds on and enlarges the scope of the definition Hunter offered.

Pastoral Care is the term Christians most often use to describe a religiously based ministry of care offered by believers and religious leaders. Pastoral Care is critically informed by authoritative sources in Christian tradition and frequently also by the resources of social sciences such as developmental theory, grief theory, and gender studies. Pastoral Care functions interdependently with other forms of ministry such as education, preaching, liturgy, theology, and ethics. It has both a restorative and transformative intent. Pastoral care in contemporary literature and practice is understood by many to include formation, support, and advocacy. As formation it enlarges believers' theological understanding and abilities assisting them to engage in personal, relational, or public challenges that call for religious resources and norms for care such as grief and loss, parenting, violence, and public policy. The role of formation increases in importance during periods of history in which believers are less literate in the resources of Christian tradition. Care as formation also recognizes that pastoral care frequently includes opportunities for constructive theological conversation. "Healing, sustaining, guiding, and reconciling" (Clebsch & Jaekle, 1964) are classic ways of describing pastoral care as *support* in times of situational or developmental crises for individuals and families such as job loss, severe and/or chronic illness, or childbirth and baptism, parenting issues, marriage enrichment, retirement, and aging. Increasing attention to the context in which care is offered has encouraged the practice of pastoral care as *advocacy* with liberating intentions for persons such as victims of violence and for shaping institutional and governmental policies as these may diminish or support the social ecology of human life.

Pastoral Counseling is defined in the *Dictionary* as a specialized form of pastoral care best understood as a form of religious ministry offered by a person who is accountable to and representative of a religious community (Patton, 1990, p. 849). Pastoral counseling is a function of the profession of ministry rather than a distinct profession though ordination is not a prerequisite. Pastoral counselors have an explicit obligation to represent the historic and contemporary resources of their faith tradition competently in their counseling. They are accountable professionally for such interpretive skills in a way that a counselor who happens to embrace a particular faith tradition is not. This accountability remains a primary issue in contemporary pastoral counseling. "Relational humanness" is the primary normative criterion for therapeutic pastoral relationships. Patton defines this as seeking to approximate the incarnation through one's counseling and to function as an interpretive bridge between contemporary life challenges and Christian tradition critically appropriated (Patton, 1983). More recently "relational justice" (Graham, 1992) is also cited as a normative criterion for care and counseling. This term recognizes the liberative, systemic, and larger public scope of contextual awareness that now frequently characterizes the literature of pastoral care and counseling. Relational humanness and relational justice are complementary, and they function concurrently in the widened scope of care and counseling.

For our purposes, pastoral counseling is a specialized form of pastoral care and accountable to religious communities through skilled representatives of such communities who practice this ministry within or alongside the communities. It is a ministry of relational humanness that intends to integrate critically and skillfully therapeutic resources with theological understanding in order to facilitate healing and justice for individuals, relationships, and communities.

Pastoral Theology, as the *Dictionary* acknowledged, has varied definitions within modern Christian theology. For Roman Catholics and some Protestants it refers to the whole sweep of pastoral practice including education, worship, polity, and homiletics, as well as care. For other Protestants it refers more specifically to theological knowledge arising from and informing ministries of care led by ordained pastors or representatives of a congregation. It emerged in its present forms as the relevance of dynamic psychology became apparent for pastoral practice in the early part of the twentieth century (Mills, 1990). Subsequently, it is often considered as a subdiscipline of practical theology. For Roman Catholics it refers to "the use of theological sources to ground, interpret, and guide the activity that constitutes the pastoral life of the church" inclusive of the ministry of laypersons (Kinast, 1990, p. 873). For many Protestants the term may refer to the theological discipline that focuses on those theories, practices, and methods that inform pastoral care and counseling (Burck & Hunter, 1990). This definition also seems prominent in the literature of the American Association of Pastoral Counselors and the Association of Clinical Pastoral Education. Alternatively, it may reflect a more direct influence of Seward Hiltner and describe a contextual form of theology that constructs theological understanding through critical engagement in acts of care by pastors or other representative religious persons. It intends to revise and inform theological understanding in behalf of the practice of care as well as for theology more generally.

In this essay, pastoral theology is understood as contextual theology that is funded by critical engagement in acts of care or response to needs posed for such care. It requires methodologies that provide for reciprocity with those discourses such as human and behavioral sciences that deepen theological understanding of and skill in promoting healing and transformation while respecting the distinctive norms and values of each "conversation partner." Indeed, what most signifies shifts in pastoral theology since the publication of the *Dictionary* is the widened range of conversation partners understood as useful for informing the work of healing and transformation, due to an enlarged vision for the scope of ministries of care. For example, largely since the publication of the *Dictionary,* liberation theology is much more frequently embraced for conversation with such new resources as critical gender and race theories, economics, narrative, and trauma theories. Further, advances in defining practical theology have led to a deepened, critical appreciation for the methodological issues inherent in pastoral theology. Practice is now more widely understood as "theory-laden" rather than merely technique. In this sense all of theology is practical. The ethical and normative assumptions grounding practice are understood in terms of the context in which it arises. Hermeneutical theory and critical postmodernity have heightened appreciation for the particularity and social location of those practicing care, the complexity of context, and the asymmetries of power in the processes of care (Gerkin, 1984; Farley, 2002; Browning, 1987, 1991).

For evangelical Protestants it continues to be the case that full reciprocity between Christian and theoretical resources is not expected in pastoral theology. Rather, pastoral theology more often functions as the application of biblical and theological resources to inform a faithful use of secular psycho-logical wisdom. The behavioral sciences are integrated into the practice of care in ways that preserve the integrity of a particular theological or biblical perspective (Johnson, 1997).

Practical Theology as used in this chapter describes an understanding of the inextricable relation of practice and theory that presumes all of theology is finally practical in its intent. Practical theology relies on a theory-laden definition of practice. Strategic practical theology (Browning, 1991) describes the concrete ministries of the church, including ministries of care, as a complex, interpretive, critical correlation of theory and theology-laden practices to inform and revise the norms and strategies of the congregation's (not just clerical) praxis in response to particular challenges and needs with-in or beyond a congregation's bounds. This definition reflects considerable revision that was anticipated in the *Dictionary* (Farley, 1990, pp. 934-36), but has been more fully developed in the intervening years.

Critical Postmodernity in this chapter refers to attitudes or perspectives critical of central assumptions associated with modernity or Enlightenment thought such as the primacy of a rational, autonomous self and "grand" narratives that carry and reproduce the power-laden assumptions of the dominant culture about authority at ethical and metaphysical levels. These critiques of modernity are associated especially with epistemology, ethics, and asymmetries of power associated with difference (Lakeland, 1997). Epistemology, for example, now acknowledges the highly relational and contextual character of the self whose knowing is socially situated rather than an objective, rational assessment of an external reality. This "de-centered self " inevitably chooses values by which to make judgments that are therefore relative rather than based on supposedly universal ethical or metaphysical standards. Similarly, a "de-centered self " encounters in the other (person, culture, religion) irreducible difference that is no longer subject to the standards of the implicit or explicit values of the worldview in which the observing self stands. The inevitable linkage of knowledge and power is now acknowledged. Evaluating among diverse perspectives and authorizing the truthfulness of one or another requires negotiating criteria for such authority or accepting some range of ambiguity and relativity. The influence of this critical sensibility has become far more predominant in the fields of pastoral care, counseling, and theology since the publication of the *Dictionary*. In fact, this critical sensibility about the self and episte-mology, the ethical challenges of a thoroughly plural civil and religious context, and asymmetries of power associated with difference provides a primary interpretive frame for understanding continuities and discontinu-ities in the field since the late-1980s, but postmodernity was not included in the *Dictionary*. However, postmodernity is embraced critically in the field as faculty and practitioners hold onto such "modern" values as human rights and justice and to "pre-modern" claims such as the authority of religious traditions and sources.

Historical Context

With more historical distance, we find the *Dictionary* published in 1990 functioned as a "hinge in time" in the fields of pastoral care, counseling, and theology. It well summarizes the best wisdom of the modern pastoral care movement in the twentieth century in the United States especially for the more liberal European American Protestant tradition. It also anticipates some of the changes frequently associated with critical postmodern sensibilities such as the relationality of the self and the ethical and conceptual importance of inclusion of gender and racial difference. In other respects even the changes it could predict have been more significant in their impact than anyone could have imagined in the latter part of the 1980s when the articles in the volume were completed.

A brief review of activity and writing in the field from the mideighties when the *Dictionary* was being readied for publication verifies the ferment by which Rodney Hunter, editor of the *Dictionary,* characterizes the state of the field during this time. Pastoral care and counseling are highly responsive to cultural dynamics. We find then initial signs of sociopolitical dynamics associated with difference from dominant values and roles such as gender, race, culture, and sexual orientation. Attention to the practice of care and counseling in other contexts around the world became more visible. For example, *The Journal of Pastoral Care (JPC)* addressed the international pastoral care and counseling movement (1983, 1984). Emmanuel Lartey (1987), a Ghanaian pastoral theologian published *Pastoral Counselling in Inter-Cultural Perspective,* a book that contributed to a new paradigm. The economics of managed care clearly emerges in concerns for marketing care and counseling with the parallel concern for maintaining integrity in pastoral identity and function in chaplaincy settings where cost and effectiveness reviews were forcing assessment strategies that challenged self and professional understanding. Ethics rises in prominence both in recognition of the need to justify norms and strategies in care and theology in the public sphere and in response to the disclosure of a seeming epidemic of clergy sexual misconduct. Attention to the abuse of power by professionals as well as by perpetrators of intimate violence emerges in the late-1980s. One of the important conceptual conversations that emerges has to do with redefining power from a singular association with dominance to an awareness of its pervasive presence as a dynamic in all relationships. Soon we see it conceptualized normatively in the service of mutuality. This discussion about power is related particularly to challenges posed by critiquing dominant norms such as patriarchy and racism. Lay pastoral care re-emerges alongside encouragement to reclaim ecclesial ties perhaps as the economic and professional identity consequences of secular settings became more apparent. Spirituality also begins to emerge as a focus—a theme that continues to prove important for current literature. New theoretical sources such as hermeneutics and systems theory are appearing while process theology and liberation theologies also become more prominent. The conceptual and methodological challenges of defining care and counseling in such shifting social contexts is apparent. Alongside this bubbling up of issues for focused attention, there were also transitions in generations. In 1984 Seward Hiltner died and a year later Carroll Wise. In 1994 Tom Pugh died.

Organizationally, the Association of Clinical Pastoral Education (ACPE) founded in 1967 and the American Association of Pastoral Counselors (AAPC) founded in 1963 were both deeply engaged by the economic challenges and the related identity issues that healthcare costs brought to specialized ministries. The toll of sexual misconduct cases was also beginning to rise in AAPC in particular. Women were entering both organizations in increasing numbers and beginning to ally with one another to increase the impact of their presence and vision (Brennan, O'Reilly, Bronersky, Burbank, McCabe, & McWilliams, 1988). AAPC was undergoing organizational expansion with the formation of regions and the beginning signs of a leveling off in membership. As the organization became more complex, it also claimed its own identity increasingly distinct from ecclesial contexts (North, 1988). Economic pressures on these independent counseling centers were certainly beginning to be felt. ACPE, like AAPC, was becoming more organizationally complex. In addition to beginning to accommodate an influx of women colleagues, it was also initiating efforts to welcome more racially and culturally diverse members and students in its educational settings—a concern it continues to address.

In 1985 a new organization, The Society for Pastoral Theology (SPT), was founded that began to affect the dynamics of the field in significant ways. Initiated by James Lapsley and Liston Mills, both clearly located in the constructive theological legacy of Seward Hiltner, the Society provided a location—otherwise absent in the academy—for faculty in the field to share ideas and generate resources. In retrospect, their publications have provided significant stimulus and direction in the changes now underway in the field. SPT arose just as European American women and some African American women and men began to enter the field. Conceptually, this widening of the horizon of voices informing the field has proven particularly significant because of the accompanying widened range of sources and perspectives these groups brought to scholarship, discussions, and practice. One of the unintended effects of this new Society was at least a temporary decline in participation by faculty in AAPC.

Of course these organizational, conceptual, methodological, economic, and professional shifts were taking place within the larger horizon of economic challenges in health care costs, the further marginalization of denominational influence in U.S. culture, the increase of emancipatory themes in theology and culture such as feminism and anti-racism, as well as the sanctions against South African apartheid. The increasing stratification of socioeconomic class lines was also beginning to be apparent with women and children bearing the brunt of economic shortfalls. The influence of Christian churches on the culture was now significantly challenged both by competing visions of various groups across a theological and political spectrum as well as an increasingly subjectively defined spirituality sometimes called "new age" and the gradual increase of Muslims whose recruiting success reshaped the former Jewish–Christian interfaith neighborhood. Hindus and other smaller faith groups were also contributing to a significant religious diversity. Chaplaincy organizations such as ACPE would feel and have to respond to this change most immediately. The rise in technological advances in communication also quietly but dramatically contributed to an emerging sense of interrelation with others around the world engaged in pastoral care, counseling, and theology. A recognition of the revised self and professional understanding that this intercultural perspective would require for pastoral practitioners and faculty in the United States would come later. Clearly, the transitions buffeting the field and its practitioners and faculty were reflective of these substantial cultural, spiritual, political, economic, and global changes. Not surprisingly, the fields of pastoral care, counseling, and theology were beginning to realize by 1990 that redefinition would be necessary in nearly every aspect of practice, method, sources, authority, and self-understanding. With hindsight, the most obvious shift or widening in focus in the fields of pastoral care, counseling, and theology lies in the paradigmatic way care was conceived. The clinical pastoral perspective that predominates in the *Dictionary* is more clinically focused on relationally conceived selves in the immediacy of their lived experience with their social context often in the background. It values an existential focus on *being* over *doing* that recognizes moral issues but does not take up their political and social consequences. While intellectually critical, it recognizes and values the authenticity of ambiguity and mystery in human experience in contrast to the hyper-rationality of modernity. This clinical pastoral perspective also is finally religious and ethical within a Christian context. Its intent is redemptive (Hunter, 1991). Relational humanness is the normative image of that redemptive intent. Healing and revelation are inextricably linked and grounded in the concrete particularity of a caring or counseling relationship. Patton is clear that the ethical context of neighbor love is the horizon of such relationality, but the foreground is deeply focused on the interpersonal and the existential experience of the one(s) receiving care.

The shift to relational justice in the next decade is suggestive of a major source of change in the field since the publication of the *Dictionary* and discloses ways a postmodern sensibility has engaged the field. Identifying justice as a prominent norm signaled an epistemological and ethical shift that brought the theme of neighbor love from the horizon to a primary diagnostic category. Relational justice, normative for the communal contextual and intercultural paradigms, shifts the understanding of the self to a far more contextual, socially located identity in which the political and ethical dynamics of asymmetries of power related to difference such as gender, race, sexual orientation, and class are prominent. From within the clinical pastoral paradigm pastoral counseling had long focused largely on liberating persons from spiritual and psychological bondage, but relational justice requires that care also includes attention to liberation from the actual bondage of oppression—the corollary of freedom from bondage is relational justice. To be in bondage is to be in an unjust relationship to an external power, or to an external power internalized psychologically and spiritually. To fulfill the image of God in human relationships, therefore, is to be liberated from internalized bondage and to create a human environment characterized by relational justice rather than oppressive structures of domination and subordination. Relational justice involves redistribution of power, resources, privilege, and risks in an equitable manner (Graham, 1996, p. 25).

The focus on being in the clinical pastoral perspective has been enlarged to include responsible agency. Meaning, long a primary metaphor of pastoral counseling and theology, is joined and transformed by attention to issues of justice and power (Poling, 1988). The attention to justice is as a corollary to the long-standing ethical centrality of love in pastoral care, counseling, and theology. However, the inclusion of justice enlivens the way love functions theologically and strategically. Concurrent with this shift is the increasing use of process, narrative, and liberation theologies. The clinical pastoral paradigm had drawn more on Barthian and existential perspectives. The humanistic and psychodynamic therapeutic models that predominated in the clinical pastoral paradigm have been joined by self-psychology, narrative, feminist, and systemic models that better disclose the intrinsic relationality of human experience. These newer models more self-consciously include contextual analysis, strategic political analysis of the larger social factors contributing to personal/relational difficulty, and a posture of public advocacy by caregivers for changing oppressive policies.

Bonnie Miller-McLemore articulated a particularly helpful reframe of the focus for pastoral care from Boisen's classic "living human document" to the "living human web." The image of web (Smith, 1982; Miller-McLemore, 1993) has emerged as an apt metaphor for describing a wider focus for pastoral care, counseling, and theology and contextualizes the self and ways of knowing. Miller-McLemore urged a broader recognition of ways public policies and practices shape the particular challenges of individuals and families seeking care. As she put it, "Public policy issues that determine the health of the human web are as important as issues of individual emotional well-being" (1993, p. 367). While this article acknowledged issues of justice, here we also find a broadening of the scope of pastoral theology to include public theology. She rightly noted that this shift would require not only competence in theology and psychological sciences but also ethics, sociology, political science, and economics. In other words these shifts carried theoretical and methodological consequences.

In 1993 Patton joined the "conversation" about the importance of context and the issues of power and justice for acts of care. He proposed the phrase "communal contextual" to describe a paradigmatic shift in definition and focus in care, counseling, and theology that had been taking shape since the 1960s. He suggested it was the most recent addition to the "classical" and "clinical pastoral" paradigms. Patton saw these paradigms as interdependent and complementary. The communal contextual is the most encompassing and most widely embraced.

The communal contextual paradigm, as Patton conceived it, includes ecclesial communities of care and the importance of cultural and political contexts shaping persons' lives. It retrieves the earlier awareness that care is a ministry of the church or faith community rather than solely a clerical responsibility. It also reclaimed the importance of social context from the influence of the social gospel on the field in the early twentieth century and the more contemporary influences of issues related to difference posed by asymmetries of power such as gender, race, and class. Several newer therapeutic models such as brief (Stone, 2001), solution focused (Kornfeld, 1998), and narrative (Lester, 1995 and Neuger, 2001) contribute to care and counseling shaped by this paradigm. In the communal aspect of the paradigm, Patton explores the normative themes that shape care offered by faith communities. In this acknowledgment of a normative context for care and counseling, Patton draws on the same biblical and ethical norm of creation in God's image that Graham took as foundational. Significantly, these pastoral theologians are identifying both the importance of an intentionality about norms and locating a biblical norm that will support and inform critical, ethically constructive attention to life in communities challenged by the abuse of power and structures that institutionalize asymmetries of power—important themes in postmodernity. Brita Gill-Austern (1995) also enlarged the ethical dimension of the communal context through the image of a web to address the mutuality of care as normative for communities of faith. The contextual dimension of this new paradigm has given rise to considerable creativity in the field. Issues such as intimate violence, gender, race, class, and sexual orientation are now readily addressed. Attention to context also disclosed the need to address ethical dimensions of care in relational and more public spheres. This attention to norms and moral and ethical foundations for pastoral care, counseling, and theology was raised first and subsequently in the most sustained fashion by Don Browning (1976, 1983, 1987, 1991). Browning, like Miller-McLemore (1993), posed this concern to raise awareness about the way in which the competing claims for moral authority in the culture required a significant shift in the depth and intentionality with which Christian caregivers and pastoral theologians reflect ethically and use resources such as theories of therapy from the social sciences. Like those named above, Browning also situates himself within Christian tradition and wants to assure that its particular moral and ethical foundations contribute to the public debates in culture such as family values and forms.

The intercultural paradigm has particular affinities with the emancipatory and ethical contextual aspects of the communal contextual paradigm. However, it arises from a particular awareness of the global dimensions of the asymmetries of political and economic power associated with racial and cultural difference. Understandably, this paradigm was voiced first from beyond the U.S. (Hollenweger, 1978). Emmanuel Lartey (2003), whose essay on these issues follows in this volume, uses the term *intercultural* to describe an approach to care and counseling that responds to the dynamic complexity of cultural pluralism around the world. Intercultural care also seeks to correct the problematic consequences of Eurocentric cultural, political, and economic hegemony. Intercultural care values the rich dynamic, interpretive complexity of interacting cultures and rejects typologies that reduce such complexity. Lartey describes intercultural care as affirming "three basic highly interdependent principles: contextuality, multiple perspectives, and authentic participation." (p. 33) Contextuality represents a shared commitment with the communal contextual paradigm in that it lifts up the multiple influences on identity and behavior from a wide range of factors such as gender, race, economics, and so on. By multiple perspectives, Lartey is naming the influence of postmodernity on our understanding of the perspectival character of knowing and the necessity of multiple perspectives if we are to have an adequate view of situations. Authentic participation is similarly informed by a critical postmodernity in its recognition of the highly political character of knowing that requires care to assure the voice of each is heard and valued. This attention to the need to empower those otherwise on the margins or silenced arises from similar biblical and political claims about mutual regard and justice to guide life in community as those that inform the communal contextual paradigm.

Intercultural care completes a continuum that moves through monocultural, cross-cultural, and multicultural approaches. Each reflects in turn a progressively more inclusive and plural understanding of difference among persons (Lartey, 2003). Borrowing from Kluckholn and Murray's (1948) description of ways we are like all others, some others, and no other, Lartey advocates valuing the uniqueness of human experience equally with universal and group traits.

This intercultural paradigm is still evolving and is sometimes described as multicultural care. However, as Kathleen Greider (2002) has noted, multicultural sometimes describes a more reductive approach that allows typologies to replace the irreducible differences among persons. How this paradigm will resolve the problematic tensive relationship between group and particular experience is yet to be seen. Meanwhile, various dimensions of this paradigm are being explored and developed. Samuel Lee (2001, 2002) has helpfully addressed the importance of intercultural sensibilities for classroom and supervisory relationships especially when the teacher or supervisor is European American because racism is inevitably a factor in the United States for those whose racial or cultural heritage is not European American. This paradigm encourages heightened attention to the dynamics of power in practices of care and the education and formation of those who give care. Also evolving is its relation to a religiously plural context. Lartey, for example, advocates redefining pastoral care beyond its Christian roots drawing on its kenotic and incarnational images (2003).

These paradigmatic shifts in the fields of pastoral care, counseling, and theology demonstrate a thoroughgoing redefinition that retrieves some earlier twentieth-century concerns for social justice as well as responding to the emerging cultural shifts that emancipatory social and intellectual movements introduce. They resonate with several newer theological sources and biblical perspectives, as well as therapeutic approaches that better serve congregational settings and a more complex understanding of relationality. They also require new skills with critical tools for cultural analysis. These paradigm shifts expand and critically adapt more than repudiate previous self-understanding. They represent a critical engagement with the emphases of postmodernity. They do not yield the goal of witnessing to religious tradition (classical paradigm) or the value of clinical skills and self-understanding (clinical pastoral paradigm). But they do recast, sometimes significantly, that witness and self-understanding. Relational justice holds onto some of the advances of modernity that assert as universally true the values of freedom, justice, and human rights, the significance of historicity, and the value of reason in public debate (Neuger, 1998). Indeed pre-modern commitments are deeply embedded in the field's continued critical reliance on religious sources of authority and symbols alongside social and human sciences. But these paradigm shifts do reflect the effect of postmodernity in its critique of grand narratives that reproduce as universally true the values of a dominant culture that oppress and obscure the particularity of all knowledge and the self-interested relation of knowledge and power. The communal contextual and intercultural paradigms engage several key characteristics of postmodernity: the concern for the self and epistemology; issues of ethics in the absence of universals; and the sociopolitical dynamics of engaging difference. These paradigms recognize the inevitably partial, particular, and political character of all knowing. Human beings are profoundly relational and social as well as unique in our identity. While the communal contextual paradigm claims a particular Christian standpoint, it seeks to engage other religious traditions respectfully with a pluralist posture toward the truthfulness of other traditions. The intercultural paradigm may provide a trajectory for care that moves beyond the boundaries of Christian tradition. Within the field, there are marked variations in strategies for engagement in a plural and complex culture. Certainly the communal contextual and intercultural paradigms both acknowledge the necessity of presenting their claims regarding care in public contexts where they must compete with alternative cultural and politically based sources of authority. Both paradigms are particularly shaped by emancipatory values that seek to hear and respond to the experience and wisdom of previously marginalized persons.

Having traced these beginnings and general outlines of these paradigmatic shifts, in the pages that follow, I will use six categories to frame briefly more specific ways the continuities and discontinuities in the field have unfolded since the publication of the *Dictionary* in publications, journal literature, and the organizations that are central to the field. These categories reflect the focus of the essays that follow: pastoral theology as public theology, issues of difference and power, internationalization, clinical pastoral method, pastoral theological method, and pastoral theology.

Pastoral Theology as Public Theology

As the field of pastoral theology and care widened its focus to include the influence of the context of human experience, its work increasingly reflected the features of public theology, a form of theological reflection that focuses critical attention on the operative norms and practices of culture in an effort to contribute to the transformation of public life (Cady, 1993). Transformation in the public sphere to enhance healing and justice systemically as well as personally is a prominent concern of both the communal contextual and intercultural paradigms. The emergence of public theology in general and as a form of pastoral theology in particular is further evidence of the influence of critical postmodernity on the field as described earlier in this essay:

- a revised notion of the self from an autonomous individual to a highly relational one and an accompanying shift in epistemology that recognizes the inadequacy of a modern, technical, universalized, rationality for complex relationality;
- a shift in ethical practice and norms necessitated by the rejection of supposedly universal norms; and
- a recognition of the sociopolitical consequences of differences such as gender, race, and class obscured by Enlightenment definitions of the public that focused on similarities in human experience.

Public theology rejects the split in public and personal sociality that characterizes modernity. One effect of that split was a compartmentalization of religion as a personal, even private, experience and theology as necessarily restricted from authority in matters regarding public welfare (Cady, 1993). Rather, a number of pastoral theologians began to argue that there is a necessary and ethical linkage between personal and public experience as the normative term, "relational justice" suggests. This widening of focus to include the public sphere required concurrent skills in discerning operative normative images and practices and a readiness to engage in conversation, if not debate regarding norms and practices that diminish our common life. Public theology, in contrast to public religion, enters such debate drawing on but not imposing in universal ways the resources of a religious tradition (Cady, 1993). One can see such differences among more evangelical sources in the field such as the journal, *Psychology and Theology (PT)* that presumes Christian tradition as normative and the more theologically liberal, *Journal of Pastoral Theology (JPT)*, the *Journal of Pastoral Care (JPC)*, or the *Journal of Supervision and Training in Ministry (JSTM)* in which largely Christian authors and readers may acknowledge the particularity of their religious worldview, but ordinarily do not presume it as universally true for all. For public theologians, particularity is understood as a bridge to more inclusive practice. Pastoral theologians who use methodologies of public theology accept accountability beyond their ecclesial bounds, while arguing for the usefulness and truthfulness of their proposals for the positive transformation of our common cultural life. This is true whether engaging in interfaith conversation about practices of care or challenging ethical assumptions of public healthcare policies.

The difference between a clinical pastoral paradigm that is focused principally by interdisciplinary reflection between psychology and theology and a more communal contextual paradigm becomes apparent when we consider Larry Graham's proposed redefinition of pastoral theology informed by public theology. His proposals suggest the emerging definitional complexity this public turn creates:

> Pastoral theology is that branch of theology that constructs theories and practices of personal and corporate care, and contributes to the constructive theological task and to the common good by identifying, evaluating, and modifying, the technical practices, core meaning systems, and normative value structures operating within and between all of the efforts of care brought to bear upon individuals and groups within our common life. To accomplish its task, pastoral theology develops for public debate and policy interpretations of our common life, norms by which this life will be lived, and practical strategies for healing, sustaining, guiding, and liberating individuals, cultures, and the natural order. (2000, p.12)

A number of factors and persons contributed to the influence of public theological methods among pastoral theologians and caregivers. A formative early and articulate proponent of widening the focus of pastoral theology and care to include critical attention to culture was Don Browning (1976, 1983, 1987, 1991, 1997). Browning has argued persuasively that theologians and pastors rightly need to address larger cultural moral issues. He contributed methodological proposals that have been critically embraced by many in the field whether to disclose the competing values and norms in the various therapeutic psychologies on which pastoral caregivers had uncritically relied or to demonstrate the ways in which theological resources could contribute to contemporary cultural debates about norms for the nature and form of family life. The latter is well illustrated in the eight-volume *Family, Religion, and Culture Series* he coedited with Ian Evison. The series is an excellent example of Browning's interests in creating occasions for reasoned debate about the helpfulness of Christian religious resources in relation to other currently operative ethical norms to inform cultural difficulties. Beyond the central role Browning's critical hermeneutics perspective has played in this shift toward a public focus, Charles Gerkin's interest in hermeneutics, and a number of faculty and practitioners who drew from liberation theology and critical theory have also contributed to the present ferment. Gerkin's work (1979, 1984, 1986, 1991, 1997) disclosed the complex sociality of human experience and proposed strategies for "widening the horizons" of care that are critically and culturally informed.

As Miller-McLemore notes in her essay on public theology in this volume, liberation theologies (Moseley, 1990) also contributed significantly to this public turn in pastoral theology and care in the U.S. and around the globe. Such theologies join macrosocial analysis to the focus on individual experience and practices—a long-standing contribution of the fields of pastoral theology, and care and counseling. Rather than focusing on the particular pain of individuals, attention shifts to naming oppressive dominant norms and practices such as patriarchy, racism, classism, and ethnocentrism as major barriers to human well-being. Leading this shift were the European American women and African American women and men who began to enter teaching and supervisory positions by the mid- to late-1980s and now significantly inform the field. These theologians and practitioners regularly draw on liberation theologies and related critical theory in the scholarship they contribute. They are joined by a growing number of European American men who also value such theory.

Feminist theory and theology has informed significant public pastoral theological engagement with the consequences of patriarchy. European American women such as Neuger (1991, 1996, 2001), Miller-McLemore (1991, 1994, 1999), Saussy (1991, 1995), and Gill-Austern (1996, 1999) named patriarchy in church and culture as problematic for the well-being of women and men in the U.S. Several European American men joined them in this way of renaming the problem of patriarchy including Graham (1992), Patton (1993), and Poling (1991a, 1991b, 1996, 1997, 1998a, 1998b).

In the work of two African American male scholars, Edward P. Wimberly and Archie Smith, Jr., we see an evolution toward a sharper critical engagement and focus on the effects of pervasive racism in culture (Wimberly, 1979, 1982, 1986, 1992, 1997a, 1997b, 1999, 2000, 2003; Smith, 1993, 1997). Womanist theologian, Carroll Watkins Ali (1999), is particularly articulate about the priority of addressing racism and classism. In the U.S. faculty and practitioners have begun to name the fact of ethnocentrism and racism as issues that must be addressed in supervision and curricula (Reyes-Netto, 1985, 1992; Lee, 2001, 2002).

Colleagues in pastoral theology and care in Western Europe as well as those in Africa, Asia, Central America, and the Pacific Islands frequently also drew on emancipatory themes that challenged any analysis that failed to acknowledge the inextricable relation of the personal and sociocultural factors. Stephen Pattison (1994), a British pastoral theologian, critiqued the influence of dominant culture in narrowing the focus of pastoral theology and care to individual well-being and argued for the corrective value of liberation theology as a resource. Sara Baltodano brings class, political, gender, and race analysis as well as liberation theology to bear on her context in Central America. The harsh political and economic realities of her context compel her to redefine the scope of pastoral care to transform the pain of inequities at both the individual and societal levels (2002, p. 205). Women in Britain (E. Graham), the Netherlands (R. Bons-Storm, A. Imbens, I. Jonker) and South Africa (D. Ackermann) joined their voices with those such as Pattison, Baltodano, and colleagues in the United States.

While this turn toward critical engagement of public norms and practices as the dynamic context for particular experience encompasses many themes and topics in recent literature, the work of Pamela Couture deserves particular attention. Hers is an especially effective voice in redefining pastoral theology to contextualize care so that it includes attention to public policy and systems. Couture has also brought careful analysis of ways public policy regarding economic issues is relevant for assessing health care and care for children and women (1991, 1995, 1996b, 2000). For example, in her recent book, *Seeing Children, Seeing God* (2000), Couture explores the work of care in relation to children who experience material poverty and the poverty of tenuous connections. She uses children's social ecology and children's rights as two normative lenses for viewing these overlapping forms of poverty in order to make proposals for enhancing the skills and resilience of adults to provide effective care. In other contexts she explores public policies and normative frameworks surrounding parenting and family life in the United States again to inform care as compassion and social and institutional transformation (1993, 1996a).

In addition to Couture's work, a number of other pastoral theologians have widened socioeconomic analyses disclosing their relevance for family life and dynamics. Judith Orr (1991, 1997, 2000) helpfully forged new awareness of the significance that socioeconomic factors have in structuring rules and roles for family members. She demonstrated effectively how these larger social structures and dynamics were especially relevant for effective care. James Poling has also extended the field's resources for analyzing the significance for socioeconomic class and economic public policies and norms in offering effective care (2002).

Pastoral theologians, counselors, and chaplains informed by public theology will require new competencies and skills to assure adequately critical engagement with the wider range of theoretical sources cultural analysis presumes. For example, as Christianity is no longer normative in the U.S., hospital chaplains must become knowledgeable about a broader range of popular spiritualities and world religions and ways their differences may matter in practices of care. Similarly, as cultural, racial, and religious differences become more significantly represented in the U.S. population, pastoral theologians, counselors, and chaplains must be aware of the ways in which these aspects of their own identities and the identities of those who differ from them are relevant for pastoral practice.

Disciplines such as ethics, political and economic sciences, cultural analysis, gender studies, critical race theory, and so forth, will be more important in the interdisciplinary work of pastoral theology and care. The multiplicity of our social identity (gender, race, class, sexual orientation), for example, will require developing new areas of political and anthropological expertise. Engaging these new resources will also require renewed attention to such topics as theological ethics, prophetic literature, and liberation theologies among others (Graham, 1995). It is likely that ecclesiology will become a significant resource as authority, boundaries, and accountability require more clarity when "personal" and "public" contexts are joined.

Broadening the focus of pastoral theology to encompass the contextual factors that are intertwined with the needs of particular individuals will also require clarifying further how pastoral theology differs from practical theology and theological ethics. Pastoral theology that includes this larger contextual awareness is distinguishable from practical theology by the attention to practices of care. When the culture appears as the "client" this distinction blurs. It is likely in the years ahead that we will be clarifying how to hold onto care for particular persons as we discern their needs within a dynamic cultural and political context.

Attending to Issues of Difference and Power

It would be difficult to overstate the impact of addressing issues of difference and asymmetries of power in pastoral theology, care, and counseling since the publication of the *Dictionary.* While the editors of the *Dictionary,* intentionally included a number of entries that addressed relevant issues such as black theology, feminist theology and therapy, liberation theology, power, and the emerging perspectives of indigenous groups around the globe, they were unable to imagine the scope of the shifts that were already unfolding at the time of the dictionary's publication in 1990. The primary perspective informing the *Dictionary* reflects the interests and perspectives of the European American, liberal, Protestant men who largely conceived and developed the dominant norms of the clinical pastoral method. The perspective of the *Dictionary* understandably reflects an "assimilationist" posture of inclusion and even affirmative recognition of the particularity of the perspectives of the "Other" (Jackson & Holvino, 1988). However, it was not able to imagine the "redefinition" of dominant theory, method, and organizational structures that would come with the influx of European American women, women and men of various other racial and cultural heritages, and the emerging indigenous pastoral care movements around the globe. Of course these changes also relied upon the contributions of a number of European American men who also value the resources of critical theory, liberation and process theologies, and accepted the implications of these sources for their own dominant status. These changes are reflected in concurrent shifts in dominant theory and methods. This claim of human rights as an ethical and religious norm for all peoples is one of the gains from modernity's value for the individual that discloses the way the field has made only a qualified or critical embrace of postmodernity that does not tolerate such universal claims.

Tracking the way in which issues of power and difference appear in the membership, literature, and structures of three organizations in pastoral theology, care, and counseling—AAPC, ACPE, and SPT—makes the scope of the changes more apparent. In AAPC for example now over one-third of the membership are women. In 2003 of the ten regional chairs, nine were women. Roy Woodruff, recently retired as Executive Director of AAPC indicated that, "not that long ago we were glad for one [woman]" (personal communication, January 8, 2003). In 1998, AAPC formed a Working Group for African American members in response to their request for better recognition and support of the distinctive needs they experienced in the largely European American organization. It seeks to offer support, empowerment, increased visibility to African American members, and mentoring to those interested in membership (N. Long, personal communication, August 13, 2003).

In ACPE seven of the fifteen new supervisors recognized in 2002 were women and six were persons of color with many from outside the U.S. At the same meeting fourteen of twenty new Associate Supervisors were women and four were international (H. Patton, personal communication, January 20, 2003). In 1988 ACPE formed the Racial Ethnic Minority Network (REM) to support members whose racial or cultural heritage differed from the European American majority. Sixty attended the first meeting. Now attendance at the meetings that are separate from the national convention averages 300. In 1998 the name of the network was changed to Racial Ethnic Multicultural Network to include a wider range of cultural difference as well as those whose religious identity differs from the Judeo-Christian majority in the organization. Since 2001, R.E.M. has become a location for certification processes for its members that has provided them a more comfortable environment for assessment (T. Snorton, personal communication, January 13 and August 13, 2003).

In the Society for Pastoral Theology, founded in 1985, participation by women and increasingly by persons of African American and Asian American heritage has been a prominent aspect of the life and direction of the organization. Its bylaws require that participation by women on the steering committee be at least equal to that of men and that persons whose racial or cultural heritage differs from the majority's be included on the committee as well. The organization's journal is coedited by women and men. A majority of the chairs of the Society have been women, and its current chair is an Asian American male.

Attention to inclusion of gay, lesbian, bisexual, and transgendered persons and the theological, theoretical, and clinical material their experiences offer differs across the principal organizations in the field. In AAPC, the ethical issues surrounding conversion therapies disclosed the potential divisions among members of more evangelical and moderate to progressive theological persuasions. In ACPE a gay/ lesbian/ bisexual/ transgendered network is in place to support members who identify with one of these sexual orientations and to educate the Association about the needs and experience of persons who claim one of these identities. In SPT interest in the theological, theoretical, and pedagogical issues appeared early (Marshall, 1995, 1997 and Graham, 1997) and now seems well accepted as significant in the widened contextual analysis that the norm of relational justice requires.

This brief review of demographic factors in these three principal organizations well illustrates the marked changes underway in equalizing participation along the lines of gender and seeking to recognize and support the participation of persons who bring racial, cultural, sexual orientation, and religious difference to conversations about theology, theory, method, and practice. As noted elsewhere in this essay, the journals serving these organizations: JSTM, JPC, and JPT have explicitly addressed these issues. It is also the case that authors who embody these societal identities increasingly bring their insights to more general articles about pastoral theology, care, and counseling.

These dramatic shifts that signal an influx of members whose voices and ideas previously were marginalized are accompanied by stories of struggles for a voice and adequate inclusion. For example, will organizations such as AAPC and ACPE move toward genuine mutuality in valuing the contributions of more Afro-centric practices and methods regarding pastoral care and counseling? It is well to remember that there can be a marked delay between the emergence of literature that signals genuine receptivity to the conceptual and methodological differences arising from another group's experience and context, and the incorporation of changes in organizational life, dominant theory, practices, and training. While the level of receptivity varies in these several organizations, the enduring effects of racism require vigilance and proactive resistance even to unwitting racism into the foreseeable future. Receptivity to the conceptual and clinical insights of feminist theology and theory appears to be somewhat more far-reaching in the literature, supervisory practices, and the body of knowledge for training and certification, but many would caution that it should not be presumed.

Educational and organizational theorists describe predictable stages in the changes that may occur in organizations that confront diversity (Marchesani & Adams, 1992; Jackson & Holvino, 1988). The pattern typically represents a movement by the dominant group from exclusion to recognition of exceptional individuals from marginalized groups, to interest in differences and ways to "level the playing field" without changing norms (assimilation), to hearing from those "outsiders" in their own voices thus introducing a multiplicity of perspectives, and finally to a transformation or redefinition of the previously dominant norms (Marchesani & Adams, 1992, pp. 15-16). This progression obviously entails a corresponding openness to relativizing and finally redefining the norms of an organization or curriculum on the part of "insiders." Less obvious but necessary for redefinition to occur, is the critical awareness on the part of insiders that their inside status or privilege contributes to the barriers that limit others. This organizational development pattern is suggestive for the process now underway in pastoral theology, care, and counseling. Experience with developmental theory would suggest both that we assume movement is not a simple progression and that transitions are particularly challenging.

From the perspective of under-represented groups, there is indeed a movement that begins with articles and books by exceptional representatives such as African American authors, Edward P. Wimberly and Archie Smith, Jr. including particularly Wimberly's *Pastoral Care in the Black Church* (1979) and *Pastoral Counseling and Spiritual Values: A Black Point of View* (1983) and Smith's *The Relational Self: Ethics and Therapy from a Black Perspective* (1983). Alongside these were articles in the 1960s and 1970s by European American women such as Emma Justes (1971, 1978, 1979), Maxine Glaz (then Walaskay) (1973), and Peggy Way (1964, 1968, 1970a, 1970b, 1972, 1981). These contributions were reclaiming a voice in ways that challenged the universality of dominant WASP norms in the field. They asserted their distinctive perspectives as relevant for effective care. In 1991 the first books emerged that claimed gender as a relevant category for analysis and practice, *Women in Travail and Transition: A New Pastoral Care* (Glaz & Stevenson-Moessner) and *Womanistcare* (Hollies). They demonstrated the initial challenge of a number of women pastoral theologians and practitioners who together offered both critique and constructive proposals for a wide range of issues in care and public theology. James Poling's *The Abuse of Power: A Theological Problem* (1991) also demonstrated the value of gender, race, and class analysis for critique and constructive proposals. In 1993 Valerie De Marinis published *Critical Caring,* the first single-author volume on feminist pastoral practice.

The decade of the 1990s was a time of tremendous ferment and productivity in the United States by women and men of both European American and African American racial identities and differing sexual orientations who together demonstrated increasing nuance and methodological sophistication in their attention to alternative theological, methodological, and practice issues in the field. Their work well paralleled the assumptions of the emerging communal contextual and intercultural paradigms. The use of critical theory widened and deepened. For example, European American women began to recognize other sources of marginalization such as race, class, and heterosexism in their work. The use of Womanist theory, for example, expanded feminist analysis (Greider, Johnson, & Leslie, 1999).

By the mid- to late-1990s the dominant (modern) theoretical norms informing the clinical pastoral method were effectively de-centered as literature in books and journals in the field demonstrated that new theological and theoretical resources more adequately disclosed and addressed the revised understanding of the self as inextricably social, relational, and political. We also see a breadth and maturity in the literature that simply presumes the necessity of contextual critical analysis and the norm of relational justice. Gender, for example, is no longer synonymous with women's issues. Masculinity itself becomes a focus of research and methodological proposals (Neuger & Poling, 1997 and Dittes, 1996). Womanist and Feminist methodological approaches are not only presumed for the practices of care (DeMarinis, 1993 and Neuger, 1996) but the range of such approaches and their value becomes a source of critical reflection in Bonnie Miller-McLemore and Brita Gill-Austern's (1999) *Feminist & Womanist Pastoral Theology.* More general books on care and counseling also increasingly presumed contextual analysis and critical theory such as Lester (1995) *Hope in Pastor Care and Counseling,* Lester (2003) *The Angry Christian: a Theology for Care and Counseling,* and Wimberly (2000) *Relational Refugees.*

Analysis of power is of course presumed in contextual analysis and critical theory, but power also became the focus of emerging attention to clergy professional ethics. Discussion of clergy sexual misconduct was framed particularly through the lens of the violation of boundaries that are intended to protect more vulnerable persons. Pastoral theologians, chaplains, and counselors all have addressed this issue. In *Taking Care: Monitoring Power Dynamics and Relational Boundaries in Pastoral Care and Counseling* (1996), Carrie Doehring well illustrates the way in which postmodern challenges to patriarchal patterns of dominance and the norm of relational justice have become central for adequate pastoral theological analysis and standards of pastoral practice and care.

Developmentally for the field, it is important to note that European American women and men have begun to name previously denied sources of privilege such as race and religion in the United States as critical issues that require revision in current pastoral theology, method, theory, and practice

(Becker, 2002; Grace, 2002; Moody, 1994; Ramsay, 2002). This self-critique marks an important elaboration in the emerging norms, such as relational justice, operative in the communal contextual and intercultural paradigms. It also suggests the effectiveness of the de-centering process that has brought those on the margins to the center of constructive conversations on pastoral theology, method, and practice.

International Dimensions of Pastoral Care, Counseling, and Theology

The recognition of truly differing interpretations of the nature of the self and ways of knowing what is true; the ethical complexity disclosed as any claim to universal norms gives way; and the sociopolitical dynamics of difference—all characteristics of a critical postmodernity—inform the story of an increasingly international contemporary pastoral care movement since the publication of the *Dictionary* in 1990. This has been a time of very productive ferment especially in non-Western contexts such as the African continent, Asia, the Pacific Islands, and Latin America. Redefinition well characterizes the corresponding period in the United States as its earlier utterly parochial posture begins to move toward recognition of the changes a truly international context will require for theory and method, training, and practices. Included in this redefinition are the consequences of religious pluralism for the largely unacknowledged Christian emphases in the structures, processes, and theological foundations of both chaplaincy and pastoral counseling.

In his essay in this volume, Emmanuel Lartey well describes the ferment in non-Western contexts. Lartey suggests that three categories help us track an emerging recognition of the value of genuine partnership between pastoral care movements around the globe in terms of theory building, practice, and training methods. **Globalization** describes an uncritical exportation of Western theory and practice with an expectation of rather simple processes of assimilation and an accompanying assumption of the normative character of these Western practices and the values implicit in them. **Internationalization** describes a more appreciative recognition that differences arising in various contexts are appropriate for such contexts and the practices of no context are universally valid. He notes that the reciprocity envisioned in this category is largely unrealized in part because of the historical and educational momentum of Western theory and practice. **Indigenization** is a term Lartey uses to describe the emerging truly non-Western theological and theoretical frames for pastoral theology, care, and counseling. According to Lartey, these categories describe a dynamic rather than linear process so that in some locations all three descriptors could be applied to various situations. At the time of the publication of the *Dictionary* it would be safe to suggest that a posture of globalization was only beginning to yield toward recognition of internationalization. However, as Lartey suggests, internationalization is now more frequently an accurate descriptor of theory and practice in non-Western settings with indigenization emerging as a factor.

We will use these same three categories to reflect on the impact of this international ferment on theory, practice, and training in the U.S. since the late-1980s. Once again, we find the *Dictionary* functions as a "hinge in time," for it well summarizes the posture of globalization that dominated as Western models of pastoral care and counseling were exported through CPE and pastoral counseling programs and graduates of such programs in the U.S., Britain, and Western Europe particularly. It also peers into the future in ways that anticipate the current ferment though, with the benefit of hindsight, some contributors also betray the limitations of this globalization posture in ways that invite humility in any evaluation of current strategies.

The International Conferences that began in Edinburgh in 1979 have continued in a way that demonstrate Lartey's claim of internationalization as a better descriptor of the current status of exchange between the now quite diverse contexts for the pastoral care movement around the world. Recent publications also demonstrate the ferment on various continents. Lartey (1996, 2003) demonstrates a largely indigenous perspective that makes theoretical and praxis proposals that challenge Western assumptions. It is striking to compare the second edition of *In Living Color* (2003) with Augsburger's *Pastoral Counseling Across Cultures* (1986) that was so crucial in helping pastoral theology and care in the U.S. move from a globalization to international posture. But Augsburger presumed a Christian theory and practice as universal and, by contemporary standards, underestimated the importance of social and political dynamics. Similarly, in 1993 Wicks and Estadt published a helpful edited volume that included descriptions of emerging care and counseling movements around the globe often authored by Western missionaries and non-Western persons who trained in the United States. It served as a valuable window for persons who were unaware of the challenges different cultures posed to Western models. A decade later we witness the emerging energy for indigenous theory building described in Farris's *International Perspectives on Pastoral Counseling* (2002) in which the predominance of contributors are speaking from their own culture and acknowledging the urgency of developing models and theory that better serve very different epistemological, sociopolitical and socioeconomic contexts. Robert Solomon (2002, p. 113) urges that in Asia pastoral care and counseling make the community its client and use issues of justice and compassion as markers of health. Moreover, he urges an indigenous model that not only draws from psychology but also a wide array of social sciences such as education and economics. Steve Shim (2002), the director of the first AAPC accredited international training center in Seoul, Korea, takes a more internationalization stance than Solomon as he argues that AAPC training and practice models will require significant cultural and theoretical adaptation to be useful, but they can be used creatively.

The ferment described by Lartey, Solomon, and Shim has been encouraged by the multiplication of regional organizations such as the African Association of Pastoral Studies and Counselling and organizations that span the globe such as the International Congresses of Pastoral Care and Counseling and the International Academy of Practical Theology. While economic differences still make such gatherings more difficult for persons in developing countries, these opportunities for conversation and theory building have made a decisive contribution to the widened imagination reflected in the internationalization and indigenization that Lartey describes. As more representatives from the United States are able to engage with those who are developing alternative models and theories, we can anticipate a parallel yielding of the cultural encapsulation that has characterized contemporary pastoral care, counseling, and theology.

Other factors are also affecting the context in the United States. Since the mid-1980s it has been increasingly apparent that the United States has been experiencing a large wave of immigration in the later twentieth- and early twenty-first centuries. The resulting demographic shifts toward an imminent absence of any racial majority hold very significant political and economic implications not yet fully realized. However, the implications for clinical theory and training and for theological foundations for care are well recognized. During this same historical period recognition of the global character of communications, economics, and politics has become commonplace along with a corresponding rise in emancipatory political movements in developing countries whether in resisting Western economic and political dominance or more local oppression. These movements have spawned corresponding liberative and ecological theological movements that have increasingly informed both emerging and U.S. based pastoral care and theology. Since the tragic events of September 11, 2001 and a large-scale confrontation of terrorism, receptivity to its increasing cultural diversity has become more complicated.

By the mid-1980s in the United States, the shift toward internationalization was becoming apparent. In a JPC editorial John Patton (1985), for example, described his awareness that addressing issues of difference had passed the "honeymoon" stage and would include hard work. He recognized the linkage between issues of cultural difference and the work already underway in addressing gender concerns. Importantly, Patton acknowledged that critical self-reflection on the formative influences in his own self and professional awareness would be part of the work for him and other European Americans. In this same volume Benoni Reyes-Netto (1985) addressed the "hidden agenda" in pastoral care and counseling in the United States, referring to the need to identify and reject the temptation to impose unwittingly the values and norms of the U.S. as if universal.

These comments from a European American and Hispanic American supervisor respectively, demonstrate the early stages of a conversation that has evolved especially in *JPC* and *JSTM*. Both journals have periodically published volumes focusing on ways a critical multicultural perspective helpfully challenges the pervasive influences of the European American norms and practices in pastoral counseling and chaplaincy training and practice. This conversation is increasingly candid about the fact of privilege and the need for European American supervisors to demonstrate the sort of fluency within and across cultural differences that is described by the intercultural paradigm.

Ferment and redefinition well characterize the status of the field with regard to the work and influence of international partners especially from outside the U.S. and Western Europe. Theory, method, and practice are undergoing sweeping changes. Organizations such as AAPC and ACPE are revising internal procedures for certification to respond to cultural and religious difference. Corresponding organizations around the world are quickly developing resources that better reflect the interface of effective care and particular cultures.

Clinical Pastoral Method

Chaplains and pastoral counselors have felt keenly the cultural and intellectual changes of the past fifteen years. They have also endured the buffeting winds of economic challenges that have dominated health care since the publication of the *Dictionary*. The Association for Clinical Pastoral Education (ACPE) and the American Association of Pastoral Counselors (AAPC) provide the primary window for our reflections as best representing the historical trajectory of theologically and clinically trained practitioners who bring interdisciplinary skills to the ministry of care and counseling, and who maintain a level of accountability with identified religious communions. Since 1985 the American Association of Christian Counselors founded by a psychologist in Mississippi and now a large professionally led evangelical group does represent an alternative voice in the emerging arena of specialized ministry. Members of AACC are unified not by standards of clinical competence but by the members' shared commitments to an evangelical, Christ-centered, and biblically based faith. AAPC has a radically different approach to education and training as well as professional identity, but these differences are more immediately apparent within the field than to those looking in from other secular groups. AACC responds to the challenges of postmodernity by embracing pre-Enlightenment understandings of the self, epistemology, and ethics.

Major change describes the past fifteen years for AAPC and ACPE. Certainly there are continuities in both chaplaincy and pastoral counseling since the mid-1980s, but even the continuities are not simple because sources informing their work, contexts for their work, certification standards, models for practice and supervision, persons seeking training, and persons seeking care have all changed. Further, the ways of responding to the challenges to their professional identity have varied in the two organizations. The different constituencies and mission of the two groups mean they've encountered the changes characterized by postmodernity and the economic shifts in health care differently. Issues of professional identity, difference, training and practice help to disclose the very dynamic years since the publication of the *Dictionary*.

Professional identity for chaplains and pastoral counselors has been complicated both from within their organizations and as each has needed to represent their interests with the health care industry and secular accrediting organizations in an attempt to secure financial and professional survival. These inward and outward journeys are highly interdependent. They are affected significantly by a concurrent cultural interest in spirituality often distinct from religious traditions. The history of both organizations includes American members who prefer a rather marginal relationship with their largely Christian communions usually because of a preference for less traditional theology and religious practice. Ironically, in the present context, it is precisely their ability to hear and respond to persons' faith and spiritual journeys that is the added value most promising for marketing and professional recognition.

In AAPC the economic challenges posed by minimal inclusion in managed care organizations for reimbursement began a variety of strategies for gaining recognition that would allow individuals and agencies to survive economically. As Roy Woodruff, then Executive Director of AAPC put it, the issue was how to sustain the "distinctive DNA" of the profession while gaining recognition in secular and governmental circles whose credentialing criteria, standards for practice, and outcome measurements were not easily matched with the history and present practices of AAPC (Woodruff, personal communication, December 16, 2002). In this context, Han van den Blink, as president of AAPC, carefully articulated an understanding of spirituality and spiritual practice that reflects the more plural and less rational influences of postmodern sensibilities. He defined spirituality as "practicing God's presence" and noted that in a plural context it was characterized by being "inclusive," "respectful," and always "invitational" rather than imposed (1995, p. 22). Organizationally, this turn to the spiritual integrity of the caregiver has led to a significant focus on formation as personal and professional grounding in the members' own tradition and attention to skills in evoking and nurturing spiritual development in themselves and their clients. While the definition of spirituality and the scope of formation are still evolving, the organization has sought to position itself in relation to other secular counseling professions as representing persons who offer, "theologically informed, spiritually sensitive, ethically sound, and clinically competent counseling as an extension of the ministry of faith communities" (AAPC Mission Statement, www.aapc.org). AAPC recently adopted a Body of Knowledge document that will satisfy major clinical certifying organizations for mental health counselors while also specifying courses that develop competence in such areas as the authoritative sources of an applicant's religious tradition (e.g., Bible and theology for Christians), the history of pastoral care and counseling, and methods distinctive to pastoral counseling (AAPC Body of Knowledge, 2002). In taking this stance, the organization has articulated a critical postmodern position that embraces an inclusive posture toward the religious pluralism of its members and those it serves while also claiming an understanding of spiritual competence for caregivers that is rooted in particular religious traditions.

ACPE has fought to secure its professional identity and survival in the arena of hospitals where profit for health care corporations and educational outcomes for the U.S. Department of Education have tested its resiliency and creativity. Unlike AAPC, chaplains have also had to engage the emerging religious, racial, and cultural diversity of the United States without lead time to prepare for the changes required in self-understanding, training, and practices. In this very dynamic context, ACPE joined other chaplaincy groups in 2001 to publish "A White Paper: Professional Chaplaincy: Its Role and Importance in Healthcare" (Vandecreek & Burton, 2001, pp. 81-98). In this document, the organization sought to redefine the competence and professional identity of its members as "spiritual caregivers" rather than the historically more familiar category of pastoral care. Perhaps because spiritual care is here described as important in healing and therefore needed in the hospital setting and because of the remarkable pluralism of the constituents chaplains may serve, the authors of the paper take a different posture than AAPC. Their inclusive strategy places no constraints on the definition or related practices of spirituality. Rather, in their definition, spirituality originates as a universally accessible dimension of human experience and may or may not include an experience of transcendence. In other words, spirituality is anthropologically framed and is inclusive of but not defined by religious experience (Lebacqz & Driskill, 2000). Spirituality in this paper is also defined instrumentally as an aid to healing and well-being, and it defines a healthcare standard. The document acknowledges that spiritual care may be provided by anyone. Chaplains then are available for "intense medical environments" and patients and families who have no other resource for spiritual care. Professional chaplains are defined as having received graduate level theological and clinical training as clergy or laypersons, and they are accountable to their religious faith group, their certifying chaplaincy organization, and the employing institution (ACPE, 2001, p. 85).

Professional identity for chaplains and pastoral counselors has also been challenged by the wider lenses of the communal contextual and intercultural paradigms. Patton, for example, on the one hand claims that central to the identity of specialized ministers is the focus on the "holy complexity" of theological and psychological depth in encounters with patients and clients

(Patton, 2000, p. 46). In the same article, he acknowledges that contextual, cultural, and international concerns inevitably modify the theories and practices of the discipline (p. 46). Others such as Herbert Anderson note that racial, gender, and cultural differences that supervisees bring require redefinition not just assimilation of these different voices (Anderson, 2000). Graham challenged pastoral counselors in a similar fashion noting that their focus needed to widen to include issues of gender, race, and class extending their historic theological concern for existential liberation to include a social and economic consciousness (Graham, 1996).

Several themes related to specialized pastoral practice have arisen more frequently in books and articles following the publication of the *Dictionary.* These themes include pastoral diagnosis, ethics, empathy, forgiveness, hope, marketing, spirituality, and cultural difference. Narrative, brief, feminist, self-psychologies, and systemic models for practice are also mentioned frequently.

These newer concerns in the practice of chaplaincy and pastoral counseling, whether in private practice or the congregation, posed new challenges for training in both forms of specialized ministry. These challenges were a consequence of a very significant increase in the diversity of students in training as well as differences in the contexts in which they would serve. The trajectories each organization has taken related to spirituality also seem relevant for current training. As Woodruff observed, AAPC membership has changed from requiring ordination to welcoming laypersons. Instead of focusing on the form of ordination, the capacity for spiritual and theological integration is a focus (Woodruff, 2002). In AAPC training centers there has been a 180-degree change as directors are more able now to presume clinical skill and must focus on students' abilities to use theological and spiritual resources (Townsend, this volume). Teresa Snorton, Executive Director of ACPE, observed that the focus of education in CPE is less on personal issues and formation or longer term interaction with patients and more on brief models for patient care, biomedical ethics, contextual analysis, cross-cultural communication, and effective care in the context of religious pluralism (Snorton, personal communication, January 13, 2003). The constituencies served in hospital and other chaplaincy settings typically do not reflect the segregation by class and race that regularly function in the U.S. culture. Thus far ACPE has had to work more intensively with racial, cultural, and religious pluralism in its training programs than AAPC. Even in ACPE, it is still unusual to find indicators of European American students and supervisors functioning from a truly "de-centered" position that relativizes the norms of the dominant culture reproduced in familiar learning theories, training models, and so forth. (Lee, 2001, 2002).

In the *Dictionary* Peggy Way (1990) anticipated very well the range of multicultural issues currently before chaplains and pastoral counselors as well as pastoral theologians such as the necessity of theories and models that are able to value diverse worldviews and encourage self-critical awareness of values and norms implicit in therapeutic approaches. She also called for training in which development of cultural fluency would be normative. She urged the development of more inclusive models and theories that built on the lived experience of cross-cultural clinical work.

In 1992 both the *Journal of Pastoral Care* and the *Journal of Supervision and Training in Ministry* devoted major sections of volumes to multicultural or cross-cultural counseling and care. The transition from Lartey's globalization with the assumption of Western norms to recognition of the need for reciprocity between equally valid perspectives can be seen among the varied articles. Augsburger (1992), for example, urges a value for a wider range of worldviews that transcends the present "monocultural" perspectives, and seems to include not only Christianity, but also alternative religious perspectives that marked a shift from his 1986 work. Other articles in this *JPC* volume, however, still invoked Christianity as normative and rejected the communal contextual and intercultural visions of a close tie between personal and cultural experience. In this *JSTM* volume, we find a quite dynamic process of revising definitions and deepening critiques of the cultural encapsulation of chaplaincy and counseling models prevalent in the United States. European American supervisors describe the new practices required for effective work with students culturally different from themselves (Ray, 1992-93) including issues of authority in supervision (Bryant, 1995).

At the turn of the twenty-first century these two central journals in the field, *JSTM* and *JPC,* once again offered important articles that demonstrate continued development of the internationalization posture with a clear appreciation of the need for indigenization on the part of partners in developing countries. Further, readers can begin to identify the kind of corresponding changes in self-understanding on the part of European Americans that progress on these issues will require. For example, Homer Jernigan (2000) argues in behalf of the need for indigenous CPE supervisors and proposes explicit strategies for effective training with students who will be returning to other cultures in order to maximize their ability to do so in a culturally congruent manner.

Clearly, cultural fluency is emerging as a requirement for supervisors as well as their students. Sam Lee (2001), a Korean American, proposes training and supervisory skills that are necessary for multicultural competence in ministry whether for chaplaincy or pastoral counseling. Lee draws from the increasing use of critical theory to discuss the barrier of unwitting racism and the fact of privilege that reproduces the monocultural ethnocentrism so problematic in the U.S. culture. This deeper exploration of the training and methodological issues and strategies continues in the 2002 volume of *JSTM*. Therese Becker (2002) calls for a training requirement in multicultural competency for CPE supervisors. An ACPE task force presented proposals in the fall of 2003. Lee (2002) urged supervisors to confront and deconstruct the effects of racial and cultural privilege in their work including leveling the hierarchy in their supervisory practices. We find in this volume a very dynamic redefinition of theory and method in the context of multicultural or intercultural experience (e.g., Greider, 2002; Grace, 2002) that suggests a correspondence to the internationalization/indigenization process Lartey describes for the field outside the West.

The range of challenges confronting training and method in pastoral counseling and chaplaincy is truly stunning. Woodruff's concern for retaining the original DNA of the field is understandable. Yet, the creativity evident in both ACPE and AAPC is encouraging, especially as each responds to the urgency of the changes posed by the two new paradigms. The trajectories implicit in their responses to the challenges of professional identity promise to yield quite different strategies for training and method in the future in the two organizations.

Pastoral Theological Method

Core values of the communal contextual paradigm include: a priority for relationality and community; a more interpersonal than intrapsychic developmental perspective; appreciation for particularity and difference and recognition of ways asymmetries of power distort these differences in communities; and a goal of mutuality and reciprocity within communities (Scheib, 2002, p. 31). Those exploring the communal dimensions of care represent quite diverse strategies, but have in common methodological concerns for fostering effective care in congregations and by lay members of these faith groups. Howard Stone (2001), for example, has noted that a consequence of the earlier clinical focus that relied on in-depth therapeutic modalities meant that in the United States a cohort of largely European American men shaped by the clinical pastoral paradigm has paid little attention to brief therapeutic approaches that are better suited for pastors with their parishioners. African American authors regularly include faith concerns in their work. A review of European American and African American women's writing in the field suggests that concern for both the well-being and resourcefulness of communities of faith has long characterized a central focus of their work (Greider, Johnson, & Leslie, 1999). Brita Gill-Austern (1995) uses the imagery of a "healing and transforming web" to describe an ecological approach to care that revalues the systems of care that can function well in congregations. She describes the losses undue reliance on professional clinical models created for effective care. She also addresses those practices and disciplines that form and deepen the communal richness of congregational life and prepare believers in communities for effective ministries of justice and compassion in a troubled world. Individual believers and congregations as a whole are the focus of her method. Karen Scheib (2002) also embraces the renewed attention to congregations as systems of care and articulates the helpfulness of communion ecclesiology to strengthen the theological foundations of the communal contextual approach. In contrast to these pastoral theologians who focus on ecologies of care within faith communities, public pastoral theological method uses the image of web (Smith, 1982 and Miller-McLemore, 1993) to focus on cultural evidences of disorder, injustice, and oppression that directly impinge on the well-being of persons and their relationships. Miller-McLemore (1993) suggested such a shift with her reframe of Boisen's "living human document" to "living human web." Her use of web imagery places the complexity of persons-in-culture as a focus for pastoral theological "investigation, interpretation, and transformation" (p. 367). As she notes, "Public policy issues that determine the health of the human web are as important as issues of individual emotional well-being" (p. 367). Alongside psychological sciences, other social sciences such as economics and political science become cognate disciplines for pastoral theologians who address public dimensions of pain and oppression such as intimate violence, public health and welfare policies, heterosexism, and debates about family policy, and managed healthcare policies. This methodology focuses our attention on operative cultural norms such as individualism and self-sufficiency. When unquestioned at the level of individual pastoral care these norms may reproduce destructive and oppressive consequences especially for those they render vulnerable by these norms such as the poor or those without health insurance (Couture, 1996). Widening the lens of care to incorporate critique of relevant cultural norms and practices suggests a more complex theory and theology of human beings as inextricably relational and political; a clearer articulation of ethical bases for critique among competing voices of authority in the public sphere; and keen attention to sociopolitical dynamics of power and difference—all aspects of critical postmodernity. These more public methodologies help to disclose problematic cultural norms that may otherwise remain obscure in more individual modalities, and they invite more systemic strategies that effect liberation and healing more widely.

Don Browning was an early and significant voice in shaping public dimensions of pastoral theological method. In *Religious Thought and the Modern Psychologies* (1987), Browning used David Tracy's (1975) notion of revised critical correlation to argue for a fundamentally reciprocal relationship between social science and theological sources. He hoped to sharpen the practitioner's awareness of the ethical issues at stake and enhance the capacity to identify and challenge problematic norms operative at the cultural level such as those mediated through the philosophical assumptions of the psychologies informing care and counseling. He (1991) has continued to develop this hermeneutical approach in what he describes as a fundamental practical theology that extends his critical theology of culture to congregational dynamics and broad public issues. Browning's hermeneutical approach to critical correlation contrasts with the more emancipatory emphases in the work of persons such as Miller-McLemore, Couture, Poling, and Graham. These scholars seek not only a richer interpretation of the Christian traditions, they also aspire to more liberatory and transformative goals. Methodologically they believe one must begin in the immediacy of public-personal dilemmas, such as intimate violence, and be open to the radical ways that these dilemmas may contest and transform conventional theological, ethical, and social science sources.

Another significant cluster of methodological innovation has come from those whose experience of marginalization has led them to draw on cultural analysis and use various critical theories such as feminist or critical race theory. They propose strategic interventions that may have larger groups of persons as their focus rather than particular individuals and their immediate relationships. These approaches are an elaboration of the emancipatory correlation method noted above as they too arise from a wider contextual analysis.

A number of African American male and womanist pastoral theologians have been particularly effective in this more contextual approach to pastoral care and counseling. Edward P. Wimberly, Archie Smith, Jr., Lee Butler, Jr. (2000), and Homer Ashby (2003) have each published books and articles that analyze the fact and consequences of racism as a primary political, economic, and spiritual contextual reality that undermines the well-being of African Americans and requires particular pastoral strategies for effective care. Such care includes transforming and liberating goals at structural and systemic as well as personal and relational levels. Womanist pastoral theologians such as Linda Hollies (1991), Marsha Foster-Boyd (1999), Carolyn McCrary (1998), Teresa Snorton (1996, 2000), and Carroll Watkins Ali (1999a, 1999b) draw on critical race and feminist theories as well as womanist theologians and ethicists. In single authored volumes or books such as those edited by Stevenson-Moessner they have brought a three dimensional critique addressing gender, race, and class to inform their strategic proposals for effective care that include broader transformative as well as particular healing goals.

Feminist theory has also informed the work of a number of European American women in the field, and has been used differently since the publication of the *Dictionary* than prior to 1990 when arguments for inclusion of women's experience itself were necessary. In 1991 and 1992 books that focused on the particular care of women—including one focusing on African American women—appeared for the first time (Hollies, 1992; Glaz & Stevenson-Moessner, 1991). Here critical gender theory and other relevant disciplines were brought to bear to begin providing resources and constructive proposals from a gendered perspective. Particularly influential were two edited volumes that elaborated feminist and womanist perspectives. Jeanne Stevenson-Moessner edited *Through the Eyes of Women: Insights for Pastoral Care* (1996) and *In Her Own Time: Women and Developmental Issues in Pastoral Care* (2000). Widely referenced in seminary classrooms and training programs, these volumes have significantly extended the reach of feminist and womanist clinical perspectives and models for care. Neuger's edited volume, *The Arts of Ministry: Feminist-Womanist Approaches* (1996), joined feminist theoretical perspectives across several practical theology fields including pastoral care and pastoral counseling to propose methodological innovations clearly informed by critical feminist and womanist sources.

Subsequently, feminist theory in pastoral theology has functioned more critically as authors have used it to challenge ideologies that marginalize and subordinate persons and groups on the basis of various essential traits such as gender, sexual orientation, race, age, and so on (Miller-McLemore, 1996b). Carrie Doehring (1999) offers a particularly careful description of feminist pastoral theological method in which we overhear critical postmodern influences as well. Doehring describes her approach as poststructural, contextual, and pragmatic by which she means she understands all knowledge to be constructed from particular locations rather than universal or absolute, and it is reflective of the particularities of such locations as well as political. She also insists that feminist pastoral theology is pragmatic. That is, it intends action rather than being satisfied with insight or interpretation. Neuger (2001) expands on the criteria Doehring shared and offers a more extended analysis of gender theories and their deconstructive as well as reconstructive implications for pastoral care and counseling. Her analyses draw on feminist and liberationist studies in psychology and psychotherapy as well as related liberation and process theological sources and careful cultural analysis of patriarchy evident in sexism. As Neuger points out, the correlation of these new theoretical resources with feminist and liberationist theologies has contributed to a truly altered body of knowledge and normative meanings of health and wholeness that inform assessment and practice.

Religious pluralism poses significant methodological challenges for practitioners of care as well as pastoral theologians. Chris Schlauch (1999) has helpfully begun what will need to be a much more extensive conversation about effective, respectful care across different religious and spiritual practices. Drawing on multiple methodologies, Schlauch develops strategies for a comparative understanding of faith as contextual praxis. He asserts that understanding faith is an intercultural and interdisciplinary enterprise (pp. 78-79).

The fact of the increasing cultural, racial, and religious pluralism in the U.S. and the postmodern and liberative perspectives that highlight asymmetries of power affecting those who differ from dominant perspectives has given rise to methodological innovation and ferment in clinical and academic settings. The editors of the *Dictionary* anticipated these changes that were already emerging as it was published, but they could not have imagined the speed and depth of change in method created by revaluing difference as contributing conceptual gain, requiring strategic variety, and prioritizing personal and professional formation especially for European Americans. Certainly there are parallels and even a kind of synergy with the contextual methods prompted by critical race and feminist theories.

Intercultural Paradigm

Authors such as Sam Lee (2001, 2002) and Emmanuel Lartey (1987, 1996, 2003) have proposed respectively multicultural and intercultural theories. Their work well represents the intention of what we are calling the intercultural paradigm to honor contextual particularities, the social and political dynamics in the construction of various perspectives on experience, and the priority of authentic participation for all persons in their own voices (Lartey, 2003). Lee, in writing for more clinical audiences, draws on critical pedagogy to advocate "multicultural competence" for supervisors and teachers. Such competence, for example, will require a European American supervisor and a culturally different student to learn collaboratively as "co-inquirers" (Lee, 2002, pp. 93-94). Moreover, his multicultural method reminds supervisors and teachers that they must become more self-critically aware of their privilege that, if unchecked, undermines this reciprocity. Further, multicultural competence requires of European American supervisors a heightened critical awareness of the influences of their own cultural and racial formation in their teaching practices. Therese Becker (2002), a European American clinical supervisor, amplifies Lee's concerns about the necessity of self-critical awareness regarding cultural norms such as individualism and the privilege that accompanies racial dominance for European Americans in this culture because of their problematic effects in supervision.

Lartey (2003) proposes an intercultural approach that draws on cultural and anthropological theory as well as theological sources. His method seeks to avoid the tendency toward reductionism and stereotypes that plague cross-cultural and multicultural models in their descriptions of typical characteristics of various cultural groups. Instead Lartey's method describes the need to hold simultaneous appreciation for the dynamic interdependence of the particular, group, and the cultural dimensions of a person's behavior in any given situation. He also proposes that intercultural care will transcend its exclusively Christian norms while holding onto its commitments to care for the other though this aspect of his method is still evolving.

Kathleen Greider (2002) extends the innovation surrounding interculturality in a somewhat different direction by framing it as an ideal goal beyond the respectful awareness of difference characterizing most multicultural strategies. She describes the fact of multiculturalism and urges supervisors and faculty to help students develop their potential for responding to it with intercultural sensibilities. The latter requires cultivating the interface between personal and social dynamics that is often plagued by false dualisms. She proposes several strategies for enhancing the potential for interculturality such as conceptualizing culture more inclusively so everyone attends to cultural characteristics; exploring the inextricable and dynamic relationship between personal and social experience by reflecting on the ways culture informs intrapersonal and interpersonal self-understanding; and conceptualizing interculturality as pilgrimage in which receptivity to difference is vital to self and other discovery.

John Moody (1994) describes effective innovations in a CPE program for addressing interfaith realities that is suggestive for the challenges of ministry in such settings where in times of crisis the particular symbols and practices of a patient's faith mitigate against "lowest common denominator" strategies. He seems to anticipate the need for intercultural sensibilities that Greider recommends, and shares her concern for developing better awareness of the reciprocity in personal and social formation. He describes the methodological challenges of supervision in culturally and religiously plural contexts. His proposal to offer religious care rather than pastoral care in interfaith settings suggests a more religiously shaped self-understanding and practice than the alternative individually defined norms of spiritual care.

Methodologically, it is important to note how a clinical skill such as empathy that is essential in the clinical pastoral paradigm is also being redefined in emerging paradigms that are searching for ways to honor and communicate effectively across differences. Marie McCarthy (1993), for example, explores how accurate empathy requires just the sort of mindfulness of the personal-social reciprocities and spiritual receptivity that Greider explores further nearly a decade later. McCarthy identifies ways in which empathy invites both conceptual and spiritual receptivity in order for us truly to engage nondefensively the possibilities another's difference presents. Methodologically, she suggests the centrality of empathy for supervisors in the formation of students' self and professional understanding for effective care in the midst of difference.

These various forms of methodological ferment and redefinition in pastoral theology, care, and counseling disclose a continued reliance on a correlational method—now critically framed—for what continues to be an interdisciplinary exploration. The large majority of current methods also continue to begin with experience rather than moving to experience from prior theologically and theoretically defined norms. Redefinition has occurred in the theoretical and theological sources on which faculty and practitioners rely as well as their much greater self-consciousness about the significance of their own self and professional understanding for their work. As noted earlier, liberation, narrative, and process theologies are far more often incorporated to inform the methods now widely used. Narrative, brief, self-psychologies, and systems theories are more often cited among the therapeutic modalities than the field's previously nearly singular reliance on psychodynamic and psychoanalytic modalities. Similarly, in addition to therapeutic sources, a breathtakingly wide array of human and social sciences now inform effective care, counseling, and theology by virtue of its revaluation of a far more contextualized understanding of the self and appreciation of the role of the public sphere for the "living human web."

In addition to widening the lens to attend to cultural and political realities, James Ashbrook (1996), Andrew Lester (2003), and David Hogue

(2003), for example, have opened the door for interdisciplinary work between theology, practices of care, and neuroscience. Alongside this growing complexity of sources and their relation, faculty and practitioners are more aware of the complex reciprocity of our personal, cognitive, spiritual, and social experience. Such awareness represents the influence of postmodern sensibilities such as a much greater appreciation for the perspectival character of knowledge and authority rather than universal absolutes, the highly relational, cultural, and political character of the self, and the significance of sociopolitical dynamics accompanying differences such as race, gender, and class.

Theology

At the time of the publication of the *Dictionary,* pastoral theology was described as being "in a time of uncertainty and ferment" (Burck & Hunter, p. 871). Questions were posed as to its viability as a discipline, whether its scope ought to be limited to the practice of care and counseling—a theology of care—or if it is more broadly a contextual theology done from a pastoral or caring perspective, that is, a theology of, for example, family, violence, hope. Now one could argue that this aspect of uncertainty is resolving toward the contextual theology definition given the operative definition in current literature.

The *Dictionary* rightly suggested that there will continue to be an ongoing need for reflection on the religious significance of human experiences that require care and that such reflection will rely on the sorts of emphases Protestant pastoral theology has brought historically to the, "interrelation of normative vision, concrete understanding of human beings, and practical wisdom about care" (Burck & Hunter, 1990, p. 872). These three categories do continue though they are significantly enriched by the critical postmodernity described elsewhere in this essay as relativizing norms, rendering human experience more complex relationally and politically, and expanding the cultural perspectives on care. Roman Catholic pastoral theology is more broadly focused by pastoral practice (Kinast, 1990), but it too has felt the effects of postmodernity and the need for more public and prophetic perspectives informing its pastoral theology.

Beginning with the midseventies, a very intentional reaction began against the well-documented psychological captivity of the field. That complaint is no longer justified though occasional illustrations of the uncritical embrace of psychology can be found. A now wider range of therapeutic sources represents a majority of the interdisciplinary partners in pastoral theological reflection. However, ordinarily, the methodological sophistication of such engagement is much improved. It is also common to find additional interdisciplinary resources for contextual analyses such as critical theory related to gender, race, or economics. As the field reclaimed the central role of theological reflection, the importance of attention to congregational contexts also increased. The influx of European American women and women and men of other racial and cultural heritages, especially African Americans, has helped increase attention to ecclesial concerns and practice (Greider, Johnson, & Leslie, 1999).

There is significant ferment in the range of theological categories addressed by pastoral theology and significant redefinition of more familiar theological categories. The redefinition going on with these paradigm shifts has included new interdisciplinary sources and relatively new areas of focus for pastoral theologians and practitioners such as violence; power; suffering, atonement, and theodicy; justice; religious pluralism; ritual; embodiment; ecclesiology; spirituality; and authority. Redefinition is also apparent in more familiar theological categories such as theological anthropology, hope, creation in the image of God, and forgiveness. These developments are addressed more fully in the related essay in this volume, but several will be explored briefly here as suggestive of these developments. Violence is a focus of pastoral theological investigation that has become prominent since the publication of the *Dictionary,* particularly with the advent of more women in the field. The focus on violence includes especially attention to various forms of intimate violence such as child sexual and physical abuse, domestic violence, and forms of rape. A number of persons have contributed to this focus such as Poling (1991, 1997, 1998), Eugene (1995), Poling and Eugene (1998), Cooper-White (1995, 2000), Neuger (2000, 2001), Leslie (2003), Ramsay (1991, 1998a, 1998b, 1999).

A brief summary of theological themes in these works suggests the ferment and redefinition in pastoral theology. Within these discussions one finds not only attention to therapeutic themes such as shame, developmental theory, and trauma theories, but also extended engagement with biblical and theological literature. Atonement theory is critiqued in favor of an understanding of God's power from the victim's perspective as compassion that empowers resistance and truth-telling. Similarly, the authors propose theodicies that better address the experience of the victim whose problem is not guilt but suffering as a result of another's sin as the abuse of power. Power, as anticipated in the *Dictionary* (Redekop 1990, pp. 931-934), is understood as potential for receiving as well as exercising influence. For example, these authors regularly bring liberative and process theology perspectives on creation in the image of God that propose relationality as essential in theological anthropology. Mutuality and relationality emerge as core normative principles for ethical pastoral practice and ecclesial life and witness. Relational justice is a normative vision lifted up from revised explorations of creation in God's image. It leads to expanded ethical assumptions for those who give care, and faith communities who need to stand with survivors of violence and advocate for justice in legal and governmental spheres. Forgiveness is reconsidered to take into account this recognition of ways asymmetries of power disclose the priority of accountability for perpetrators of violence. Hope is expanded to include the practices of resistance and empowerment. The range of revised and new theological and biblical proposals reflects pastoral theologians as contextually focused and generatively engaged with emerging biblical and theological scholarship as well as critically adapting current psychological theory and therapies. These sources certainly represent the field's historical concern for the needs of particular persons, but they also develop their analyses and proposals with a much wider frame in which to interpret those needs and propose effective strategies. These proposals do not apply theology to the practice of care nor do they limit the focus of pastoral theology to care for individuals. Rather, they offer theologically informed reflections on the complex contextual dynamics of violence and on the needs for care created by experiences of violence and develop their implications for practice.

Care for families is a concern that developed in diverse directions after the publication of the *Dictionary*. A majority of these sources illustrate a significant public theology component while also critically engaging ways that cultural norms sometimes undermined more faithful ecclesial care and life-giving forms of spirituality. Contributors such as Anderson et al. (1993a, 1993b, 1994, 1995, 1997), Couture (1991, 2000), Miller-McLemore (1994), Graham (1997), Marshall (1997), Browning et. al. (1997), Smith (1997), Wimberly (1997), Townsend (2000), and Butler (2000) represent a spectrum of methodology, sources, definitions of family, and definitions and goals for care. The two series represented in this list, for example, demonstrate well the widening scope of the field and the overlap that public theology themes for care create with practical theology. *Family Living in Pastoral Perspective,* edited by Herbert Anderson, who also was coauthor of each of the five books, is an excellent resource for pastors and other congregational caregivers. It draws on family life cycle developmental theory and family systems models for care principally with middle-class nuclear family structures. The series embraces themes familiar in North American culture such as individuation and autonomy correlated with theological themes of relational and congregational commitments of care. *The Family, Religion, and Culture* series funded by the Lilly Endowment and edited by Don Browning and Ian Evison, represents a wider ranging critical theological engagement with culture around issues of care for families. Like the Anderson series, it too presumes a context that is quite challenging for families and finally endorses a nuclear family structure. But this series represents the pastoral theology as public theology end of the continuum. In this series caregivers and persons in specialized ministries do not find specific clinical resources, but they do find careful analyses of stressors in the larger context that directly inform marital and parenting crises. Christian and Jewish sources are correlated with sociological, ethical, economic, political, critical gender, race, and culture theories, as well as psychological theory to generate a wide range of proposals regarding family life in the United States.

Miller-McLemore (1994) in *Also a Mother: Work and Family Life as Theological Dilemma* demonstrates a more focused constructive, critical theological engagement with the cultural dilemmas posed to families by traditional interpretations of gender roles for women as wives and mothers and those expected of husbands and fathers. Traditional interpretations of such doctrines as love, self-sacrifice, creation, vocation, and community are reworked in light of more liberative theological interpretations, sociological and political analysis, and critical theory. More of a pastoral theology as public theology resource, *Also a Mother* certainly makes a substantive contribution to Christian theological resources for families as theology done pastorally.

Care for different forms of family is also addressed by pastoral theologians. Larry Graham in *Discovering Images of God: Narratives of Care Among Lesbians and Gays* (1997) develops a public theology of care for gay and lesbian families that critiques and revises more traditional interpretations of creation in the image of God. Joretta Marshall in *Counseling Lesbian Partners* (1997) also critiques and revises more traditional public and Christian interpretations of marriage covenants. Marshall proposes specific strategies for pastoral care and counseling not only with lesbian partners, but for anyone who wishes to enter into covenanted relationships. In *Pastoral Care with Stepfamilies: Mapping the Wilderness* (2000), Loren Townsend broke new conceptual ground when he developed proposals for care with stepfamilies. Once again, we find some aspects of public theology as Townsend critiques and revises cultural norms as well as theological ones. Moreover, like Graham and Marshall, Townsend challenges congregations to care differently for an increasingly common family form.

Care for African American families and marriages represents a somewhat different pastoral theological strategy. Archie Smith, Jr., Edward P. Wimberly, and Lee Butler, Jr. each described the challenge for African American marriages and families in a culture where racism, violence, economic hardship, and spiritual impoverishment have become too common. All three authors critically engage the way racism undermines African American relationality and spirituality. Each also seeks to retrieve critical earlier insights that can serve African Americans well. They rightly acknowledge that while the focus of their work is on the experience of African Americans, their proposals are also more widely useful.

These two topics, care in response to violence and care for families, are suggestive of the kind of vitality and methodological creativity evident in current pastoral theology. It is well to identify some characteristics that regularly appear across diverse topics and methodologies. Typically faith contexts are presumed though not necessarily Christian ones. However, as illustrated above, authors critically engage ecclesial practices as well as norms and practices evident in secular spheres. Their goals for care include the practices and public witness of communities of faith as well as resources for those in specialized ministries. Occasionally, as with James Poling's *The Abuse of Power* (1991) or Bonnie Miller-McLemore's *Also a Mother* (1994), pastoral theologians develop constructive theological proposals that are deeply shaped by a pastoral perspective and contribute to strategies for care while also contributing to larger theological conversations. In most cases the authors cited here relied on more than psychological disciplines for the inter-disciplinary aspects of their work. Where therapeutic resources are cited, they represent theories that presume a relational and contextual identity. Christian tradition and scripture typically function normatively in theological resources developed by pastoral theologians since the publication of the *Dictionary.*

Trajectories

Throughout this essay I have described the *Dictionary* as "a hinge in time." It summarized the clinical pastoral paradigm and anticipated changes that were underway even as it was published in 1990. By the last decade of the twentieth century two new paradigms were emerging: the communal contextual paradigm in the U.S. and an intercultural paradigm that has been articulated within and well beyond the borders of the United States. As described in this essay these paradigms have occasioned considerable ferment because they require new sources, norms, interdisciplinary methods, practices, and training approaches. A variety of models are evolving within these paradigms. Their implications are startling including, for example, the need for a remarkably revised body of knowledge for practitioners and pastoral theologians. Competence to engage several psychological theories was once sufficient for effective care and counseling. Now competence in a much broader range of tools for contextual analysis is necessary.

Theological anthropology continues to be a significant theological theme and resource. However, as several of the essays that follow note, the self to whom we attend is conceived as necessarily relational and social so that analysis must include broader relational and public spheres. Both new paradigms deepen the complexity of honoring the differences in and continuities across human experience.

Both the communal contextual and intercultural paradigms disclose a significant shift in the way power is understood. They signal appreciation of a more dynamic and complex definition of power. It is explored as agency, as an intersubjective, dynamic reciprocity of influence, and functioning politically through privilege as well as marginalization and subordination. Similarly sweeping is the need for cultural competence that attends not only to racial, cultural, and religious difference, but also to critical self-awareness regarding the asymmetries of privilege.

The levels of redefinition carried by these two paradigms is suggested by an emerging identity issue for the field forced by both the economic pressures of managed care and the reality of increasingly plural understandings of religions and spiritual identity in the United States. For example, given the fact of an increasingly plural religious context in the U.S., is "pastoral" the best adjective to accompany care? As this essay suggested, there is considerable debate about alternatives such as spiritual care, religious care, soul care, and ministries of care. Currently ACPE has chosen to define itself as offering spiritual care with religious traditions being secondary to spirituality. AAPC has taken a different strategy of locating care for spiritual well-being within the practices and rituals of particular religious traditions. What approach is essential to secure the DNA of the field, as Roy Woodruff put it? Such pluralism also requires a very significant revision of seminary and graduate instruction where Christian norms are frequently presumed and function as the parameters of the field.

Care in the context of faith communities, relatively obscured by the professional focus of the clinical pastoral paradigm, is now receiving attention both for the resources needed by pastors such as brief therapy models and as the involvement of laity in care is reclaimed in care team models and other similar approaches. A dimension of this trajectory appears to be a renewed appreciation for the place of ecclesiology alongside the field's long-standing value for theological anthropology.

The influx into the field of pastoral care by European American women and women and men of other racial and cultural heritages and persons whose sexual orientation is not heterosexual has obviously contributed greatly to the changes described in this essay and elsewhere in this volume. However, in the years ahead it will be important to assure that the organizations helping to structure the field such as AAPC, ACPE, and SPT truly reflect a reordering of their norms and practices in light of the new ideas and processes these persons bring.

Both the communal contextual and intercultural paradigms envision a wider horizon for the practice of care. Yet, currently, training for care is largely defined by individual or systemic therapeutic models and congregational care models. Yet to be seen are models that conceptualize and guide training and assessment of practices such as advocacy for the public and political dimensions of care in relation to institutions that participate in the living human web.

Formation and Professional Identity

These various trajectories suggest an additional concern that is new to pastoral care. What professional identity do we seek to present to the public as theologians and practitioners of care? How can we honor religious pluralism and adequately represent the wisdom of particular traditions? In supervision and teaching, how will we help to form the self-understanding of students adequately for them to be able to engage multiple levels of difference effectively? Loren Townsend, for example, in his essay in this volume, notes that where clinical training centers once had to be certain students knew psychological theories, now their attention needs to assure adequate grounding in a theological worldview.

Currently, creative work is being done to assist this grounding that relies on skills related to empathy. In other words, it appears that models relying on moving from particularity to engage difference self-consciously will serve us well. This suggests, for example, that helping theologians and practitioners of care develop a sense of rootedness in a particular religious tradition, will assist them in building bridges to engage difference respectfully. As we've noted in this essay, African Americans such as Edward P. Wimberly, Archie Smith, Jr., Homer Ashby, and Lee Butler, Jr. are also proposing strategies that encourage self-conscious grounding of identity in the values and practices of particular ecclesial communities.

Another important formation strategy that is new to pastoral care could be described as *de-centering*. This strategy emerged with the recognition of the need to deconstruct patterns of privilege that were carried in the assertion of universal or absolute status for particular groups, worldviews, religions, and so forth. Now, for example men's experience is not typically considered normative. Similarly, when European American students become more self-aware of their particular racial and ethnic heritage and the dynamics of power related to that experience, they are more likely to be effective in embodying care and deconstructing racial and cultural barriers to care. This shift to self-critical awareness entails a de-centering of racial or cultural privilege that is internalized in racist cultures. The dominance of Christian values, norms, and practices in the field also suggests that the years ahead will necessarily involve developing much more self-awareness on the part of Christian theologians and practitioners. However this dominance has typically reflected a liberal Protestant perspective. Now de-centering needs to happen among Christians as well as between them and those who offer care from within other religious traditions. Such de-centering will require more generous engagement with differences among evangelical and more liberal Protestants and Roman Catholics as well as those differences that arise among Christians in various racial and cultural groups. It will also be important in order to assure both the adequate care of those whose religious experience is not Christian and the enrichment that mutual engagement with different religious traditions will bring.

At the close of this essay we find ourselves coming to terms with the complexity that is introduced by the scope of redefinition underway in the field of pastoral care. Not only has our focus widened so as to comprehend more fully the contextual realities of a social, cultural, and political self, our own self-understanding as pastoral theologians and caregivers must also reflect a similar complexity and range. Formation is at once more difficult and crucial.

CHAPTER 2

Pastoral Theology as Public Theology: Revolutions in the "Fourth Area"

Bonnie J. Miller-McLemore

Significant shifts in the subject matter of pastoral theology, care, and counseling have occurred in the United States in the last decade. Several years ago I described one of the notable changes as a move from "care narrowly defined as counseling to care understood as part of a wide cultural, social, and religious context" (1993, p. 367; 1996, p. 14; 1999, p. 13). Anton Boisen's wonderful 1950s metaphor of the "living human document" as a prime text has mutated into the "living human web." Pastoral theologians and counselors today are more accountable in study and practice to the political and social factors that impinge on people's lives on local and global levels than previous definitions of the field have acknowledged or allowed. Other scholars have also called attention to this development (Graham, L., 1992; Patton, 1993; Gill-Austern, 1995; Couture, 1996; and Louw, 2003). My own particular social location as a White mainstream Protestant educated at the University of Chicago in the 1980s especially provoked and reflects this change. Chicago has had a significant impact on the move of pastoral theology toward public theology, as has the liberation theology to which I turned when I began teaching in 1986 and found conventional pastoral resources ill equipped to understand women's plight in sexist societies.

The *Dictionary of Pastoral Care and Counseling* appeared on library shelves in 1990 after many years of organization just as pastoral theologians rounded the corner on this reorientation. The *Dictionary*'s only entry under "public" is "Public/Private Interface." And it simply tells readers to "*See* Personal, Sense of. *See also* Prophetic/Pastoral Tension in Ministry; Shame." The former describes the mid-twentieth-century pastoral care and counseling movement as focused on the personal. Pastoral theologians and counselors were distinguished by their close attention to an individual's "full uniqueness," made known through intimate, emotional self-disclosure. This emphasis diverts important attention away from the "public self" and its social responsibilities (Hunter, 1990b, p. 893). The entry on "Prophetic/ Pastoral Tension in Ministry" attempts to correct this powerful leaning toward individual subjective experience (Seifert, 1990, pp. 962-966). The pastoral should not be equated without remainder with the personal. But even here the focus is on the interdependence of "personal health and social improvement" and not yet upon pastoral counseling's public responsibilities or upon the ways in which the very core of the personal is socially constructed.

Rodney Hunter's editorial preface briefly notes that the *Dictionary* appears at a time of historical ferment. Major representatives of the field "have begun to advance new understandings" that challenge its "subjective individualism" as well as its "sexism, racism, psychologism, . . . clericalism, ahistoricism, and lack of moral and religious criticism" (1990a, p. xii). Indeed, the attention given to each of these concerns has stretched the field's horizons from a discipline centered primarily on individual well-being to one centered on the close connections between private and public. It is important to document the factors that have contributed to this transformation.

How has pastoral theology gradually shifted in the past two decades toward new subject matter and methods related to public theology? What distinctive contributions do pastoral theologians have to offer? And what does pastoral theology as public theology mean for the discipline's future and for theological education and the church more broadly speaking? This essay will begin the task of answering these questions, exploring factors that have ignited concern about public theology and examples of pastoral theology's reconceptualization as public theology. I will conclude by suggesting ramifications for pastoral care and formation.

"Public theology" is itself a phrase needing more explanation. In broad terms, "public theology" attempts to analyze and influence the wider social order. It has received considerable attention in the past two decades by a variety of theologians wanting to challenge religion's modern privatization and affirm its wider public relevance. Different from civil religion's generic universal appeal, public theology attempts to make a recognizably valid and self-critical claim for the relevance of specific religious beliefs and practices. The entire essay, especially the first section on the trends behind its pastoral emergence, traces ways in which those outside and within pastoral theology have redefined both public theology and the field itself. Many scholars to whom I refer, such as Paul Tillich, use the term "practical theology" more than "pastoral theology" to talk about the broad area in theological study that encompasses pastoral care, counseling, preaching, educating, and so forth and their academic disciplines, such as pastoral theology, homiletics, and religious education. This conventional definition of practical theology, however, has itself undergone revision in light of developments in public theology. Its mission now extends well beyond ministerial practices to theological engagement of public issues of significant practical and pastoral consequence, such as child welfare or economic justice.

My focus throughout is primarily on the United States. This does not mean that a similar movement of pastoral theology toward public theology is not occurring in other places around the world. Although space does not allow close examination of the latter, I will attempt to indicate critical places of intersection and parallel developments outside the United States.[1] There are also important intercultural differences in conceptualizing public theology that require more attention than I can give them. The United States context is especially shaped by divergent interpretations of the First Amendment's constitutional separation of church and state. Public theology looks different in other countries where religion is either established by the state (e.g., Britain) or disenfranchised (e.g., China). Moreover, whereas European practical theologians are troubled about Christianity's decline, many mainstream pastoral theologians in the United States worry more about the growth of conservative evangelical forms of Christianity. Even mainstream Christianity still does fairly well in some parts of the country, such as the South. An extensive religious pluralism, accentuated by the liberalization of immigration laws in the 1960s, also characterizes U.S. society. Although the dominant religion of the past—Christianity—professes to do and have a "theology," many dominant religions in other societies do not make such claims or seek a public theology.

Trends Behind the Push for Public Theology

Several economic, political, and cultural developments external to religious and theological studies have encouraged the development of public theology in the United States. On the economic front, major funding organizations, such as the Lilly Endowment, Pew Charitable Trusts, and Henry R. Luce Foundation, have made Christianity's public role a major initiative, supporting programs that have engaged significant public dilemmas, such as the family. These organizations have funded innumerable conferences, projects, publications, and university centers aimed at bridging academy, church, and the wider public around a number of pressing issues (see Miller-McLemore, 2000). In part, these foundations are concerned about the post–civil rights decline in Protestantism's social activism and, as troubling, the new Christian Rights' increased prominence and ability to influence society through large conglomerate operations. The desire is not for a return to mainline hegemony but for greater understanding of Christianity's proper role in public policy formation in an increasingly diverse and religiously plural society.

On a more political front, politicians and public intellectuals have renegotiated the delicate lines of state and church separation by proposing an enhanced role for "faith-based organizations" and "faith-based initiatives" supported by taxes to deliver social services. Moreover, some public spokespersons talk about the need to bring faith perspectives to bear on national moral issues, such as overcoming racism or strengthening the family, where government efforts have essentially failed. The expectation that religious communities might provide both service and values has increased pressure on theologians to reconsider religion's public role.

Finally, religion's de-privatization is also related to cultural shifts. Public intellectuals no longer have faith in the power of value-free science or even the state and the market to solve all dilemmas. Problems, such as the growing poverty of the Two-Thirds World and international interreligious conflict, call for serious deliberation. Instead of labeling particular religious beliefs as arbitrary, unimportant, or irrational, many people suggest that they now have a legitimate, even if necessarily delimited, place in public discourse and decisions (see Carter, 1994). New talk about "civil society" is not a return to a generic civil religion but a reclaiming of the importance of beliefs and practices in all their particularities. Public theology offers critical and constructive reflection upon the civil relevance of particular religions (see Cady, 1993, pp. 21-25).

While not usually acknowledged, dire pastoral needs stand behind the aspiration for public theology. As sociologist Robert Wuthnow remarks, the debate about religion and civil society is not so much about "preachers in politics or even about First Amendment freedoms; it is about the quality of social life itself" (1996, p. 2). The lure of public theology arises from deeper questions about how people with many differences and serious religious convictions can live together well in an increasingly perilous world. Christians, among other religious groups, face complex dilemmas as they attempt to live lives shaped by religious values. Dilemmas previously considered private and sometimes trivial, such as whether to get married and have children or how to dispose of one's trash, are now seen as having unavoidable national and even international implications. Religious leaders can no longer bracket pastoral needs from public consideration.

Theological trends internal to religion have also influenced pastoral theology toward public theology. In particular, debates between Chicago's David Tracy and Yale's George Lindbeck about Christianity's place in society have had a considerable role. Ronald Thieman, for example, pursued such questions to distinguish his position from the more sectarian approaches of Lindbeck and Stanley Hauerwas (Thieman, 1991, p. 12). He describes more than defines public theology as a theology "based in the particularities of the Christian faith while genuinely addressing issues of public significance" (p. 19). Victor Anderson condenses descriptions of Thieman, William Joseph Buckley, and Roger Shinn to characterize public theology as the "deliberate use of distinctively theological commitments to influence substantive public debate and policy" (1996, p. 20).

These wide-ranging definitions, however, could potentially refer to almost any socially conscious theological position, as the rest of Anderson's essay illustrates. My interest here is to focus on one place where the term got codified in the Chicago-Yale debate. In the debate, the Chicago school gets accused of compromising Christianity's distinctiveness in its revisionist efforts to participate in public deliberations. The Yale school, on the other hand, is charged with lacking a genuine public theology in its postliberal attempts to preserve the unique language and rules of the Christian narrative and community. Thieman and others, such as William Placher and David Kelsey, have responded to such allegations with their own versions of how a confessing Christian who takes Christianity as authoritative can effectively address political and social issues (Placher, 1985; Kelsey, 1990).

Several prominent scholars in the "Chicago school," such as Tillich, Tracy, James Gustafson, and Don Browning, influenced pastoral care and counseling toward public theology through their sway over doctoral students. They joined a gestalt of interest in the public church, public ministry, and public intellectuals among other early twentieth century Chicago scholars, such as Shailer Mathews, and more recent figures, such as Martin Marty (1981), Robin Lovin (1986), and Clark Gilpin (1990, 1996). Tillich's correlational method (1951) and his theology of culture had a fundamental impact through his influence on his Chicago colleague, Seward Hiltner, on Hiltner's students, such as Browning, and even on Browning's students, such as Pamela Couture and myself. More recently, Tracy's efforts to refine the correlational method and to assert the essential public responsibility of fundamental, systematic, and practical theology in an increasingly pluralistic world provided powerful impetus for pastoral theology to develop its public contributions (1981, 1983). Most pastoral theologians and counselors today employ some version of this liberal model, however modified by revisionist, liberation, or postmodern theology.

Liberal views of the public, however, came under attack by liberation theology. In Rebecca Chopp's words, "while liberal-revisionist theologians respond to the theoretical challenge of the nonbelievers among the small minority of the world's population who control the wealth and resources in history, liberation theologians respond to the practical challenge of the large majority of global residents who control neither their victimization nor their survival" (1987, pp. 121, 128). The public is no longer the modern scientific audience that worried Tillich or the scientifically disenchanted postmodern audience that plagues Tracy. Instead, liberation theologians address those previously marginalized, silenced, and erased from social history, political voice, and theological mediation.

Liberation theology began in the early twentieth century in Latin America as a Roman Catholic movement focused on liberating the poor from systematic economic exploitation and securing justice for the oppressed (Gutiérrez, 1973; Segundo, 1976; Boff & Boff, 1987). Since its inception, liberation theory has been taken up by Protestants, the women's movement, black power consciousness-raising, German critical theory, and others around the world and applied to many kinds of social oppression besides poverty, such as racism, sexism, heterosexism, and colonialism. It seeks to free or liberate those who suffer from social inequities and oppression not merely through discourse but through practical grassroots strategies for social structural change. Problems previously defined along private lines as signs of personal weakness and moral turpitude such as drugs, alcoholism, depression, poor academic performance, and even failed marriages or delinquent children, are redefined in broader public and political terms as a result of unjust patriarchal social structures and racist ideologies. Recent feminist, post-structuralist, and postmodernist theory takes the premise that the "personal is political" to a new level: The personal is not only political, it is socially constructed. That is, power relationships in history and society construct the self. Theologians must take seriously the social location of the self, the ways language constructs reality, and the impact of power on language and subjectivity.

While the Chicago school affected central pastoral theologians who came within its orbit, liberation theology's transformation of pastoral theology was more widespread. Few, if any, contemporary pastoral theologians or counselors have escaped its impact. Although the influences on pastoral theology are many, liberation theology helped transform pastoral theology toward public theology by identifying the ways in which society indelibly constructs selfhood in oppressive ways, by redefining the nature of the public, and by demanding a prophetic reorientation toward it.

Developments in Pastoral Theology

Different Representations of the Changes

Pastoral theologians have described the development of pastoral theology as public theology in different ways. In 1993, in an introductory overview John Patton announced a "paradigm shift" (pp. 4-5). Prior to the mid-twentieth century, pastoral theology adhered to a "classical paradigm" that, as Hunter puts it, "concentrated primarily and often exclusively on the gospel message" (2001, p. 20). Clergy diagnosed problems in religious terms and responded with Christian solutions, often relying on rituals, such as prayers, the laying on of hands, or confession and absolution of sins.

Both the "clinical pastoral" and the "communal-contextual paradigms" have appeared in the last half-century, each one representing what Patton sees as a major redefinition of focus and method. The clinical paradigm that arose midcentury and shaped the *Dictionary* drank deeply from the wells of modern psychology, using its insights into emotional dynamics and its therapeutic techniques to shape a new kind of spiritual care attentive to the inner needs of individuals in crisis. Diagnosis relied heavily upon psychological categories, amended with theological reflection, and solutions almost always included some kind of empathic listening, however modified by more directive techniques.

The most critical aspect of the new communal-contextual paradigm, according to Patton, is its fresh commitment to the community rather than the pastor or pastoral counselor as the heart of pastoral care. The audience is "no longer . . . the male clergyperson of European ancestry." Both clergy and laity—" 'all sorts and conditions' of God's people"—offer care in a variety of contexts and Christian communities (p. 3). Pastoral care has yet to tap the community's rich resources, according to Brita Gill-Austern. She uses the metaphor of web to describe the importance of nurturing the interconnections or the "ecology of care" within congregations (1995, p. 234). Pastoral theologians in non-Western contexts have long recognized the significance of the community in care giving (see Lartey, 1987; Wicks & Estadt, 1993; Wilson, Poerwowidagdo, Mofokeng, Evans, & Evans, 1996). Conferences overseas in the last decade have actually convinced scholars in the U.S. about this.

In contrast to Patton and Gill-Austern, I use the image of the web to depict a major change in the field as a whole, and I describe that change in terms of a modification in primary subject matter from the "living human document" to "living human web" (1993, 1996). My focus is less on who offers care (clergy or laity) or how care is offered (hierarchically or collaboratively) and more on what care involves today. Genuine care now requires understanding the human document as necessarily embedded within an interlocking public web of constructed meaning. Clinical problems, such as a woman recovering from a hysterectomy or a man addicted to drugs, are always situated within the structures and ideologies of a wider public context and never purely interpersonal or intrapsychic. Where Patton credits Vatican II and ecumenism as major factors broadening pastoral care's context, I see liberationist perspectives as more instrumental. Criticism of pastoral care's individualism and the necessity of confronting systems of domination have come largely from feminist, black, and more recently, Asian, Latino/a, and African theologies. To think about pastoral care from this perspective requires prophetic, transformative challenge to systems of power, authority, and domination that continue to violate and oppress individuals and communities nationally and internationally (Graham, L., 1992; Pattison, 1994; Couture & Hunter, 1995; Graham, E., 1996; Poling, 1991, 1996; Neuger, 1996; Lartey, 1997; Ackermann & Bons-Storm, 1998; Miller-McLemore & Gill-Austern, 1999).

Pastoral theology brought to theory-bound doctrinal theology a wealth of vivid, concrete human experiences through a new tool. The case study or verbatim, developed in clinical programs mid-twentieth century shaped by the medical and social sciences, focused closely on particular interchanges and emotional, theological dynamics between and internal to an individual and a caregiver. Even today one rarely finds pastoral theological reflection that does not include some kind of "case" material. What has changed, however, is the way in which the case is understood, analyzed, and positioned. Pastoral theologians now work hard to locate material publicly, as part of a wider social and cultural web.

In 1992, Couture also described a new "social ecological foundation" for pastoral care and counseling which positions personal suffering within its wider "web" and Larry Graham called for a new "psychosystems approach" to replace what he named the previous "existential-anthropological mode." He saw in the latter a progressively "widening split between care of persons and care of the larger environments in which persons live" (p. 12). In addition to liberation theology, he finds family systems theory and process theology suggestive. Just as liberation theology contends that troubled persons, families, and groups reflect serious problems in the cultural context, so also does family systems therapy argue that individual symptoms are simply signs of serious dysfunction in the larger family social system.

Couture worries in particular about the individualistic premises that almost completely determine economic and political policy. She finds expertise in public policy, history, and particular religious traditions requisite for adequate publicly oriented pastoral theology. In her words, "to offer adequate care beyond the 1990s we will want to become as expert about public policies affecting the family and health as we are about the workings of various personality types" (1996, p. 103). Nothing less than a reformulation of the "basic commitments of our discipline" is needed (Couture, 1996, p. 103). When pastoral theology attempts to engage the "social context, economics, cultural meanings and practices" in its understandings of pastoral care, it has affinity with other kinds of public theology (Graham, 2000, pp. 6, 9).

Historical Complications

Every historical typology has the danger of oversimplification. Pastoral theology and care has never been quite as individualistically or personally focused as often portrayed. Historian E. Brooks Holifield's frequently cited history (1983), for example, depicts the discipline's development primarily along one declining trajectory—the widely lamented growth in American individualism. Anxieties about the church's love affair with psychology and counseling led him to characterize the field as evolving from an emphasis on salvation in the pre-modern world to a modern obsession with self-realization. Yet even the early twentieth-century pastoral care movement held other social and religious commitments in tension with psychology. Moreover, a great deal has transpired since he completed the book. His otherwise well-documented history positions women, slaves, and "others" primarily as the objects of care, rarely as caregivers, and seldom as the source of new ideas. Many pastoral theologians and counselors have been attracted to new psychologies that are not inevitably individualistic even if focused on the individual, as evident, for example, in family systems theory, feminist psychology, or theories of selfhood in object relations.

One could even argue that the original turn to psychology by pastoral theologians included a public dimension. As Hunter notes, "pastoral counseling represents a profoundly important expression of the liberal churches' social mission" (2001, 2003). By this, he means that pastoral counselors opened their doors as inclusively as possible. Pastoral counseling "reaches persons who might otherwise not venture near a church or pastor," and who might benefit from religious wisdom without the fear of "proselytizing or moralistic judgment" (p. 23). Most counseling centers began as ecumenical ventures and still pride themselves on their receptivity of believers and nonbelievers. While indiscriminant tolerance loses sight of specific Christian beliefs, this does not negate the ideal of public service and witness with which many centers began.

Hunter's positive assessment of the therapeutic tradition's public inclination is quite different from Holifield's. Hunter argues that a social concern about the destructive nature of a highly industrialized society motivated the pastoral movement from the beginning, partly through the influence of the Frankfurt School of social theory. The movement changed the previously narrow pastoral focus on individual moral behavior into a wholistic view of healing that involves persons' needs in their totality (1995, p. 20). Chaplains were actually uniquely positioned to offer a prophetic critique of modern medical establishments "from within" (p. 22). And they realized a level of public cooperation with other health professionals that challenged the modern specialization of health care long before medicine's recent fascination with spirituality. The movement also made a prophetic social demand on churches to engage more authentically as a community. Indeed, "when done artfully," therapeutic intervention enhances a person's public moral capacities and self-examination. Therapeutic confrontation itself can be "a powerful and significant moral practice" (p. 25).

By the early 1980s, Edward Wimberly and Archie Smith had already made a clear case for the communal and public nature of pastoral care (Wimberly, 1979) and the inextricable connection of social ethics and psychological therapy in the Black church (Smith, 1982). Perhaps ahead of his time, Smith testifies powerfully to the ways in which the social oppressions of racism create personal suffering and call for care that involves social activism. And Wimberly's *Dictionary* essay on Black American pastoral care reminds readers that it has had a long commitment to attending to "social structures and conditions" and to the "corporate" dimensions of both church and wider society (1990, pp. 93-94).

As these observations indicate, the history of pastoral theology as public theology is more complex than one might guess initially. One might even argue, as does Couture, "twentieth-century education in pastoral care had its roots in the social gospel, and after intense work on various forms of personal relationships in the decades after World War II, has made natural strides toward returning to that heritage" (2001, p. 161). An edited volume, *Pastoral Care and Social Conflict,* makes precisely this point. The "core identity" of the field lies in the ways in which "its twin emphases on persons *and* society . . . inform theology" (Couture, 1995, p. 13, emphasis in the text). Current problems sustaining a public voice for pastoral theology go right back to the bifurcation of an effort that, with Walter Rauschenbusch's immersion in New York soup kitchen ministry, once joined social ethics and pastoral care as two sides of the same coin.

Whether this return to the social gospel is as "natural" or as steady as Couture hopes waits to be seen. Some of the difficulty has to do with a tension notable from the beginning between those who supported the development of pastoral counseling as a specialized ministry, such as Carroll Wise and Howard Clinebell, and those who thought this was fraught with problems. Both Hiltner and Wayne Oates disagreed strongly with pastoral counseling as a "private" practice. Instead, they insisted it remain located within the church and refused to join in the formation of the American Association of Pastoral Counselors (AAPC) in 1963 (Holifield, 1990, p. 848).

Oates and others protested the medical or clinical model of intervention precisely on the grounds that it distorted the intricate relationship between private and public. It placed undue blame on the individual rather than seeing symptoms as a "magnifying glass for the sickness of a community as a whole" (1974, p. 163). Personal needs arose precisely out of some kind of public failure. In fact, pastors who do counseling stand in a unique position. They have " 'a microscopic lab report' on the massive social injustices that need changing" (p. 160). Moreover, church structures provide the corporate means and position to initiate public transformation. The very nature of ordination "rules out the luxury of a *purely* private ministry that ignores society [and] removes the distinctly prophetic element from the counseling" (p. 21, emphasis in text). Perhaps more needs to be done to recover some of these initial inclinations in the field toward public theology.

Pastoral Theology Turns Public

This interest in retrieval of public dimensions itself, however, is what makes the contemporary situation distinctive. Figures like Oates still regarded clinical training as one of their mainstays. Broadly speaking, two primary factors distinguish the most recent move toward public theology: concern about the public silence of mainstream Christianity on key social issues and awareness of the serious limitations of the pastoral focus on the individual alone. Recent pastoral theologians and counselors have attempted to shape public discourse on a wide range of dilemmas that have critical social and political implications, such as health care, the family debate, welfare policy, Western economic imperialism, and domestic violence. This shift in focus goes against the grain of the stereotypical understanding of pastoral care and counseling as merely focused on personal, spiritual care of parishioners and of practical theology as only knowledgeable about clerical skills.

Explicit ideas about pastoral theology as public theology made their way into the field initially through Browning. Both his earlier work (1976) and a later publication (1983a) position pastoral care as a ministry of the church within the world. In the former, Browning actually says pastoral care has become "impaled" upon the division between "private and public" in its focus on personal problems without "sensitivity to . . . larger social-ethical questions" (p. 17). Restricting pastoral care to assistance to individuals in crisis fails to socialize believers to particular understandings of the church, and, most important for this essay, ignores the critical task of interpreting modern culture and articulating a social ethic relevant to public problems (p. 21).

Perhaps more influential than James Gustafson's advocacy of secular sciences in understanding the church was his portrayal of the church as a "community of moral discourse" (1970, pp. 83-97), a phrase Browning adopts as his own in his claim that pastoral theology is responsible for public moral understandings. For Browning, pastoral care occurs as part of the church's dialogical mission related to both faith and society. It is not simply care of persons but also must involve care of systems as well as attention to the dominating public or cultural constructions of care.

This stance evolved in response to two problems—pastoral restriction to what Farley called the "clerical paradigm" (or pastoral care defined around the skills of individual clergy) (1983a, p. 26; 1983b, p. 85) and pastoral substitution of psychology for theology. A pastoral theology whose subject matter includes "more encompassing social systemic and policy issues in care" broadens the range of pastoral care to the "care of the congregation and the care of the laity, both for one another within the congregation and for the world around the congregation." It requires skills not just in facilitating care within the local church but also in creating strategies to shape society and culture (Browning, 1987b, pp. 14-15; see also 1983, p. 19; 1988, pp. 103-118).

The pastoral task with regard to the world is twofold. In the manner of a good theology of culture, it involves discerning the quasi-religious norms and assumptions behind all acts of care, pastoral and secular alike. Second, it requires articulating alternative public norms derived from the Christian tradition. The task here is not just "to state the norms . . . for the faithful (although certainly for them), but also to determine whether these norms have general public meaning, that is, whether they have general significance even for those who are not explicitly Christian" (Browning, 1983b, pp. 194-195).

Although this shows the influence of the Chicago school, Browning largely fails to credit liberation theology. In Romney Moseley's *Dictionary* entry on liberation theology and pastoral care, he succinctly captures the change it inspires:

> From a liberationist's perspective one should conceive of pastoral care fundamentally as the care of society itself. That is, one should understand the needs and hurts of individuals in their primary relationships—the primary focus of pastoral care and counseling—in terms of the macrosocial power relationships of domination and exploitation. For these larger relationships structure selfhood, personal experience, and individual behavior in fundamental, if usually unrecognized, ways. Thus pastoral care must always

engage in a mutually critical conversation with theological and social scientific methods informed by an emancipatory praxis. (1990, p. 646)

Even though Moseley's article and a few others on feminist and black theology appear in the *Dictionary*, the volume reflects an assimilation mentality characteristic of early stages of consciousness-raising in general. It insightfully includes new voices, inviting a number of African American men and European American women to contribute articles on race and gender with the hope of fostering greater interest in and attention to these issues. But by and large pastoral theologians could not foresee the major conceptual redefinition of pastoral theory that has occurred since the *Dictionary*'s publication, particularly in regard to its public responsibilities posed by particular marginalized groups. The allure of the clinical pastoral method tended to obscure the emerging significance of these other movements and newer literatures.

A great deal has happened under liberation theology's influence that goes beyond the public theology of most pre-1985 texts, as the next section will demonstrate. Today most pastoral theologians recognize problems of sexism and racism as a central consideration in conceptualizations of pastoral care. In an impressive survey of women's contributions over the past four decades, Kathleen Greider, Gloria Johnson, and Kristen Leslie, in fact, contend that women "contributed precisely and significantly" to the evolution of the new contextual communal paradigm. Under this fresh rubric, pastoral theologians give more attention "to caring communities and the impact of context on human experience and care" than in the typical clinical pastoral psychology of the 1970s and 1980s (1999, p. 22). But more important for public theology, women address the *ekklesia,* the human community in God writ-large, as distinct from the institutional church. That is, women are more prone to address "more culturally diverse 'congregations' . . . beyond the walls of church buildings," such as hospices, hospitals, prisons, and universities. They attempt to bring Christian ideas into public deliberation over such issues as service, covenant, ritual, and the common good (pp. 27-28).

Beyond the United States, others argue for similar changes in language, pastoral identity, and action. Danilo and Valburga Streck assert that within the incredibly diverse mosaic that shapes the heritage of those in Latin America, pastoral theologians have a mandate to create social solidarity among those excluded from political, economic, and religious power (2002). Similarly, British pastoral theologian Steven Pattison claims that only a "socio-politically aware and committed pastoral care" can liberate the field from its "therapeutic captivity" (1994, p. 221). Dutch pastoral theologian Riet Bons-Storm and South African pastoral theologian Denise Ackermann presume that social analysis of the construction of gender is absolutely necessary for adequate pastoral care. In many of the chapters in their edited book, this leads almost inevitably to concerns about corporate justice and communal action (1998, p. 5). And John Redwood contends that pastoral care in the Caribbean must attend to economic pressures and take an active stand against insidious capitalistic greed and hopelessness in the face of poverty (2000).

New Subject Matters of Public Relevance

Pastoral theology as public theology has appeared most distinctively around prominent public issues that have irrevocable pastoral dimensions. Although the issues are many, I mention briefly three prominent concerns as examples: violence, families, and public health. Pastoral theologians have played a public role in reshaping understandings of sexual violence as not simply a personal or familial issue but also a social and religious matter. It has little to do with sexual desire and everything to do with destructive perversion of social power as a consequence of sexist and racist ideologies and institutions (Ramsay, 1991; Lebacqz & Barton, 1991; Fortune & Poling, 1994; Adams & Fortune, 1995). James Poling's work on abuse nicely illustrates the transformation (1991). Repeatedly, he uses the phrase "personal, social, and religious" to describe the necessary scope of pastoral work. He, along with the considerable efforts of Marie Fortune and others, have helped institute regular programs of education and policy formation that have raised the consciousness of the wider public.

Poling names this pastoral issue a specifically public and theological problem closely related to Christian views of sacrifice, God's omnipotence, human impotence, and women's necessary submission. Moreover, pastoral theology must give public voice to those least heard. Indeed, "those with the least power can reveal the most" (p. 14)—a major premise from which Poling has not wavered as he has ventured into explorations of the evils of racism and market capitalism (1996, 2002). Pastoral care then requires responding on each of these public levels. It must challenge public ideals and structures, listen to those publicly silenced, and reconstruct religious beliefs and practices that perpetuate major social problems, such as racism, sexism, and economic exploitation.

The ideology of the family as a private, patriarchal institution has contributed significantly to the problem, hiding abuse from public view. Other pastoral theologians have answered the call of Poling for a "reformulated family mythos" that establishes the equality between the sexes and the rights of children (1991, p. 133). Couture's (1991, 2000) and my own work on mothers and children (1994, 2003) and our joint research on the family along with Browning, project director of a major Lilly Grant on Religion, Culture, and Family offer another important instance of pastoral theology going public. On each account—with mothers, fathers, children, and families—the case is made that Christianity has a formative role to play in shaping public discourse and policy.

The family project involved cross-disciplinary conversations between those in pastoral theology and scholars from historical, ethical, systematic, and biblical disciplines and the publication of a series of books geared to a wider public audience. The capstone volume of the initial grant, *From Culture Wars to Common Ground* (Browning et al., 1997), authored by five pastoral theologian all schooled at Chicago, draws on the other books to develop a publicly and pastorally sensitive evaluation of and response to contemporary family dilemmas. As with violence, families are understood in "psychocultural-economic" terms. They are not just psychological realities based on human needs or private interests grounded in individual freedoms. They are cultural, religious, and economic institutions with wide-ranging public ramifications. Consequently, the book considers a diversity of public voices that have dominated the family debate. And the concluding chapter articulates not only what churches can do internally to strengthen families but what they must do in the realm of public policy, such as advocating for family-friendly workplace policy or critiquing distorted media images.

To make a public difference, one can distance but not remove particular Christian claims, such as equal regard as part of God's covenant love for creation, from their specific Christian location. The goal at its broadest level is to "define the role of religion" in "America's struggle to strengthen its families" (p. viii). More specifically, the book attempts to fashion a new public family ethic of equal regard or mutuality that has relevance not only for confessing Christians but also for wider society at a time of great cultural need. It is not triumphalist about Christianity's virtues—at best "'a treasure in earthen vessels.'" But Christianity, carefully reinterpreted, does have distinctive contributions to make to public ideals of democracy within families (p. 3). Lifting up its gifts to believers and nonbelievers alike does not require finding generally agreeable truths that just happen to correspond with the Bible or whittling down religious convictions to a generic love or justice. Rather, one mines the richness of particular Christian attempts to understand love to determine what, if anything, they might add in all their specificity to the greater good. In fact, the hope is to contribute to a religious and cultural revolution on par with past social revolutions with which Christianity had a major role (p. 25; see also Pasewark & Paul, 1999, p. 306, footnote no. 97). As reiterated boldly in an appendix to the second 2000 edition, ultimately the book tries to "overcome the marginalization of Christian theology in public discourse" and establish the value of Christian norms (2000, p. 341).

Finally, as a last and significant example, a great deal has happened in healthcare to propel pastoral care and counseling into public theology. Pastoral counseling's presence has changed dramatically in the last ten years in terms of both its public prominence and its health policy activities. As Roy Woodruff, fifteen-year executive director of AAPC, remarked in personal conversation, "Five or six years ago, I had to explain pastoral counseling and AAPC. I virtually never have to do so anymore" (personal communication, July 18, 2002).

Rather than distinguishing pastoral and secular counseling, Woodruff now spends more time clarifying the difference between the interfaith efforts of pastoral counseling and the more conservative, biblically literalist, evangelistic perspective of the newly formed American Association of Christian Counselors. At this point, pastoral counseling's looser organizational church connections—something about which Hiltner and others originally worried—have proved an advantage. The wider public appreciates pastoral counseling and the AAPC precisely because of its recognition of diversity and its efforts to inform rather than convert the public to any particular Christian position.

A major turning point came with the Clinton administration's efforts to reform the United States health care system in the early 1990s. It drew pastoral counselors and their representatives onto public roads previously less traveled. AAPC and pastoral counseling are now regularly recognized simply because representatives showed up for meetings and kept showing up. Differently from even a few years ago, when national tragedies and issues arise, such as September 11 or the sexual abuse scandal in the Catholic Church, AAPC responds with public pronouncements and receives phone calls from news organizations for comment and reflection.

A prime motivation for showing up on Capital Hill was to establish pastoral counselors as recognized health care providers. To garner additional support for its proposal that pastoral counselors be included in Medicare's roster of approved caregivers, AAPC commissioned a national political survey of one thousand likely voters. Following up on a 1992 Gallup Poll, Greenberg Quinlin Research asked respondents about the connections between their religious beliefs and counseling. Results revealed not only clear affirmation of the links but also confirmed that a high percentage of respondents "would prefer to seek assistance from a mental health professional who recognizes and can integrate spiritual values into the course of treatment" (Greenberg Quinlin Research, 2000). More people choose pastoral counselors and others with religious training than any other type of counselor.

Whereas AAPC had no representatives on the Hill when the *Dictionary* appeared, today lobbying efforts have become a prime responsibility. Regular legislative consultation occurs between pastoral counseling representatives, legal advocates, and members of Congress. Pastoral counselors attempt to influence health care spending in faith-based initiatives, working, for example, to obtain a counseling training grant for minority persons. Other efforts in public theology have arisen at the state level with the growth of managed care. Pastoral counselors have sought licensure and third party payments as a profession with comparable credentials to other recognized clinicians. Perhaps most symbolic of the overall change, pastoral counseling appeared for the first time in the government publication of *Mental Health, the United States, 2002* alongside other mental health professionals (see http://www.mentalhealth.org/cmhs/ MentalHealthStatistics/default.asp).

Changes in chaplaincy are a bit less dramatic, perhaps because chaplains have had a longer-standing investment in public issues related to health care than pastoral counselors. There are, however, still markers of advances in public theology and recognition. For the first time in the late-1980s and early 1990s, the Joint Commission on the Accreditation of Healthcare Organizations (JCAHO) required institutions to establish that they care for patients' spiritual needs. Current lobbying efforts on the part of Association of Clinical Pastoral Educators (ACPE), in fact, concern exactly how this requirement can be met. According to Teresa Snorton, executive director of ACPE, they hope to get JCAHO to specify clinically trained individuals as providers (personal communication, August 1, 2002). Similarly, in recent years ACPE has worked with Medicare to establish clinical pastoral education as equivalent to medical residency in providing care and with the federal Health Care Financing Administration (HCFA) to specify pastoral care as a reimbursable expense. In a final ruling in 2001 after a nearly two decades long governmental process, including debate about the separation of church and state, the HCFA named clinical pastoral education and pastoral counselors as allied health care professionals and included them in allowable Medicare costs.

Recently, the five largest chaplaincy organizations worked together on a document that establishes chaplaincy's role and importance in public health care (Vandercreek & Burton, 2001). The paper draws on empirical studies to demonstrate the health-related benefits of religious practices and the positive difference of professionally trained chaplains. There are also changes in the ways chaplains interact with the public. With the relatively new recognition of palliative care's significance, physicians and others have become more receptive to the religious care offered by chaplains. The *Journal of Pastoral Care* regularly features essays deliberating on the legal, political, and moral implications of such dilemmas as assisted suicide, withholding nutrition and hydration, AIDS, and hospice care.

Growing public interest in spirituality opens up doors to chaplains. Some have begun to use the terminology of spiritual, religious care rather than pastoral to describe their work, not as a cheap imitation of popular trends but to make it more accessible to the wider public. Pastoral care is often equated with particular traditions whereas spiritual care is more inclusive of diverse perspectives (see Anderson, 2001; VanKatwyk, 2002). Of course, this change in terminology is not without its hazards and problems. Sensitivity to other religious cultures, for example, requires knowledge and training. Eclectic spirituality often ignores to its detriment the value of specific institutional commitments, religious communities, and particular traditions and rituals. Nonetheless, the use of the term "spiritual" care signals a move toward a more inclusive, publicly accessible activity than "pastoral" care, which has traditionally been associated primarily with ordained Christian ministry.

Implications for Pastoral Care, Counseling, and Formation

What are some of the specific implications of these moves toward public theology for the practice of pastoral care and counseling and the formation of its practitioners? With the "living human web," on what or whom does the caregiver focus—the person or the web? Scholars in the field have not wholly resolved this question. For several decades, pastoral theologians have learned well how to teach students about personal interventions in the midst of pastoral crises. Pastoral theology has spawned congregational programs focused almost entirely on individual care, such as Stephen Ministries or Parish Nursing. Such programs consume significant resources to reach a relatively small population in need. They do not do much at a public level, such as challenging God imagery that perpetuates abuse or addressing harmful health and welfare policies.

Learning how to intervene pastorally on a congregational, social, or cultural level now needs the same kind of extended attention, discussion, and programmatic strategizing. It will require closer allegiance with other areas of study, such as social ethics, and investment in other forms of practice, such as public networking or community action. Ministers will now have to know how to analyze communal resources, enter and organize communities for action, and balance ministry to individuals in crisis and social advocacy (see McWilliams, 1996 as an excellent example).

This presents new challenges in pastoral formation, adding to the already demanding need to understand intrapsychic and interpersonal dynamics the need to understand social location and identity, political policies, and public responsibilities. Emmanuel Lartey's "intercultural approach" nicely illustrates this new attempt to bridge the wisdom in both "private care" or individual counseling and "public struggle" or social liberation praxis as the two crucial bookends to adequate pastoral care (1997, pp. 103-104). Distinct from pre-1990 texts that focused almost solely on the former, he spends time exploring alternative methods that require pastoral engagement in concrete experiences with the poor, situational analysis, and social transformation. Nancy Ramsay's work on systemic White complicity in endemic racism also reflects this shift in focus and method. Identifying and resisting collusion on individual, institutional, and cultural levels is a moral mandate within the classroom, requiring a second look at curricula and syllabi, a rigorous investigation of one's own racial and cultural history, and a good grasp of social analysis and models of antiracist action (2002, pp. 24-25).

Clinical supervision and training programs certified by AAPC, ACPE, and other bodies will now have to consider such methods as part of clinical training and determine new means by which to encourage and assess self-awareness of social location and social identity. Pastoral identity now involves more than intrapsychic awareness, psychological insight, and religious inter-pretation. It demands cultural and political sensitivity, social activism, understanding of the congregation as a social institution, and faithful, some-times prophetic, convictions.

Close work with the individual continues; the individual is simply under-stood in new, possibly more complex ways. Psychology and counseling remain significant, but their singular status has changed. Most pastoral the-ologians today believe that pastoral caregivers must add to their repertoire other disciplines, such as political science, economics (e.g., Couture, 1991), sociology (e.g., Furniss, 1992, 1994), and feminist theory (e.g., Miller-McLemore, 1994, 1999). These other bodies of knowledge help disclose not just how individuals function but how congregations and the wider public shape individuals. Affecting public rhetoric and policy issues that determine the health of the human web is as important as addressing impediments to individual emotional well-being. This broadens the scope of pastoral respon-sibility and action beyond its conventional boundaries of individual coun-seling and personal care to the public arena.

Redefinition of pastoral theology as public theology also means new delineation of pastoral care's central functions of healing, sustaining, guid-ing as defined by Hiltner (1958) and then refined by William Clebsch and Charles Jaekle to include reconciling (1983). Certainly emphasis on individ-ual healing, sustaining, guiding, and reconciling still stands as critical to good pastoral care. But again and again, in publications over the last decade one hears new phrases that point toward a different set of priorities with greater public ramifications: resisting, empowering, and liberating.

Resistance, empowerment, and liberation all entail a deconstruction of limited definitions of reality and a reconstruction of new views of the world and one's valued place within it. While these new functions do not replace the prior ones or exhaust the implications of pastoral theology as public theology, they provide a good sense of the direction toward which pastoral theology as public theology points caregivers. These functions provide alter-native means to achieving healing, guidance, sustenance, and reconciliation that require fresh public understanding and response.

Carroll Watkins Ali was among the first to argue explicitly that previous metaphors are inadequate when considered within the African American context. It is almost ridiculous to talk about sustenance when many poor Black women face more serious questions of sheer survival. And reconcilia-tion as previously understood ignores core questions of public compensation for and correction of racism's injustices. Pastoral care aimed at reconciling individuals is "premature and futile until the inequities between Blacks and Whites have been removed" and the dominant culture finds a way to acknowledge and atone for the "dehumanizing injustices" of the "last four hundred years" (Watkins Ali, 1999, p. 55). Individual healing cannot take place until, as Wimberly said more than two decades ago, it "takes place in the structure of the total society" (1979, p. 21).

Other pastoral theologians have made similar claims more recently in pastoral situations of sexual abuse, domestic violence, and depression. With abuse, rushed forgiveness short circuits recovery and avoids the inevitable rage that deserves recognition. Effective pastoral care must "be broader than care for those immediately affected" (Ramsay, 1991, p. 121). In depression, "cultural and theological messages of worthlessness and weakness need to be dispelled" (Neuger, 1991, p. 158). And for the battered woman, the "basic need is empowerment" (Garma, 1991, p. 136). While these are only examples, they represent the public language that has grown common in pastoral scholarship of the last decade. It is rare to find an article today that does not refer to social advocacy or to a common range of interventions that involve greater reach than individual counsel, such as "breaking the silence" within congregations and beyond, active confrontation of abusive behavior, false stereotypes, and unjust situations, public education, support groups, preaching on hard biblical passages that deal with these issues (e.g., the rape of Tamar), and more conscientious pastoral use of ritual and liturgy in public situations as far-ranging as those of abuse, divorce, and child-rearing.

Pastoral work on new public fronts alters its position in what has been narrowly conceived as the theological school's "fourth area." As defined by nineteenth-century theologian Friedrich Schleiermacher in his attempt to make a place for Christian theology in the modern university, the first area is Bible. Many schools in the United States, including the one in which I teach, began as Bible schools. The typical curriculum adds Christian history and systematic theology as areas two and three. In some university settings where it is difficult to legitimize doctoral studies in religion, the "fourth area," with its greater proximity to the church, is the first to drop out. Even in self-standing seminaries, all three areas are commonly considered prior to and more fundamental than the fourth area which is, despite a couple of decades of protest, still often characterized as the application of what is learned in the other three arenas to ministerial practice. As a rule, pastoral theologians have not been happy with this designation, especially when it implies marginalization, devaluation, and trivialization and ignores the theological construction that occurs within pastoral theology. Asserting the public value of pastoral insights—pastoral theology as public theology—participates most immediately in the protest against such misunderstandings.

Many implications of this shift remain to be seen over the course of the next decade. While some of the *Dictionary*'s articles reflect initial hints of the changes described in this chapter, significant developments have occurred since its publication that reflect broader trends in society at large. Today, changes in the cultural climate, as illustrated by the increased receptivity to spirituality as a part of health, have opened up new public space for pastoral care and counseling. Pastoral theology remains accountable to particular persons in need. But now it involves analyzing power and social constructions of selfhood, giving public voice to the socially marginalized, and arguing for alternative theological understandings of the social context as essential for adequate care not only in congregations but also in society at large. Its unique contribution to public theology will lie precisely in its ability to use what it knows best—intimate understanding of individual religious experience and its religious significance—to shape wider public policies and ideals.

Note

1. For further investigation of the trends in U.S. theology that have influenced this conceptualization of pastoral theology, see an essay that builds on this chapter, "Pastoral Theology and Public Theology: Developments in the U.S." (Miller-McLemore, 2004).

CHAPTER 3

Power and Difference in Pastoral Theology

Christie Cozad Neuger

The dynamic of power and difference is a central concern of pastoral the-ology in the postmodern context. No other topic has received more attention over the past twenty years of research in this field. The study of power and difference has redefined the way that pastoral theology looks at the kinds of problems and decisions that people bring for care and counsel-ing. Hence, all situations involving pastoral care require a thorough analysis of how cultural power and difference function in the lives of those who have come for care.

Pastoral care practice now takes as central the impact of living in a world in which access to power and resources is either made available or limited based on cultural designations of normativity and difference. The issue at stake is justice. Whether we are looking at individuals or a culture, the way power is arranged, and the way that difference is defined, have a crucial impact on the well-being of all. As certain individuals and groups are given the power to define "truth" or "reality" and, thus, create norms and rules about what that truth is, other individuals and groups are often defined as deviant and less-than the dominant group. In this way, power hierarchies specific to particular cultures arise and operate. The notions of power and difference are a defining element of postmodernity and are key to under-standing and facilitating the emotional, spiritual, and physical health of all of us.

Yet, we don't accept the premises of postmodernity uncritically. Many would say that we live in an in-between time in pastoral theology, claiming many of the values of modernity even as we take the claims of postmoder-nity seriously. The deep belief in the inevitable situatedness of human thought within human culture and the importance of historicity in the inter-pretation of ideas are modern claims that continue into the postmodern world. The belief in individual rights and in the pursuit of liberty is part of a modern legacy. As David Tracy summarizes, "All of us who speak an emancipatory, liberating language are modernists at heart" (Tracy, 1995). Yet, these ideas of liberty and equality have been qualified in the ordering system of the grand narrative of modernity. The postmodern contribution has been not only to look to the importance of standpoint in observations and theories, but also to recognize that value and truth claims have been based on criteria grounded in the ordering of power in the culture. What is truth and what is myth, what is health and what is sickness, and what is reality and what is fantasy have been normalized by criteria determined by those with the power to do so (Neuger, 1998).

So, although power and difference have always existed in human culture, with the more culturally dominant groups able to define what makes a group different and to define those traits as deviance, postmodernity has given us new lenses for identifying the systematic character of dominant power and working to undo its damaging effects on both theory and practice. The purpose of this chapter is to explore these emerging perspectives as they have impacted and will continue to impact the nature of pastoral theology and the practice of pastoral care and counseling. Since there has been an enormous body of literature on these issues generated over the past twenty years, this chapter will be suggestive rather than comprehensive in delineating that literature. In addition, this chapter is both informed and limited by the author's social location as a European American, middle-class, heterosexual woman from the United States, ordained in the United Methodist Church. While taking into consideration the literature on this topic that has emerged from a variety of international perspectives, this article primarily addresses pastoral care and counseling dynamics in the United States.

Defining Terms

Six primary ideas will be discussed here: social identity/social location, power, difference, method, essentialism, and constructivism.

Social Identity/Social Location

The notion of social identity or social location is a crucial concept for any discussion of power, difference, and postmodernity. If, as postmodern notions claim, truth, norms, and assumptions are all largely dependent on who one is and one's position in the dominant culture hierarchy of value and power, then it becomes very important to be able to identify those aspects of a person that the culture uses to assign them value and place. Those aspects tend to include things such as race, ethnicity, class, gender, sexual orientation, able-bodiedness, and age, although there are other factors that could be identified. This combination of factors in the lives of people, including their places in the various cultural discourses and the other more particular contexts of their lives, is what is generally referred to as a person's "social location" or "social identity." All of us live within a variety of cultural discourses and so have different amounts of cultural power in different contexts.

Power

The use of the word *power* in contemporary pastoral care and counseling literature can range anywhere from the mundane to the prophetic. On the one hand, *power* means no more or less than the ability to act and, more abstractly, the ability to receive action. Power can be psychological, physical, relational, institutional, and cultural. In postmodern conversations, the emphases have been primarily on institutional and cultural power that impact and are carried out through physical, psychological, relational, and economic means. The notion of power has generally been expanded to include the ability (or inability) to act and to have (not have) an intended impact in any given situation. Power implies the ability to have agency in a situation in such a way that one's intent is carried out despite possible resistance to the intention. Power is not always easily discerned or claimed. Access to many kinds of cultural power, for example, is often based on essential characteristics such as sex, race, ethnicity, sexual orientation, age, physical ability, and so on. And, yet, often persons may hold such power unwittingly and even feel as if they are lacking in power and influence. Similarly, groups to whom access to cultural power has been reduced may define that lack of access to power as something else such as appropriate social role, complementarity with others of greater social power, or even as attributable to personal flaws.

So, in summary, power in postmodernist theory is looked upon as the ability to assert knowledge and authority as forms of social control. Power is claimed and used by those who have been given, by the culture, the right both to name and to shape cultural reality. In that reality, power is used to grant some groups the ability to have greater access to resources, including physical resources, psychological resources, and social resources, and to deny some groups equal access. This greater and lesser access to resources traditionally has been seen as part of the "natural order" or as due to the nature of reality itself. So, women often have been seen as less able (by virtue of being women) to be rational, to be intellectual, to be strong, to contribute to the public world of meaning, to defend themselves and others from threat, and so on. People of darker color (in the dominant European American culture) often have been seen as less intelligent, less capable of leadership, physically stronger so as to be more suited to physical labor, and so on. These became defined, by virtue of cultural power being granted to men, people of lighter color, and so forth, as part of the natural order and not open to analysis. This approach to "truth" and to "natural order" has been shattered by postmodernist ideas that take as central the analysis of power and difference as key to both personal and cultural health. Issues of power and difference have been brought together in various discussions of cultural oppression, its impact on individuals and populations, and the work of liberation and empowerment. This analysis has become central to contemporary pastoral care and counseling.

Difference

Difference, as a key postmodernist concept, has been implied by the prior discussion. Difference, although a common concept indicating a focus on characteristics that are not shared in common whether by individuals, groups, or cultures, has taken on a political meaning in postmodern conversations. In the context of power analysis as described above, *difference* has come to mean the way that these characteristics not shared in common become a way of distinguishing the place of individuals and groups in the social hierarchy of value. In other words, difference becomes a way to locate populations or portions of populations in terms of their rights to power and agency and to the shape of power appropriate to those groups. And, because certain populations are defined as normative (the normative human is white, male, heterosexual, and middle class in the dominant European American culture), those populations that are defined as different are also defined as deviant, that is, unlike the norm. Part of the role of cultural power is to find ways to define difference as deviance and, thus, justify the assignment to individuals and populations who are different/deviant, less access to power and resources. In addition, cultural power assigns privilege to groups that fit dominant culture norms of superiority and grants to members of those groups greater access to resources. Even more important, it grants to those privileged groups, the right to have their experiences named and remembered in cultural history. These groups have the power to name, to designate what is important and what is not, as well as to set the rules and the norms for the culture. These issues will become clearer as we trace the movement, through the literature, regarding power and difference in pastoral theology.

It is important to say that individuals can lose their cultural rights to power granted through their social identity in a variety of ways. Access to power is amazingly fragile for individual members of these populations. Since all people are members of multiple reference groups, anyone can lose access to power by also belonging to a less powerful reference group. Two of the most obvious examples are African American men and gay men. African American men often are seen as "lesser males" because of the stereotypes associated with them that are assigned by the dominant culture as part of the rationale for depriving them, as males, of power. Gay men are often seen as having "chosen" to give up their male privilege of dominating/protecting a female partner and, thus, are a threat to the assumptions of patriarchy.

People can also sacrifice their access to culturally granted power by refusing to follow the rules of their dominant reference group. For example, a man who chooses to be the primary homemaker and child-rearer in a family sacrifices some of his access to power by challenging the essential definitions of maleness, again a threat to the assumptions of patriarchy. Men who make choices both to step away from and to be held accountable for their male privilege are generally punished vocationally, financially, and socially. Although these rules may be less rigid than they once were, they still have considerable impact on access to power. And, people who have lost certain forms of access to cultural power may ameliorate the effects of those losses, in part, by the kinds of countercultural supportive communities in which they have been raised or in which they choose to operate. It is important to look at the systemic way that various populations are deprived of power, based on their differences from the dominant cultural norm.

As noted above in the definition of power, an analysis of this sort needs to draw distinctions between individuals that belong to defined populations and those populations themselves. There are many factors that influence access to power, and every person is a member of more than one reference group. As a woman, I belong to a socio-cultural reference group that has been systematically deprived of certain forms of cultural power. As a European American, well-educated, middle-class, middle-aged, heterosexual person, I belong to reference groups that offer me many avenues to power and resources. These dynamics are further complicated by my own unique history, psychological makeup, personal gifts and limitations, and so on. Persons are, at one and the same time, both oppressed and oppressor, depending on their immediate context. However, in order to look at some of the important notions of power and difference and their cultural roots and dynamics, there will be times in our theory-building when we will be creating a more monolithic identity for a population, as if every member of that population (women, African Americans, older people, and so on) experience the same kinds of culturally designated possibilities and limitations. This is in contrast to modernist conversations in which individual dynamics took center stage over membership in any population or reference group. We will attempt to walk the balance between "the rock and the hard place" (Jones, 1997) in analyzing the cultural meaning of power and difference in a postmodernist understanding of pastoral theology.

Essentialism

Essentialism is a philosophical position that either implicitly or explicitly claims that certain traits, abilities, behaviors, or "vocations" belong universally to a certain group and, as such, become defining qualities for that group. There are a variety of ways to ground essentialist claims. Although the place of earliest debate has been of essentialist claims grounded in biology, the more relevant issue of essentialism is when it is based on looking at a reference group's experience as universal. In other words, the tendency has been to look at some women's experience, for example (usually women of some privilege—white, educated, middle class, heterosexual), and conclude from that experience that it fits most or all women. Most feminist research began with this set of essentialist assumptions. As women discovered that male perspectives and power dominated the formation and maintenance of culture, they began to focus on the reclaiming of women's voices and experiences, as both unique and generally unheard. This focus on "women's" experience allowed for a body of knowledge to be built that was extensive enough to stand as significant critique to male-based knowledge revealing it to be partial and nongeneric. Revealing the false generic in language was a very important movement in feminist theory building. However, over time those women whose experiences were not represented by the claims of "women's" lives challenged these more privileged perspectives. Women of darker color and lesbian women, especially, began to develop research that revealed different kinds of experiences and the essentialism of "all women's experience" began to be deconstructed. European American women in pastoral theology began, albeit slowly, to recognize the claims being made by other women's perspectives and join in a more complex process of deconstructing the normative truth claims of the dominant culture. Despite the problems of essentialism, it is important not to abandon this philosophical and methodological position completely because focusing entirely on particularity will diminish or potentially eliminate the solidarity that has made and continues to make political and societal change possible.

Constructivism

The counter position to essentialism is the philosophical claim of constructivism. Constructivism posits that traits, abilities, behaviors, or vocations do not belong to a group in any universal way and that cultural notions like gender or race or sexual orientation are constructed and socialized in people according to the rules of the culture. A constructivist position would argue that the experiences that seem to be universal to a particular group are often challenged when that group is analyzed from different cultural perspectives and categories.

The constructivist approach addresses the problems of essentialism by acknowledging the deep and fundamental particularity of each life experience. The strength of the constructivist position is that each person's story is seen in its uniqueness and within its own particular context. Generalizations are avoided, which then limits the power any one story (or cultural narrative) can have over another. In this way, the power to oppress any one group by another becomes limited. However, in a similar fashion, any chance for a shared narrative within a group and the resultant possibility for solidarity is also limited. These are central issues for pastoral theology as we seek to walk a line between paying attention to particularity and difference while still allowing enough commonalities within and between groups to facilitate theory-building and the development of useful pastoral practices.

Methodology

Pastoral theology has a complex methodology that is helpfully explored through the use of a spiral image. The methodological spiral that characterizes pastoral theology is one that begins in particular and cultural experience and then uses that experience both to critique and utilize the traditions and theories of pastoral theology. Those traditions and theories include insights from Scripture, church traditions and doctrines, the social sciences, and clinical theories. From that dialogue between experience, understood broadly, and theory/theology, new and relevant pastoral practices are generated. Those practices are brought into the pastoral care and counseling process with the particular individuals and situations to see if they are, indeed, useful in offering liberating, empowering, and healing directions for those seeking help.

This spiral is important for pastoral theologians—it keeps the traditions in dialogue with particular contexts, and it holds practices accountable to both. In a time when cultural analysis and liberation movements have revealed both the limitations of what we had thought to be true and the distortions within many of our core theories and theologies, we have to approach these theoretical and theological conversation partners with a great deal of suspicion and critique. These various dialogue partners in pastoral theological method, that work together to generate our theories and practices of pastoral care and counseling, are in very different stages of critique, deconstruction, and reconstruction. Thus, we can often engage in harmful counseling practices, even when we think we are committed to postmodern and liberationist ideals, because we have inherited unexamined assumptions from one or more of the conversation partners of our discipline—often psychology or clinical method, sometimes theology and Scripture, or even unexamined life experience. This means we need to recognize the complexity of what we are doing, and we need to carry both a self-conscious set of criteria for liberating pastoral practice and a constant awareness of the contexts (both large and small) of the people who come to us for care and counseling. It is the self-conscious application of value-laden criteria to these various disciplines in pastoral theology that helps to surface assumptions and allow for appropriate deconstruction.

Not only are the various conversation partners of pastoral theology at differing levels of deconstruction and reconstruction, but also different groups have done more or less analysis of their own place in the cultural soup of power and difference. For example, there is considerably more literature from European American perspectives than from African American, Hispanic, or Korean perspectives (although this literature is growing rapidly). There is more literature from women's perspectives than from (self-conscious) men's perspectives, in terms of power and difference, and more African American racial analysis than European American (White) racial analysis. There has been very little work published on class difference.

Yet, a significant percentage of the current literature in pastoral care and counseling deals with these issues of power, difference, and diversity as central to the theoretical and theological tasks of the field. It is helpful for our purposes to look at the development of the field's current focus on power and difference by surveying the pastoral care and counseling literature over the past twenty years or so. In this way we are able to get a glimpse of the movement from a tendency to the generic, one size fits all, model of pastoral care to the focus on particularity and interconnectedness more characteristic of contemporary pastoral theology. One of the primary questions at stake in a literature survey of this nature is that of "how did we get here?" It is to that question that we now turn.

History

It's important to acknowledge that contemporary work on power and difference in pastoral theology owed some of its roots to the secular liberation movements, especially feminist and African American analyses, and to works in biblical and constructive theology. Historically, the most important of these was the 1960 article by Valerie Saiving (Goldstein) entitled "The Human Situation: A Feminine Viewpoint." This article, originally printed in the *Journal of Religion,* went well beyond an analysis of sexism (analyses had begun to surface already in the current feminist wave) to a compelling look at power and difference in terms of the culture's role in creating and maintaining gender differences and the theological collusion with this. This article broke new theological ground as it provided an analysis of gender in light of both culture and theology.

Saiving's insights were not evident, to any significant extent, in the pastoral theology literature of the following twenty years, although there were occasional exceptions. Particularly noteworthy are Peggy Way's "Community Organization and Pastoral Care: Drum Beat for Dialogue"; Don Browning's "Religion, Revelation, and the Strengths of the Poor"; Emma Justes's "Theological Reflection on the Role of Women in Church and Society"; Maxine Walaskay's (Glaz) "The Liberation of Women in Theology and Clinical Pastoral Education"; Edgar Ripley's "Pastoral Care and the Black Community"; and Calvin Bruce's "Nurturing the Souls of Black Folk." Each of these articles had a significant element of cultural analysis that began to challenge the notion of universal goods, norms, and truths and to look at the role of culture and theology in setting up and maintaining power differences that take shape in the systemic dynamics of oppression. They helped move the field from an awareness of difference and injustice to the role of cultural analysis and deconstruction.

In the 1980s the use of critical theory from the perspective of gender, race, class, sexual orientation, and ethnicity began to be more evident in the pastoral theology literature. We began to move from a sense of awareness about injustices in the theory and practices of pastoral care to a more persistent analysis of the role of culture in the assignment of power and resources to different groups of people. This analysis generated literature that saw culture and the assignment of power in the culture as forces to be considered when developing pastoral care practices for marginalized groups of people. There are several early and important illustrations of this phase of development in pastoral theology. Edward Wimberly's two books, *Pastoral Care in the Black Church* (1979) and *Pastoral Counseling and Spiritual Values: A Black Point of View* (1982), significantly moved from an anti-prejudice approach that tended not to challenge universal norms and rules to a place of claiming a particular (Black) perspective and the important value of that perspective for theory and practice. Archie Smith's book, *The Relational Self: Ethics and Therapy from a Black Perspective* (1983), was another example of seeing culture as an important aspect of a person and the issues they bring to pastoral counseling. Anne Ulanov's book, *Receiving Woman* (1981), would also fit into this category. It drew heavily on traditional psychological and sociological resources but focused on the role of culture in the formation of women's lives and on both their strengths and their vulnerabilities. These books, along with several articles on similar topics, built a solid foundation for two important dimensions of power and difference. They first made compelling claims for the importance of hearing and privileging previously marginalized voices in generating pastoral care theory and practice. Rather than dominant culture theorists writing about the contexts of European American women or African Americans, European American women and African Americans themselves took on the project of making their own perspectives heard in the pastoral theology guilds. This was the work of *reclaiming voice*. Second, these books and articles revealed that culture needs to be taken seriously, when looking at the problems and concerns brought to the pastoral counselor. In other words, psychospiritual issues aren't all products of unconscious conflict or idiosyncratic problems of development. These theorists helped the discipline of pastoral theology begin to understand that problems and vulnerabilities were often the product of a life lived in the context of cultural oppression. This was the work of *cultural analysis*. However, most of this literature did not yet seriously challenge pastoral theology at the level of epistemology. In other words, the knowledge bases of psychology, clinical theory, and pastoral methods went largely unchallenged. Theological premises, especially in the feminist literature, were beginning to be challenged but thorough epistemological analysis was yet to come.

By the mid-1980s another layer of the work on power and difference began to develop and that was in cross-cultural/multicultural/intercultural theory building. In 1986 David Augsburger wrote an important text entitled *Cross Cultural Pastoral Counseling*. In this text, relying on the centrality of culture and social location developed in the earlier literature, Augsburger developed perspectives and theory about pastoral counseling work between people of differing cultures. Similarly, Emmanuel Lartey, a pastoral theologian from Ghana, wrote *Pastoral Counseling in Intercultural Perspective* (1986). Both Augsburger and Lartey lift up the importance of the complexity of social location and the multiple strands of culture in each person. These complexities call for more than just knowledge about different kinds of culture. The ability to build the kind of counseling relationship that allows for the differences in the nuances of meaning to surface and be understood. This work not only developed important theory in pastoral counseling between people of different cultures, but, in essence, it asked the field of pastoral theology to take seriously that social location deeply shapes the nature of reality for each of us. This was a key move away from a sense that there was one normative reality—a reality that was generally defined in the way the dominant culture saw it to be. Questions of epistemology began to be introduced in this literature.

At about the same time as this intercultural/cross-cultural work was happening, thematic work, particularly in feminist pastoral theology, emerged. Good summaries of the early phases of this research and its foundations can be found in two articles in the *Dictionary of Pastoral Care and Counseling:* "Feminist Theology and Pastoral Care" by Pat Zulkowsky and "Feminist Therapy" by Charlotte Ellen. The primary focus of this literature was on violence against women, especially wife/partner battering and rape. In 1986 Rita Lou Clarke wrote *Pastoral Care of Battered Women* and in 1987 Mary Pellauer, Barbara Chester, and Jane Boyajian wrote *Sexual Assault and Abuse: A Handbook for Clergy and Religious Professionals*. Also in 1987 Marie Fortune's book for battered women in the Christian tradition (especially those in the more evangelical traditions) was published and became a primary resource for many pastors. *Keeping the Faith: Questions and Answers for the Abused Woman* was written in order to help women who were struggling with doctrinal and faith positions that tended to keep them from seeking safety from their abuse. These three books all addressed the collusion between theology and the epidemic of violence against women, suggesting that, at best, most (available) theology didn't help women resist or get free of violence against them and, at worst, it reinforced a cultural mind-set and gender practices that supported violence against women. These books also identified the kinds of norms that kept women and men from being able to identify the theological and cultural underpinnings that supported this kind of intimate violence. In 1989 Carole Bohn and Joanne Brown edited *Christianity, Patriarchy, and Abuse,* which took the theological analysis of intimate violence against women even further. The authors in this text used a *deconstructive* agenda to lay bare some of the most problematic elements of Scripture, theology, church structure, and pastoral practice. In 1992 Annie Imbens and Ineke Jonker published *Christianity and Incest,* a powerful work based on a series of interviews with 19 women in the Netherlands who had experienced incest. Eighteen of them had grown up in strict Christian homes. Imbens and Jonker were able to make visible these women's experiences of their faith in relation to their experiences of incest and to ask some hard questions of theology. In a later addition to the literature, Riet Bons-Storm in *The Incredible Woman: Listening to Women's Silences in Pastoral Care and Counseling* (1996) used a similar method of making abused women's stories available and allowing the reader to see how women were generally disbelieved by their pastoral care providers when they shared stories of abuse with them. In both cases, the women's stories serve as the deconstructive vehicle for pastoral theology and pastoral practice.

As is evident from the above titles, new approaches to theology began to surface regularly in this literature on power and difference. Both process theology and liberation theology became more visible in the pastoral care and counseling literature of this time. One can particularly see the influence of liberation theology in the deconstructive work of gender analysis in pastoral care. As Romney Moseley states in his article on Liberation Theology and Pastoral Care in the *Dictionary of Pastoral Care and Counseling,* "Liberation theology thus brings to pastoral care the same concerns offered by critical social theory but mediates these concerns theologically through the church, as it struggles to ensure the fullness of life" (Moseley, 1990). Many of the authors of these works in power and difference took on central theological concepts in terms of their impact on the theory and practice of pastoral care and counseling. In particular, pastoral theologians studied the doctrines of the atonement and Christology (Poling, 1991), the nature of forgiveness (Fortune, 1987), and the image of God (Saussy, 1991; Imbens & Jonker, 1992; Neuger, 1993).

The early 1990s saw an amazing influx of deconstructive work in pastoral theology from a variety of perspectives and viewpoints. Two very important books were published in 1991: *Women in Travail and Transition: A New Pastoral Care,* edited by Maxine Glaz and Jeanne Stevenson-Moessner and *The Abuse of Power: A Theological Problem* by James Poling. These were landmark books, each in their own way. Glaz and Moessner gathered a number of women pastoral theologians and asked them to address key issues in the lives of women. They were to deconstruct current theory, theology, and practice and propose new directions for the pastoral care. This book set an expectation for pastoral theologians about both the range of issues needing to be discussed and the inclusion of reclaiming, deconstructive and *reconstructive* themes. In *The Abuse of Power,* Poling uses a complex critical analysis through the lenses of gender, race, and class to explore pastoral practice in the context of sexual abuse. The complexity of this analysis, which includes theological, social, and practical deconstruction, again brought the field into a deeper commitment to the kinds of hermeneutical lenses that need to be used when exploring power and difference and pastoral practice. The value of this deconstructive project was immense.

Between 1992 and 1994 a significant amount of literature using reclaiming, deconstructive, and reconstructive methods emerged from gender (DeMarinis's *Critical Caring;* Graham and Halsey's *Life Cycles: Women and Pastoral Care;* Adams's *Women Battering in the Church;* Miller-McLemore's *Also a Mother*); race (Wimberly's *Using Scripture in Pastoral Counseling*); disability (Eiesland's *The Disabled God: Toward a Liberatory Theology of Disability*); and global (Wicks, Estadt, & Van Engen's *Pastoral Counseling in a Global Church: Voices from the Field*) lenses. These texts and two, more theoretical, texts (Patton's *Pastoral Care in Context* and Graham's *Care of Persons: Care of Worlds*) put the reconstructive agenda front and center for the guild without sacrificing a persistent attention to both reclaiming and deconstructive elements. Miller-McLemore's text, in particular, combined these various approaches to power and difference in very effective ways, by explicitly asking the epistemological question, "How do we know what we know?" By explicitly asking this question, Miller-McLemore was able to challenge pastoral theology to examine all of its assumptions about psychology and clinical practice along with those of theology and culture. Elaine Graham's book, *Making a Difference,* was also a landmark text for pastoral theology in terms of exploring epistemological questions. Working through the perspective of gender, Graham asked three levels of questions: how does gender get constructed and progressively reconstructed over the life cycle; what does gender mean for the social arrangements between people and the power implications of those; and how do the symbolic, deep cultural structures shape and define our knowledge base and our ways of knowing? In this text, Graham invited us to question our most deeply held assumptions about truth. These works in epistemology served an important role in deepening the analysis of power and difference in pastoral theology.

The primary journals in pastoral theology were also carrying cutting edge articles during these years. As noted above, the *Journal of Pastoral Care* and the *Pastoral Psychology* consistently addressed issues of power and difference from the late-1970s on. In 1991, for example, the *Journal of Pastoral Care,* had a special issue, edited by Holliman and Neuger, dedi-cated to collegiality and diversity in which issues of gender (both women's and men's voices), race, and class were addressed. The article on class ("Ministry with Working Class Women" by Judith Orr) was particularly significant. Class continues to be one of the most neglected perspectives in pastoral theology and Orr's work here and in two edited collections (Neuger & Poling's *Care of Men* and Stevenson-Moessner's *In Her Own Time*) are among the most significant class analyses in pastoral theology to date.

Also in 1991, The Society for Pastoral Theology (1985) started its own journal, the *Journal of Pastoral Theology*. This journal, like the Society, was committed to the deconstructive and reconstructive projects around power, difference, and diversity. One can see from the 1991–1994 tables of contents of this journal that its core commitment was to these issues and methods (Poling, "Hearing the Silenced Voices: The Work of Justice in Pastoral Theology"; Glaz, "Gender Issues in Pastoral Theology"; Taylor, "Black Experience as a Resource for Pastoral Theology"; Neuger, "Feminist Pastoral Theology and Pastoral Counseling: A Work in Progress"; Van den Blink, "Empathy Amid Diversity: Problems and Possibilities"; McCarthy, "Empathy Amid Diversity: Problems and Possibilities"; Streaty-Wimberly, "Narrative Approaches to Viewing and Addressing African American Spirituality and Sexuality"; Wimberly, "African-American Spirituality and Sexuality: Perspectives on Identity, Intimacy and Power"; Marshall, "Pastoral Theology and Lesbian/Gay/Bisexual Experiences"). In these same years, the other guild journals were producing similar works, although not in as focused a way as the *Journal of Pastoral Theology*. Most noteworthy of these was "Feminist Perspectives on Pastoral Care: Implications for Practice and Theory" by Nancy Ramsay and "Developing Models of Feminist Pastoral Counseling" by Carrie Doehring. Both of these articles continued to develop the methods of deconstruction and reconstruction through the critical lens of gender theory.

The mid-1990s brought an increasing volume of literature on these matters and, more significant, an increasing complexity of method. The more essentialist approach to power and difference, which tended to look at broad stroke categories like gender and race, gave way to a better articulation and reclaiming of the particularities within those broad categories. So, instead of just talking about women, for example, the literature began to take seriously that different groups of women had different kinds of locations and experiences in the culture. African American women's experience with depression or with pastoral care in the church could not be conflated with European American women's experiences. And, even within the African American women's experience, there were many layers of experience based on issues of economics, education, geography, and so on. Lesbian women, older women, women of diverse ethnicities, women of diverse abilities and disabilities, and so forth were able to make their own perspectives heard and European American, educated, heterosexual women (who had tended to write most globally about "women's" experience) recognized the privilege they had been claiming when they collapsed important differences within reference groups. The tensions of the essentialist-constructivist debate became more evident in pastoral theology publications of the mid-1990s. Books such as Stevenson-Moessner's *Through the Eyes of Women;* Neuger and Poling's *Care of Men;* Eugene and Poling's *Balm for Gilead;* and Miller-McLemore and Gill-Austern's *Feminist and Womanist Pastoral Theology* attempted to be both very conscious of the particularity of social location *and* of the need for finding ways to build theory out of shared experience.

Also in the mid- to late-1990s previously under-represented populations began to publish in greater quantities. For example, more Womanist pastoral theology emerged in books such as Anne Streaty Wimberly's *Honoring African American Elders: A Ministry in the Soul Community* and Carroll Watkins Ali's *Survival and Liberation: Pastoral Theology in African American Context,* and articles such as Watkins Ali's "A Womanist Search for Sources" and Foster Boyd and Bohler's "Womanist-Feminist-Alliances: Meeting on the Bridge" (in *Feminist-Womanist Pastoral Theology*). Joretta Marshall's several articles "Pastoral Theology and Lesbian/Gay/Bisexual Experiences," "Covenants and Relationships: Pastoral Counseling with Women in Lesbian Partnerships," and "Pedagogy and Pastoral Theology in Dialogue with Lesbian/Bisexual/Gay Concerns" along with her book, *Counseling Lesbian Partners,* are noteworthy examples of the kind of constructive work done from a lesbian perspective. Work by Rick Mixon, Larry Graham, and others also reflected on gay and lesbian experience and analyzed the cultural and theological power issues in developing appropriate pastoral care practices for the gay/lesbian/bisexual community.

Another important focus of the power and difference literature that ran through the 1990s was the work done around the issues of ministerial boundaries, especially in pastoral care and counseling. Here the issues of power and difference were sharply focused by careful analyses of the different kinds of power that might reside in the caregiver as he or she engaged in the work of pastoral counseling. Marie Fortune's case study of a church pastor who sexually abused members of his congregation (*Is Nothing Sacred? When Sex Invades the Pastoral Relationship,* (1989) was a watershed book in terms of creating very powerful norms for ministry that mandate the analysis of power in pastoral relationships. The debates about pastoral power and boundaries were frequent and accessible in the literature throughout the 1990s (Rambo's "An Interview with Marie Fortune," 1991; Lebacqz and Barton's *Sex in the Parish,* 1991; Fortune's "The Nature of Abuse," 1993; Capps's "Sex in the Parish: Social Scientific Explanations for Why it Occurs," 1993; Clark's "Lessons from Feminist Therapy for Ministerial Ethics," 1994; Neuger's "Establishing Boundaries for Clergy Well-Being," 1999; Ragsdale's *Boundary Wars,* 1996). Boundary issues also surfaced with intensity in the pastoral counseling guild meetings of the mid- and late-1990s. These debates about pastoral power brought the power dynamics of gender and race into common parlance in ministry, even if they didn't add to the complexity of the analysis.

The late-1990s also brought a focus to the links between pastoral theology and public theology. Much of the literature on power and difference began to be more self-consciously political. Some key examples of this would be Pamela Couture's *Blessed Are the Poor?* and her later book, *Seeing Children, Seeing God: A Practical Theology of Children and Poverty* as well as Couture and Hunter's *Pastoral Care and Social Conflict;* Steinhoff-Smith's *The Mutuality of Care;* and Poling's *Render Unto God: Economic Vulnerability, Family Violence, and Pastoral Theology.*

Finally, the late 1990s literature brought a continuing focus on multicultural and intercultural work and on global perspectives on power and difference. The early literature on cross-cultural counseling (Augsburger's *Pastoral Counseling Across Cultures,* 1986 and *Conflict Mediation Across Cultures,* 1992; Bohn's *Therapeutic Practice in a Cross-Cultural World,* 1995; and Van Beeks's *Cross Cultural Counseling,* 1996), focused on what it meant for a pastoral counselor and counselee from different cultures to work together. The task was to build a relationship that would allow a mutual sharing of difference and meaning. The assumption often was that the counselor was from a dominant culture perspective and the counselee was from a more marginalized perspective. The notion also developed that all counseling was cross-cultural in some ways since all people have particularities and differences that make shared meaning a difficult task. Again, as the analysis became more developed, cross-cultural counseling moved toward a more intercultural definition, which, according to Emmanuel Lartey, means the "attempt to capture the complex nature of the interaction between people who have been influenced by different cultures, social contexts and origins, and who themselves are often enigmatic composites of various strands of ethnicity, race, geography, culture, and socioeconomic setting" (Lartey, 2003, p. 13). The move has been similar to that of other analyses of power and difference that move being from a monolithic understanding (of race or gender or ethnicity or culture) to a more complex and multilayered understanding of those realities. People have multiple memberships in cultural groups and diverse kinds of access to power. Conversations about power and difference today need to walk that fine line of particularity of social location and the meanings of that particularity with a larger sense of a shared meaning and experience. However, that shared meaning and experience among people based on a shared social location must always be held lightly because boundaries of that membership are fluid and multiple. Recognition of the complexities is a key development in the pastoral theological conversations about power and difference.

As one can see from the above discussion, pastoral theology has developed, as normative, the analysis of power and difference in generating its theory and practice. There has been movement in the methods and emphases of these analyses. The movement started with greater and greater awareness of the problems of injustice and exclusion, often with dominant culture practitioners writing on behalf of those who were excluded. Over time, those who had experienced exclusion began to have the access and the

confidence to write on behalf of their own experience. The early representatives of marginalized populations often wrote as if there were a generic
experience to be described. This was a very helpful stage of the process as
it allowed the concrete reality of experience to have authority and as it facil-
itated the development of a critical mass of critique against the dominant
"truths" of the day. However, those members of marginalized groups whose
realities didn't fit the experiences being described and who were aware of
their multiple memberships in diverse marginalized groups (e.g., gay men,
African American women) began to add to the conversations. This created
a move to a more constructivist emphasis in the literature. It also generated
a greater sensitivity to the systemic and interlocking nature of power and
difference. The notion that one could be in a position of dominant power in
one context and disenfranchised of power in another context became woven
into the analyses and allowed a necessary complexity to develop.
Practitioners began to recognize that their well-loved theologies and clinical theories needed to be held in suspicion and that they were likely to do
harm if they didn't learn how to deconstruct the foundations of their practices through the lenses of diversity, power, and difference. Family systems
theory helped pastoral practitioners understand the multiple layers that
needed to be considered in pastoral counseling, widening the systemic circles to include institutions and cultural discourses as key in understanding
counseling problems. Pastoral care guilds like the American Association of
Pastoral Counselors (AAPC) and the Association for Clinical Pastoral
Education (ACPE) took the more theoretical foundations for reclaiming and
deconstruction and worked conscientiously at guild meetings, in journals,
and in supervision and training to develop appropriate practices and ongoing theory for the tasks of pastoral care and counseling. Throughout the
1980s and 1990s especially, annual guild meetings frequently focused on
issues of diversity and on the dynamics of power and oppression relevant to
their pastoral work and within their own guilds. Leadership and guild structures changed to reflect their growing commitment to diversity, collegiality,
and justice. These issues continue to be central to the major guilds in pastoral care. Diversity, power sharing, and justice were founding principles
behind the Society for Pastoral Theology and have played a central role in
the other mainline guilds.

As deconstructive methods became available and as their diversity began
to reflect the realities of the culture, pastoral theologians recognized that
they were better at exposing the dominant culture assumptions and practices
than they were at generating new proposals for theory, theology, and practice. Especially in the mid-1990s reconstructive proposals began to develop
and the reconstructive project took on priority for the guild. New ways for
understanding psychological and spiritual health developed that better
reflected the way people respond to living within dominant discourses that
don't reflect their experiences or needs. Postmodernist ways of understanding clinical practice (e.g., constructivist and narrative counseling theories),

theological reflection, and teaching and supervision practices emerged and were enthusiastically discussed and explored. Guild meetings began to reflect these new approaches. Some in pastoral theology found that a break from traditional practices (clinical, theological, psychological) was necessary for the new knowledge about power and difference/diversity to be enacted. Others worked (and continue to work) to critique adequately more traditional approaches so that the riches of those traditions do not get lost. This process is ongoing and will continue indefinitely as we seek to embrace both diversity and justice.

It is important to note that the material in this article regarding power and difference in pastoral theology reflects a mainstream track. There are subgroups within pastoral theology where some of its foundations are off-limits for deconstruction. Particularly in more conservative groups the tension of fidelity to traditions (especially biblical and theological, although sometimes to therapeutic schools) with commitment to diversity and justice result in differing theory-building priorities. Conversations between subgroups in pastoral theology need to continue so that all may participate in these important conversations without perspectives and wisdom being lost.

Future Trajectories

Obviously the guild of pastoral theology is still very much in the middle of this story. Ongoing awareness of diverse perspectives and realities, and active efforts at justice are of high priority. Consequently, the deconstructive project is very much alive and necessary for pastoral theology. Yet, it is reconstructive efforts that are the priority at the current time and that continue to claim the bulk of theoretical and practical energy. Those reconstructive efforts focus on four primary themes and serve as a statement of both current practice and future trajectory.

First, there is a strong move toward a greater focus on the global spectrum of experience and a need to understand and build in knowledge and wisdom from the perspectives of other international communities. Several important books have been published recently that either focus directly on global voices or that integrate global perspectives into the text. Representative examples of these works would include *International Perspectives on Pastoral Counseling* edited by James Reaves Farris; *The Blackwell Reader in Pastoral and Practical Theology* edited by James Woodward and Stephen Pattison; *Render Unto God* by James Newton Poling; and *Liberating Faith Practices: Feminist Practical Theologies in Context* edited by Denise Ackermann and Riet Bons-Storm. These are only a few of the books in current publication that represent global perspectives in pastoral theology. There are also numerous articles on this topic being published. This global emphasis is changing the kinds of analyses being done in pastoral theology.

Critiques of capitalism and general economic practices, class structures and distribution of wealth and resources, continuing imperialistic practices and impositions of dominant norms, especially by the United States around the world, as well as other kinds of cultural investigations are moving pastoral theology into an increasing position of public theology. Guilds have emerged with a strong global emphasis (e.g., the International Council for Pastoral Care and Counseling and the International Academy for Practical Theology). Pastoral theologians are recognizing that care for individuals and families are integrally related to care for communities at the national and global levels and to the pursuit of peace and justice for all people. Pastoral theology as public theology and the development of practices that focus on care of persons at the same time they focus on care of the world (including the natural world) will continue to be a top priority in the future.

A second emerging priority is the shift from an exclusive focus on populations that have been marginalized and disenfranchised by dominant discourses in the culture to a growing awareness and focus on those who have benefited and continue to benefit from those dominant discourses. In other words, there is increasing focus on the nature of cultural privilege, its origins and dynamics. We can see some of this in earlier writings such as those by James Poling *(The Abuse of Power: A Theological Problem),* Larry Graham *(Discovering Images of God: Narratives of Care Among Lesbians and Gays),* and Paul Hopkins ("On Being a Compassionate Oppressor"). However, pastoral theologians are working to address both the identity of dominant group membership and the various practices that support that identity. Nancy Ramsay's work in white identity formation ("Navigating Racial Difference as a White Pastoral Theologian") is a clear illustration of this trajectory that is gaining considerable momentum in the field.

A third area of current publication is that of cross-disciplinary interest in and commitment to the issues of justice in creating models for theory and practice. Pastoral theology as a field has gained enough identity and clarity to engage in cross-disciplinary conversations that draw productively on differences in method and perspective. This work is enlivening for all disciplines. Two recently published books illustrate this cross-disciplinary pollination: Ramsay and McClure's *Telling the Truth: Preaching About Sexual and Domestic Violence* and Eugene and Poling's *Balm for Gilead: Pastoral Care for African American Families Experiencing Abuse.* In addition, work directly applicable to these emphases in pastoral theology is coming out of other disciplines. For example, Emmanuel Lartey states that some of the best global perspectives for pastoral practice are coming out of the work of African biblical scholars (e.g., Musa W. Dube, "Postcolonial Interpretation of the Bible," 2000 and Musimbi Kanyoro, *Introducing Feminist Cultural Hermeneutics: An African Perspective,* 2000). The deconstructive/reconstructive project around power and difference for the sake of relevant and just pastoral care practice requires the collaborative and cooperative efforts of all the theological disciplines as well as those of the secular helping professions.

Finally, a fourth, and more abstract, trajectory is the continuing integration of these methods and agendas into the general theories and practices of pastoral care and counseling at every level. Theory building and new methodological frameworks for pastoral care and counseling are emerging at a rapid rate. Nancy Ramsay's book, *Pastoral Diagnosis: A Resource for Ministries of Care and Counseling,* is an excellent example of the integration of these methods into general pastoral care theory building. Other recent examples would include Neuger's *Counseling Women: A Narrative Pastoral Approach* (2002) and Culbertson's *Caring for God's People: Counseling and Christian Wholeness* (2000).

Pastoral Identity and Formation

There are profound implications of these theoretical shifts for the practice of pastoral care and counseling. The history of pastoral care has been so individually and intrapsychically focused that a move to looking at social identity and the centrality of power and difference is challenging. Since the practice of pastoral care and counseling is based on a complex methodology where theology, psychology, clinical theory, spirituality, sociology, anthropology, and the traditions of pastoral counseling are brought into dialogue with each other, the deconstructive and integrative task is substantial. As these conversation partners in pastoral theology continue their move through this process of deconstruction, the practices that they generate will also continue to change. One of the challenges for education, training, and supervision is to keep this dialogue between the deconstruction and reconstruction of new theory and theology and the generation of more liberating practices visible to students and practitioners. If practitioners and students are exposed only to new practice, they will not be able to play a significant role in the ongoing development of the field. Similarly, theorists in pastoral theology need to pay careful attention to new practices that are emerging as these are the primary source of deconstructive lenses and serve to hold new theory accountable to the ministry needs of those who seek pastoral care. Since pastoral theology still has much work to do to end its collusion with dominant cultural discourses that harm marginalized individuals and groups, all who engage in pastoral care and counseling should continue to carry a strong hermeneutic of suspicion into the practices of our work. We are in a time when complacency in our forward progress of empowerment and liberation in pastoral theology is vastly out of place. There is much still to be done.

This means that teachers of seminary students must consistently employ a deconstructive lens in their teaching of the traditions of seminary. This is a challenging prospect when many seminary students today come to seminary without a firm grasp of the traditions themselves. Yet, even as students are exposed to the theological and practical traditions of ministry, they also need to be exposed to the voices that have not been a part of making those traditions. They need to be immersed in the perspectives and communities that have been named by dominant culture as different. They need to be made aware of the various levels of privilege in which they have operated as well as those arenas in which they have been disempowered and marginalized. And, they need to understand the methods of social deconstruction. Seminary teachers need to face their fears of risking "doctrinal purity" as they boldly explore what it has meant for the Church to take shape in cultures organized around designations of normativity and difference. And, all seminary students need to be helped to integrate the important values of the traditions with the deconstructive and reconstructive tasks of today's global community.

In addition, for those students who move into more specialized training in pastoral care and counseling, the complexities increase. Since modern pastoral counseling has relied so heavily on psychological and clinical theories, these disciplines, too, have to be examined and deconstructed through the lenses of difference, power, and established norms. Questions like diagnosis (who defines what is ideal, normal or deviant and in what contexts, for example), the goals and processes of counseling, and the nature of health all have to be ruthlessly explored as constructs that have been developed by people of immense privilege and, often, monolithic perspective. One of the tasks of pastoral counselors who engage in training and supervision is both to engage in this deconstructive work themselves and to help new pastoral counselors integrate these liberating perspectives into the everyday work of pastoral counseling. The implications of this are beyond the scope of this article. It is enough to say that it requires courage and commitment by training supervisors to deconstruct the clinical theories they have assumed to be true so that new pastoral counselors do not participate in reproducing pastoral practices of harm. Loren Townsend develops these themes further in his essay (in this volume) on supervision and training.

These educational commitments will assist in the formation of religious leaders and specialized pastoral care providers who are able to see the needs of their congregants and care receivers in light of the impact of the dominant cultural discourses in their lives. They will be able to identify those same dynamics in themselves. This will lead, hopefully, to the continued deconstruction of disempowering pastoral strategies and the reconstruction of truly liberating pastoral practices. It will also result in the increasing representation of diverse perspectives and global participation.

We are making progress in these endeavors. It is noteworthy for example, in looking at recent journal issues of the *Journal of Pastoral Care and Counseling, Pastoral Psychology,* and the *Journal of Pastoral Theology,* that, although there is a decrease in topic-oriented articles that, by their title, signal a focus on diversity, power, and difference in pastoral theology, many articles provide powerful articulations and applications of reclaiming, deconstructive, and reconstructive methods in the generation of more "mainstream" pastoral care theory and practice. In addition, there is increasing focus on teaching and supervision as they embody these methods in both the teaching itself and in the classroom content and process. In other words, the navigation of power and difference for the sake of enhancing both diversity and justice is moving into deeper and more foundational layers of pastoral theology.

This is not to say that there aren't always temptations for any discipline to fall back into dominant culture discourses and practices. The seduction of the dominant discourses, especially for people who have access to dominant culture power, is potent. It would be easy to become complacent and claim that we have accomplished the major elements of this project in the discipline of pastoral theology. But, it is important to remind ourselves that we are very far from our hopes and dreams about justice and diversity and that persistent vigilance in theory building and practice are absolutely necessary. The hermeneutic of suspicion is our greatest ally and that suspicion needs to be aimed at all who participate in generating knowledge and norms for the field. The emphasis to look at privilege, dominant culture identity, and accountability will continue to be an important dimension of the movement forward. All of the methods—gaining *awareness* of injustice, *reclaiming* a diversity of perspectives, *deconstructing* dominant culture norms and practices, *reconstructing* new theory, theology, and care, and maintaining *persistent accountability* for all who have access to privilege and power—will be necessary as we continue to respond to God's call for mutuality, love, and justice for all of creation.

CHAPTER 4

Globalization, Internationalization, and Indigenization of Pastoral Care and Counseling

Emmanuel Y. Lartey

This essay explores global developments in pastoral care and counseling since the mid-1980s and surveys various organizations that reflect international concerns. The United States is the context out of which this chapter is written, and the influence of theories and practices of pastoral care and counseling from this region is evident. This influence is inevitable since any survey of theories and practices of pastoral care and counseling demonstrates the central place the United States occupies in these disciplines.

My aim here is to inform a largely North American audience about worldwide developments, based on a firm belief that knowledge of global trends and practices can enhance theory and practice in the United States. Achieving this enhancement will entail critically developing our understanding of relevant and useful practices in pastoral care and counseling throughout the world. As such, processes and developments in different parts of the world that are related to or depart markedly from those of North American origin are examined here. These explorations allow deeper reflection on North American and Western European assumptions and practices and potentially make the theory and practice that is developed here in the United States more inclusive and beneficial to a wider public.

I survey developments in the following geographical regions—Africa, Asia/Pacific, South America, and Europe—following my own familiarity with pastoral care and counseling in these areas, having resided in Africa, Europe, and North America, and having participated in conferences and meetings in all the other regions. I will identify well-known institutional as well as less familiar indigenous practices of pastoral care and counseling. This essay will extend our knowledge and understanding of global issues and fill lacunae in the *Dictionary of Pastoral Care and Counseling* (1990).

I am a native of the West African country of Ghana and received my formative training in psychology and theology there. In the mid- to late-1980s I was a practitioner and seminary teacher of pastoral care, counseling, and Christian ministry in Ghana. In the early 1980s I was graduate student, and then in the 1990s, a University lecturer in Britain, where I resided for more than fourteen years. Currently, I am a seminary professor in the United States where I have lived for the last few years. The denominational background with which I am most identified is Methodist. However, all my formative and subsequent years have been in ecumenical settings, and I have benefited tremendously from a wide range of religious and cultural influences—not the least of which are African liberationist impulses that for me always have had primacy.

I was involved in the founding of the African Association of Pastoral Studies and Counselling and have served on British and European bodies in these disciplines. I have also been a participant at several of the International congresses I write about and have followed closely the development of pastoral care and counseling in different local and international contexts. Drawing upon such varied and enriching experiences, this chapter seeks to be informative as well as to provide critical appraisal in the hope of encouraging globally informed, reflective practice of pastoral care and counseling.

Major Processes in Evidence Globally

Three types of processes seem to characterize developments in pastoral care and counseling on the global scene over the past two decades. These can be described as *globalization, internationalization,* and *indigenization.* Although each of these historical processes is identifiable and describable by itself, there is mutual influence among them. All three may be, and often are, present in any given locale. However, there is not always respect or dialogue between practitioners whose practice could be labeled as exemplifying one or the other. There appears to be a progression from globalization through internationalization toward indigenization in many areas of the world, although by no means is this true everywhere. Moreover, one particular current practice in a given place in the non-Western world may manifest elements of all three processes.

Globalization, in pastoral care and counseling, entails the exportation or importation into different cultures and contexts, in whole or in part, of the worldview, values, theological anthropology, lifestyle, paradigms, and forms of practice developed in North America and Western Europe. The term *globalization* is itself ambiguous and has been used in many different ways. Nevertheless, there are some realities that appear to underlie all usages of the term. Globalization has been described as "the closer integration of the countries and peoples of the world which has been brought about by the enormous reduction of costs of transportation and communication, and the breaking down of artificial barriers to the flows of goods, services, capital, knowledge, and people across borders" (Stiglitz, 2002, p. 9). While this general definition would seem to be adequate, it does not specify the general direction of the flows it describes. Clearly that movement in products, lifestyle, and values has been from the economically advantaged toward those who have much less. In economic terms, the rich and powerful nations and international institutions write and enforce rules that apply to all, but benefit the affluent. Globalization in pastoral care and counseling has followed similar social and economic patterns.

In pastoral care and counseling globalization occurs where the practices that are encouraged and in which local people are trained, become the dominant approaches and models of the United States and Western Europe. For example, globalization occurs when a counseling center is established in a non-Western context and the accreditation, recognition, inspection, standards, and models of practice in this enterprise arise in the United States. When the mentality of local people is such that they believe implicitly that things imported from the First World are *ipso facto* superior to what is locally produced, the soil is fertile for globalization to grow. Globalization is an inexorable fact of international relations at present and has certainly been beneficial in some respects to all concerned. A great deal of ambivalence also exists in non-Western contexts, especially concerning culture and identity, about the processes of globalization that all realize are at work.

Internationalization is the process in which an attempt is made at dialogical engagement, where American understandings interact with non-Western ones in a quest for practices that are more contextually appropriate. Internationalization is premised upon an increasing recognition and valuing of "difference" between cultures and contexts, together with respect and interaction between cultures, nations, and social groups. In this process there is an attempt to facilitate the development of creative and/or integrative approaches relevant to the local contexts by placing Western theories and practices alongside non-Western, local ones. As will be evident later in the chapter, the International Council on Pastoral Care and Counseling (ICPCC), formally established in 1979, encourages such dialogue, as does the Society for Intercultural Pastoral Care and Counselling (SIPCC), inaugurated in Germany in 1995.

The orientation to international work in and through these associations is intercultural in that attempts are made to give voices from different contexts an equal position in decision making and practice. Nevertheless, those who come to the table in the first place are trained in the theories and practices of pastoral care and counseling favored in the West—especially the United States. The tacit assumption is that the practices developed in the West are normative. Dialogue is premised upon theories and practices of pastoral care and counseling as they are envisaged in Western Europe and the United States.

The International Academy of Practical Theology (IAPT), which came into being in 1991, is illustrative of some features of internationalization.

This is a body of academic scholars drawn from different countries around the world, united around research, teaching, and practice of the disciplines of Practical Theology, namely Christian and Religious Education, Worship, Preaching, Christian Ethics, Pastoral Care, Counseling, and Pastoral Theology. The focus of the Academy, quite distinct from the more practice-oriented movements mentioned earlier, is on theory building. Practical Theology is understood as a "theory of praxis" and membership is open to academic scholars with a publishing track record. Biennial conferences have been held in Princeton (1993), Bern, Switzerland (1995), Seoul, Korea (1997), Quebec, Canada (1999), Stellenbosch, South Africa (2001), and Manchester, England (2003). Representation from the northern countries of the West is international, although there are a few members from the Third World and IAPT continues to seek ways of encouraging more global participation. Collections of papers presented at conferences wrestle with the nature of difference in theory and practice in the disciplines of Practical Theology (Ballard & Couture, 1999, 2001).

Indigenization, the least recognized of the processes, is occurring on the margins of the global movements. In this process, models and practices indigenous to non-Western contexts are beginning to be re-evaluated and utilized in pastoral practice. In line with postcolonial cultural, social, linguistic, and political criticism, indigenous practitioners of healing are increasingly encouraged to impact the halls of power in the practice of pastoral care and counseling in several places in the world. This is happening at various levels within countries as well as between them.

A study of developments in pastoral care and counseling throughout the world quickly picks up broad differences between Western and non-Western thought and practice. Wicks and Estadt (1993) gathered together the experiences of pastoral counselors, trained in the United States, at work in ten different countries, namely Australia, Ghana, Kenya, Korea, Malawi, Netherlands, Panama, Thailand, Venezuela, and Zambia. In all cases these practitioners have found it necessary to modify the Western-based training they received with its assumptions and presuppositions in order to practice effectively in their culturally distinct contexts.

Counseling developed in the United States is largely individualistic, rationalistic, and promotes the self (ego) above all else (Halmos, 1965; Lambourne, 1974; Wilson, 1988). This is in line with a system of thought that is essentially materialistic and consumerist, and which, as a result, places the greatest value on acquisition. As Colin Lago and Joyce Thompson have argued (Thompson & Lago, 1996), Western forms of knowledge have tended to be external, the result of counting and measuring, with knowers distancing themselves from the objects to be known.

On the other hand Asian conceptual systems tend to emphasize cosmic unity and place much more value on the cohesiveness of groups. Both inner and external ways of knowing are important. The aim of knowledge, learning, and healing practices is the integration of body, mind, and spirit that are considered to be different aspects of the same oneness (Thompson & Lago, 1996, p. 86). Most Asian contexts are religiously plural, with Christianity historically being a relatively late addition. Asian cultures and religions espouse rich and ancient heritages of healing, care, and guidance.

African systems of thought and practice are based on a spiritual ontology and pragmatic philosophy, which place greatest value on relationality. Knowledge is acquired through intuition and revelation that comes through participation in ritual, symbol, ceremony, and rhythm. The focus of healing and counseling is upon the relationship existing between persons and among groups whose intrinsic worth is to be found within the network of spiritual, familial, and intergenerational bonds within which they are embedded. Religion and views of transcendence are pervasive and resilient in all of African life. There is little or no separation between a "sacred" and a "secular" realm. All life is both sacred and secular. These beliefs are expressed most clearly in rituals that are meant to foster and enhance harmonious relations between humans and the unseen world of ancestors, gods, and spirits. Ceremonies, rites, and rituals emphasize the importance of participation, symbolic representation, and celebration.

Historical Developments

Historical studies, such as those undertaken by Clebsch and Jaekle (1964), John McNeill (1977), and Culbertson and Shippee (1990), point out that Egyptian sages, followed by philosophers, and finally the Early Church, all sought to heal, sustain, guide, and reconcile persons and communities using *iatroi logoi* (healing words). Forms of what we now describe as pastoral care and counseling, which seeks to integrate theological and psychological insights in bringing relief to suffering people, have been practiced in many cultures for millennia.

The earliest roots of pastoral care and counseling lie in the healing and restorative rituals and arts practiced by priest-healers in antiquity. These ancient traditional healers often combined the roles of priest, therapist, and physician. Such persons were the ones to whom people would turn in crisis, danger, or when seeking guidance. They were consulted with the expectation that they would offer words, rites, or rituals grounded in culture, worldview, and belief, that would be effective in bringing relief or else offering meaning, explanation, and treatment strategies for traumatized persons and communities. Traditional priest-healers, as such, were knowledgeable concerning a wide range of physical, emotional, spiritual, social, cultural, and psychological phenomena.

Present-day Western pastoral caregivers appear very different from their historical predecessors; however, the needs and expectations that propel people to seek care today are similar across history and cultures. The integrative, diagnostic, and therapeutic activities of pastoral caregivers today reflect similar practices in past ages.

Pastoral care is dependent upon the cultures, reigning philosophies, and psychologies of the periods in which it is practiced. Forms of pastoral care and counseling practiced in Western societies in the twentieth century and now the twenty-first century reflect the dominant social, cultural, theological, and psychological theories of the West. There are real differences between theories and practices of effective pastoral care and counseling in different parts of the globe.

International Exchanges

International conferences of Christian clergy and Jewish rabbis with physicians, psychotherapists, social workers, and other counselors mainly from the United States and Europe have contributed significantly to the current disciplines of pastoral care and counseling. Dutch pastoral theologian, the late Heije Faber, has offered an important sketch of the early European-based conferences in the *Dictionary of Pastoral Care and Counseling* (1990, pp. 589-590).

It was in 1979 that the first "truly international ecumenical council" on pastoral care and counseling was convened in Edinburgh, Scotland on the theme, "Risks of Freedom." This hugely successful gathering was compared by the Moderator of the General Assembly of the Church of Scotland to the great Ecumenical Mission conferences of 1910 and 1937. The conference, with more than 400 participants from all the continents, saw the formal birth of the International Council on Pastoral Care and Counselling. Werner Becher, a past president of the International Committee, offers analysis and comment on the international trends in the disciplines of pastoral care and counseling following the first meetings:

> The influence of psychotherapy and the clinical setting of many specialized ministries have supported a pastoral care for people in sickness, suffering, grief, and other crises and conflicts of life. However, together with the support of people in various stages of life a pastoral care is now developing which leads from crises to growth, from conflicts to innovation, from healing to prevention, from remediation to the discovery of gifts and talents. (Becher, 1993, p. 5)

Already at this time Becher noticed "a general trend" toward "the reappraisal of the biblical, theological and pastoral traditions" (p. 6) in the emerging international movement for pastoral care and counseling.

The following chart outlines the International congresses that have been held since then.

Date	Location	Theme
1983	San Francisco, USA	Symbols and Stories in Pastoral Care and Counseling
1987	Melbourne, Australia	Pastoral Ministry in a Fractured World
1991	Noordwijkerhout, Holland	Pastoral Care and Context
1995	Toronto, Canada	Babylon and Jerusalem: Stories for Transition in a Strange Land
1999	Accra, Ghana	Spirituality and Culture in the Practice of Pastoral Care and Counseling

Figure 1: International Congresses

A highpoint of the Melbourne Congress illustrated the potential of processes of internationalization leading to indigenous voices impacting a global audience. It occurred on the final day of the gathering when Carolee Chanona and Jose Marins from South America made a presentation on pastoral responses to "the oppressed and the oppressor." The two are an itinerant pastoral team that emerged in response to the Roman Catholic Bishops Conference of Medellin in 1968, the conference that saw the formal birth of Latin American Liberation Theology. This is how they began:

> We will speak to you from the special vantage point of the Basic Ecclesial Communities as they grapple with this challenge and seek to respond pastorally to the situation of oppression. Our presentation will in part be using the language of our people who at the grass-roots level are classified as illiterate and who thus have recourse to the language of symbols. We will allow them to speak of and to their realities as experienced in their day-to-day living and then reflect with you upon the theological implications and pastoral challenges of this reality in our part of the world. (*Pastoral Ministry in a Fractured World,* 1987, p. 94)

Behind the speakers were banners, paintings, pictures, and icons from Panama, Bolivia, Haiti, Brazil, and the Dominican Republic. Commenting on the power of this presentation, British pastoral theologian John Foskett writes, "for once words fell into place as a simple commentary on the message born across oceans of space and experience, and yet immediately striking chords within us" (Foskett, 1988, p. 9). The presentation won a standing ovation from the congress. Participants had been taken through the now classic stages of experience to observation to reflection and thence to understanding and action—and it all made huge pastoral sense. Indigenous voices had been "heard" through symbols.

The main presenters at the Holland meeting in 1991 were diverse in terms of culture, gender, and religious tradition. Participants attempted to wrestle with the realities of their individual contexts against a background of the situations of others. A result of these discussions was the sense that Third World participants were still, by virtue of the inequalities of the global economic scene, largely marginalized and treated as guests, rather than as full participants at the congresses. In Holland a strong call was made for a Congress to be hosted and held in the Third World. A clear struggle was emerging between those who insisted that the function of pastoral counseling was very different from social work or political action, and those whose view was that pastoral counseling could not be seriously practiced in a social and cultural vacuum.

The rather unusual theme of the Toronto Congress was a deliberate invitation "to pursue ideas which, in important ways, were different from those of previous meetings. . . . The global movement was being invited to consider 'a much more universally inclusive understanding of pastoral care and counselling'" (from the First Announcement brochure of the Congress). The main presentations at this meeting were offered from within Jewish, the Anishinabe (a native Canadian) nation, Muslim, Buddhist, and Christian religious traditions. This congress sought to propel the movement on into the reality of pluralism in the religious and cultural contexts in which pastoral care and counseling is engaged throughout the world today. It presented pastoral practitioners with the ambiguities and difficulties in communication, learning, method, and culture for the practice of pastoral care and counseling.

The Sixth Congress, held in Accra, Ghana, in August 1999 was the first to be held in the Third World and to that extent fulfilled the aspirations of those who had called for such a gathering eight years before in Holland. This congress was perhaps the most diverse of all, with participants drawn from more than 40 countries. The majority of the 175 participants, for the first time, came not from the United States but from African and Asian countries. Issues of contextualization, pluralization, and globalization of pastoral care and counseling were very evident. In many respects, this congress represented a real step forward in the process of internationalization of the worldwide movement for pastoral care and counseling. However, indigenous voices and those of different religious traditions were not significantly present in the program of this gathering. The independent former British colony did not feel free enough to enable the "native" voices truly to be heard.

Regional Trajectories

Pastoral Care and Counseling
in the Asian-Pacific Region

By reference specifically to three Asian cultural contexts (Filipino, Korean, and Chinese) I will characterize the current state of the theory and practice of pastoral care and counseling within these regions of the world. I will also make brief reference to India where indigenization has a long history and continues to impact recent developments in pastoral care and counseling. Tsyugikazu Nishigaki's entry in the *Dictionary* (1990) on the "East Asian Pastoral Care Movement" draws very briefly on Japanese, Korean, and Taiwanese historical developments (pp. 329-330). Here I will highlight issues that indicate the importance of contextual thinking for pastoral care and counseling in the twenty-first century.

Methodist Bishop of Singapore and medical doctor, the Right Reverend Dr. Robert Solomon, in a keynote address at the 2001 Asian-Pacific congress on pastoral care and counseling, highlighted seven concerns for pastoral care and counseling in Asia as follows:

- Globalization
- The growth of technology
- Knowledge explosion
- The New Economy
- Violence
- Poverty
- HIV/AIDS

In order to respond in helpful ways to these contextual realities in the face of rapid and relentless social change, Bishop Solomon urged Asian Pacific pastoral practitioners to "take serious consideration of the part played by sociocultural forces in shaping the values and personalities of people." "Counseling," he continued, "cannot be confined to the counseling room in Asia or be organized simply along a clinical professional approach. Helping people cannot be relegated to the privatized sphere. It must be a personal act in a public world" (Solomon, 2002, p. 111). In line with Asian cultural anthropology, Solomon places pastoral care and counseling squarely in the communal arena. The care of the individual in this model needs to go hand in hand with the care of the community.

Solomon argues that in the Asian Pacific region, tradition and modernization exist side-by-side and in a mutually influential relationship. As an illustration Solomon mentions the Iban, an indigenous people of East Malaysia, who traditionally live in communal long houses where their lives and economies are organized in terms of this form of communal living. As a result of rapid urbanization, young Iban people are moving to towns and cities where they suffer disorientation and other forms of psychological and social distress. As a pastoral response, attempts are being made by the church to build communal housing for these Iban in the cities in order to minimize the disruption of their social and cultural lives in the new urban environment. Significantly, Iban Christian leadership is re-examining Iban traditional rituals and customs to recover pastoral aspects of these so that the community can be helped to cope with modern pressures. Indigenization is beginning to take place as these traditional people try to draw on their ancient heritage and customs to find ways of dealing with modern and even postmodern realities. Bishop Solomon's thoughts about a future shape of pastoral care and counseling in Asia are illuminating:

> For the future we may have to rethink our approaches in pastoral care and counseling. *The community itself may need to be seen as the client or patient.* Theory-building activities must take place and we will have to help communities in the way we have been helping individuals and families. We may have to think of how communities experience stress, anxiety, grief, loss, identity crisis, and depression, and of how they develop, and suffer dysfunction. We will have to study the secret of resilient communities, communal myths, scripts, coping styles, and so on. We will also have to deal with issues of justice and compassion for these are important markers of the health and well being of a community. (p. 113, my emphasis)

Solomon's new paradigm of seeing whole communities as the clients of pastoral care and counseling embraces a Christian theology of the cross as described in Eph. 2:14-16, where the enmity between Jews and Gentiles is resolved by the discovery of a transcending corporate identity and reality in Christ. "This spirituality of finding larger transcending identities that can bring healing by bringing people together in peace is central to a pastoral care approach to communities that are divided and estranged from other communities" (p. 115).

Asian emphasis on the communal within a context of religious pluralism raises important questions for pastoral therapeutic practice in general.

The Philippines

The Philippines is mentioned as the first Southeast Asian country in which American styles of pastoral counseling took root. Clinical Pastoral Education began in the Philippines in 1964, when Albert Dalton, an American Episcopal Chaplain and CPE supervisor, began work at St. Luke's Hospital in Manila. The Clinical Pastoral Care Association of the Philippines (CPCAP) was started in 1965 (Dumalagan et al., 1983). CPCAP maintained membership and training centers in church-related as well as nonchurch hospitals and universities throughout the country. Numerous denominations from the Roman Catholic majority through mainline and evangelical churches have been involved in this enterprise. The Asian Clinical Pastoral Education Association offers CPE training in Metro Manila and Baguio, as does St. Luke's hospital, under the direction of the Reverend Narciso Dumalagan. These centers attract students from many other Asian countries thus having a significant effect on the shape of the practice of pastoral care and counseling throughout Asia following the model of practice that I have described as globalization.

However, Fred Gingrich's research (2002) points to several distinguishing features of counseling in the Filipino context.

- Because Filipino culture tends to be less time-bound, directive, and linear, counseling in that context may not always fit into the fifty-minute hour slot.
- Counseling in this context needs to be more flexible, relational, and concrete.
- Clients prefer to see counselors they know personally rather than complete strangers.
- In view of the high value placed on family decision making, family honor, and authority, counselors need to give special attention to the role of authority figures and family support.
- The belief in the influences of the unseen world of spirits and powers is strong and needs to be taken seriously in pastoral counseling. An important instance of this is the fact that pastoral counseling in the Philippines inevitably faces the issue of *sinapian* (possession or oppression) by the demonic. In Filipino life there is little problem with the interface between the psychological and the spiritual. Pastoral counselors need to articulate theologies that will assist them in engaging in contextually appropriate responses to this phenomenon. (For a brief and thoughtful reference on this see the entry by Richard Woods on "Exorcism" in the *Dictionary*, pp. 387-388.)
- *"Hiya"* (shame, embarrassment, losing face, having a sense of propriety) is a pervasive cultural dynamic that is one of the determinants of valued social behavior. Pastoral counselors often have to help clients "save face."
- In the face of colonial denigration, economic deprivation, and social pressure there is a widespread sense of pain, anger, powerlessness, and helplessness which constitute the psychological framework within which much pastoral counseling is done. Gingrich writes, "Sikolohiyang Pilipino (Filipino psychology) represents the desire to develop a Filipino identity and consciousness apart from colonial heritage" (Gingrich, 2002, p. 16).

An important reference point is the work of Filipino psychologist Enriquez especially articulated in a book entitled *Indigenous Psychology and National Consciousness* (1989, 1994), which, through the use of linguistic and field survey methods, rejects the continuation of a colonial mentality among Filipinos and the imposition of oppressive foreign psychologies upon local people. In place of these culturally and psychologically destructive impositions, Enriquez develops a Filipino psychology based on what he describes as a core Filipino value, namely *kapwa* (shared identity) that is related to the interpersonal value of *pakiramdan* (shared inner perception).

Evidence of indigenization has already been presented in a book edited by Mercado (1977) entitled *Filipino Religious Psychology*, which describes medico-religious therapy and counseling in popular Catholic practices and in indigenous churches and sects. More recent evidence can be found in the work of Salazar-Clemena (2000), who was president (1996–1998) of the Association of Psychological and Educational Counselors of Asian Pacific.

Korea

Korea is a country in which Christian faith and practice has seen spectacular growth in the last century. As regards pastoral care and counseling, the tensions between globalization and internationalization are very clearly in evidence there. Dr. Steve Sangkwon Shim has been involved in pastoral care and counseling in the United States and in Korea for many years. There is no lack of organizations for practitioners of counseling in Korea. Shim (2002) lists seven significant associations involved in secular and Christian counseling, psychotherapy, and training in Korea currently.

In 2000 the Seoul-based Korean Christian Institute of Counseling and Psychotherapy (KCICP), which Shim founded in 1993, became the first service and training center outside North America to be accredited by the American Association of Pastoral Counselors (AAPC). KCICP provides pastoral psychotherapy and in-depth training for interns and residents with different religious backgrounds.

Critical issues facing the practice of pastoral counseling in Korea identified by Shim include:

- The lack of adequate integration of theory and practice. This concern arises through the historical emphasis, for various cultural and linguistic reasons, on theoretical training (especially for Koreans in the United States) to the neglect of therapeutic practice.
- The tendency to "copy American theories and methodologies without criticism or cultural adaptation" (Shim, 2002, 84).
- The absence of distinction, in both identity and training, between pastoral care/CPE and pastoral counseling.
- The absence of competently trained Korean supervisors. Shim identifies two factors: the greater responsiveness to group rather than individual supervision, and the cultural preference for dependence and compliance on the part of trainees in the trainee-supervisor relationship.

Globalization tends to be the main model at work in Korea, although internationalization is on the increase, not least through the efforts of Shim and others. Shim realizes that the AAPC mode of pastoral counseling is more suited to North American individualism and lifestyle than it is to Korean familism, veneration for the elderly, filial piety, harmony, relationality, and interdependence. He emphasizes the importance of avoiding simply "transplanting" Western models without taking the deep cultural differences between East and West into consideration. Nevertheless, he remains convinced that, "An American-made piano can be quite useful for the benefit and well being of people in the global village as long as the piano player is sensitive to variations in culture and lifestyle" (p. 95).

Chinese Cultural Developments

In Chinese traditional thought the self cannot attain wholeness except through integration with others and the surrounding context. Thus, following Confucius's (551–497 B.C.) writings and teachings *Jen*, translated as benevolence, perfect virtue, goodness, and love (Simon Lee, 2002, p. 123), is the basis of all goodness. Etymologically the Chinese characters for *jen* comprise the word for "man" and the word for "two" (community). Persons, then, find their identity—and the ethical basis for their lives—in society. "A virtuous man is one who lives in harmony with others" (Lee, p. 123). As a result of this way of thinking, it is evident that pastoral counseling that emphasizes collective harmonious relationships and family well-being is better suited to Chinese persons than overly individualistic approaches.

According to Confucian teaching regarding psychological health, composure, satisfaction, calmness, and poise are crucial. The traditional Chinese sign of maturity is the ability to appear calm, cool, and collected—containing rather than expressing one's emotions. Such Chinese "reserve" should not be interpreted as an absence of feeling.

Another important Chinese concept with huge implications for pastoral care and counseling is that of *Li* which means rules of propriety, ritual, and good form. Making reference to the classic Chinese text, *The Works of Mencius* (Book III, Part I, Chapter VIII), Lee asserts,

> *Li* is the code of propriety in the five dyadic relationships: Between father and son, there should be affection; between ruler and minister, there should be righteousness; between husband and wife, there should be attention to their separate functions; between old and young, there should be proper order; and between friends, there should be faithfulness. (Lee, p. 124)

The term *methodological relationalism* has been used to describe the reciprocity, interdependence, interrelatedness, and good order that are envisaged within Chinese traditional communal life. Challenges in families and society arise where male positional power, in what is a largely patriarchal social structure, is misused leading to chauvinism and spousal abuse, among other forms of oppression.

Simon Yiu Chuen Lee (2002) has studied pastoral care and counseling within Chinese culture focusing on Hong Kong and Chinese immigrants in Canada. The pervasive influence of traditional Chinese culture upon the lifestyle, personalities, and practices of Chinese people is recognizable in these communities. Family therapy is recommended especially because of the pivotal place of the family as a unit. Simon Lee finds the work of Berg and Jaya (1993) with Chinese Americans offers useful insights for family therapy among Chinese people everywhere. Factors emphasized in this work include (1) problem-solving techniques need to be used that emphasize negotiation rather than confrontation, with the therapist acting as an authoritative mediator; (2) clients need to be seen separately before family members are seen together in family sessions; (3) due respect needs to be given to the head of family; (4) the vertical, hierarchical structure of the Chinese family differs from the more horizontal, "democratic" style of most North American families; (5) family members should never be embarrassed in front of each other; and (6) family relational approaches often prove more useful.

Internationalization appears as the main process for ministries of pastoral care in Chinese contexts. Historical and geographical location appears to be the key to culturally sensitive pastoral care and counseling among these communities. Discernment is also needed to determine the extent to which specific people, generations, and communities are affected by the interplay of traditional and nontraditional ideas regarding issues such as relationships, individualism, power, authority, and societal roles. Family therapeutic models of care are most fruitful in the dialogue with Western approaches.

Indigenization in India

Indigenization in the Asian context is perhaps most marked in India where ancient Hindu and Yogic rites of meditation and therapy continue to enjoy widespread interest and practice. An example of this can be found in the *Swami Vivekananda Yoga Anusandhana Samsthana*, a global movement active in more than 24 countries, with headquarters in Bangalore, India. This association aims at bringing the benefits of yoga to the whole society and through scientific research to demonstrate and prove medically the health benefits that may accrue from meditation. Scientific research is conducted by highly qualified medical and scientific personnel trained in Western medical sciences into the effects of the practice of yoga. The Pastoral Care and Counseling Association of India (PCCAI), revived and renamed at a national conference held in Bangalore in July 2001, recognizes work that has been done before in the dialogue between Hindu philosophy and Christian faith. Among other things, PCCAI is exploring ways in which this rich heritage may inform philosophical, theological, and therapeutic models for a more relevant and effective practice of pastoral care and counseling in India and beyond.

Pastoral Care and Counseling in African Contexts

Traditional African life and thought provide the framework and backdrop against which the practices of pastoral care and counseling across the continent may be appropriately understood. Centuries of interaction with European and American philosophies and understandings have resulted in modification but not vitiation of the traditional African mind-set. It is possible to speak of an African cultural milieu that is manifest in assumptions and practices. This milieu is observable within diasporan African communities such as can be found in the Caribbean, South and North America, and Europe. (See articles by Edward Wimberly in the *Dictionary*, pp. 93-98.) Among the most obvious of these assumptions and practices are the following:

- A pervasive and enduring place of religion in life. So embedded is religion in life that many African languages do not have a specific word for "religion." Religion is not a distinct compartment. Instead, it is a discernible strand in the tapestry of life. The "sacred" and the "secular" cohere strongly without contradiction or confusion. Life at all points is both sacred and secular.
- The cosmos is inhabited and animated by numerous unseen forces, spirits, and gods, among which are the ancestral spirits—human spirits of departed members of the living human community. These forces have a crucial relationship with the physical and material forces of humanity and society. People may acquire knowledge and skill in interacting with the unseen forces. Such skill may be used for good or ill.
- For human well-being and flourishing there has to be harmony throughout the cosmos. The ancestors as intermediaries between the seen and unseen forces of creation are arbiters of this harmony
- A holistic and synthetic view of life prevails. The different aspects of human, social, and spiritual life are connected and interpenetrate.
- A communal view of life prevails that emphasizes a sense of belonging, rather than an individualistic one that values aloneness.

The African Association for Pastoral Studies and Counseling (AAPSC) was formed in 1985 following an ecumenical consultation on African pastoral studies organized largely at the initiative of Congolese pastoral theologian Dr. Masamba ma Mpolo. The consultation, jointly organized by the World Council of Churches Office of Family Life Education and the Conference of African Theological Institution (CATI), was attended by thirty-eight delegates and visitors drawn from the Protestant, African Independent, Roman Catholic, and Orthodox churches. Countries represented were Benin, Central African Republic, Egypt, Germany, Ghana, Jamaica, Kenya, Lesotho, Nigeria, Sierra Leone, United States of America, Zaire, and Zambia.

Masamba ma Mpolo's article in the *Dictionary* on the "African Pastoral Care Movement" (pp. 11-12) makes mention of earlier meetings held in the 1950s and 1960s that were important precursors to the founding of the Association.

The African Association's objectives include promoting pastoral studies and counseling from a "distinctly African" perspective, and fostering awareness of the "spiritual, psychological, and social processes taking place in Africa as they relate to pastoral studies and counseling" (Masamba ma Mpolo & Daisy Nwachuku, 1991, p. 5). In keeping with the worldview where spiritual forces are seen as crucial in life and therefore in any form of pastoral practice, the spiritual is primary in the processes considered important for pastoral studies and counseling in Africa.

Two books published under the auspices of the African Association capture the emphasis of African pastoral care and counseling. These are

Pastoral Care and Counseling in Africa Today (1991) and *The Church and Healing: Echoes form Africa* (1994). An earlier work edited by Masamba and Kalu (*Risks of Growth: Counseling and Pastoral Theology in the African Context,* 1985) contains relevant insights into the nature of pastoral dynamics in various parts of Africa. In these works, responses to globalization are offered though internationalization and indigenization are very much the preferred processes.

Masamba offers an integrative vision bespeaking internationalization, in which pastoral practitioners,

> work towards the integration of the cultural, psychological and theological disciplines, helping us to explore the insights of these disciplines in relation to the ministry of the Church in today's Africa. (Masamba and Nwachuku, 1991, p. 27)

He nevertheless remains convinced that pastoral counselors in Africa "have to take into account the African dynamic interpretations of illness and health" (p. 27) in diagnosis, as well as in treatment strategies giving voice to indigenous sentiments. Masamba's work thus revolves around beliefs and practices that have occupied a central place in much African discourse, especially having to do with illness, misfortune, anxiety, and mental ill health— namely, African "witchcraft." His approach seeks to be quintessentially African:

> Disease in Africa is thought of as also having spiritual and relational causes. It may be ascribed to bewitchment, to the anger of mistreated and offended spirits, to possession by an alien spirit, or to broken human relations; pastoral counseling should therefore also use spiritual means of letting people deal with their emotional needs, even through ecstasy, rituals, and symbolic representations. (p. 28)

Two books written by Ghanaian pastoral theologian, Abraham Berinyuu, *Pastoral Care to the Sick in Africa* (1988) and *Towards Theory and Practice of Pastoral Counseling in Africa* (1989) also helpfully explain contextual pastoral issues faced by pastoral practitioners in Africa. In the latter, Berinyuu presents divination as an African form of therapy, because it is a model that seeks to respond efficaciously to the question on the minds of traditional Africans when confronted with any form of suffering or misfortune: Why did this happen? The African diviner not only diagnoses but also offers effective remedies for the condition (Berinyuu, 1989, pp. 38-49). This work highlights and questions significantly the theological underpinnings of African pastoral practice, thus illustrating the need for pastoral practitioners to engage in *both* religiocultural and theological reflection upon the data, beliefs, and practices nascent within their context.

What seems significant about all researchers and writers on African pastoral care and counseling is that they engage with indigenous people's beliefs and the practices of traditional healers in their attempt to evolve a truly African approach to pastoral care that is relevant and effective. Berinyuu's "divination" and Kasonga wa Kasonga's "African Christian Palaver" (in Lartey et al., 1994, pp. 49-65) are illustrative of this. The overriding model is that of indigenization. In almost all cases there is also a desire to engage Western theory and understanding in an international, dialogical approach, often reflecting the framework of training or education that most African pastoral caregivers have had. To this end it can be argued that African approaches to pastoral care and counseling are largely indigenous and international.

Latin American Developments in Pastoral Care and Counseling

An exploration of pastoral care and counseling in Latin America is best approached from two arenas—Protestant and Catholic. Protestant or Evangelical Pastoral Care has largely followed the process of globalization. James Farris, an American who is professor of practical theology at the Methodist University of São Paulo, Brazil, points out the lack of organizations in Latin America for pastoral counselors and outlines the extent of dependence on U.S. and European sources by reference to the texts used in seminaries and universities almost all of which are translations from Spanish speaking countries, the United States or Europe (Farris, 2002, p. 245).

It is in Catholic or what is known as *Pastoral Popular* (Popular Pastoral Care) that one hears the voice of the *pueblo* (people)—especially the poor— in Latin America. What is common to both Protestant and Catholic forms though, reflecting the reality of the context, is that "there are no private practice models for Pastoral Counseling" (Farris, p. 245).

Sara Baltodano, Professor of Pastoral Care and Counseling at the Universidad Bíblica Latinoamericana in Costa Rica, helpfully draws on translations and indigenous publications, as well as booklets and pamphlets by Latin American organizations to illustrate the nature of the practice of pastoral care and counseling in the region. Three local Latin American organizations that have published materials on pastoral care are:

1. ASIT (Asociación de Seminarios y Institutos Teológicos del Cono Sur or Association of Theological Institutions of the South Cone of South America). This association organized the first Latin American congress on pastoral psychology in Buenos Aires in 1981 and publishes the journal *Psicologia a Pastoral* (founded in 1972 in Argentina).
2. The Corpo de Psicólogos e Psiquiatras Cristãos (Body of Christian Psychologists and Psychiatrists) founded in Brazil in 1977.
3. EIRENE (Latin American Association of Family Pastoral Care) founded in Argentina in 1979, now has educational institutions in Mexico, Venezuela, Colombia, Brazil, Ecuador, and Peru. EIRENE teaches a systemic approach to the family.

While Protestant approaches to pastoral care in Latin America have tended to follow a globalization route, Catholic approaches have been more closely tied to Latin American Liberation Theology. To that extent, Catholic approaches have been more indigenous in method and ethos. With the exception of a growing interest in systemic approaches to pastoral care in some organizations, Protestant pastoral care in Latin America has followed the largely individualistic approach of American Protestant models. Baltodano points to ecumenical and evangelical bodies such as CEDI (Centro Ecuménico de Documentacão e Informacão) in Brazil; CELEP (Centro Evangélico Latinoamericano de Estudios Pastorales), a continental organization with its headquarters in Costa Rica; and CEDEPCA (Centro de Estudios Pastorales en Centro America) located in Guatemala that aim to broaden the concept of pastoral care and counseling to include collective action by the church (Baltodano, p. 204).

Influenced by *Guadium et Spes*, the famous papal encyclical issued at the beginning of the 1960s that studied the role and function of the church in the modern world, a new Catholic approach to pastoral care in Latin America, based on Liberation Theology, has emerged. This form is defined by its focus on the care of the Latin American poor, who are, in fact, the majority of the population (hence it's being called "popular"). Although not necessarily the form adopted by Catholics across the continent, Popular Pastoral Care is increasingly well developed especially in Brazil and Nicaragua.

Brazilian Protestant philosopher, theologian, and psychoanalyst, Rubem Alves, arguably the first to articulate a theology of liberation, has been in the forefront of the ecumenical dialogue around Liberation Theology in Latin America and beyond. Alves argues persuasively that "pastoral care is determined by its institutional setting." "Pastoral care," Alves declares, "is located institutionally. It can only exist within a specific social organization that has certain problems to be solved" (Alves, 1977, p. 127). Hence,

> If pastoral care is socially determined by the functional relationship between, on the one hand, individual-congregational needs and, on the other, its ability to respond to these needs, the ultimate criterion for its success is whether it contributes to the unity, well-being, and growth of the congregation. (Alves, p. 130)

Popular Pastoral Care, recognizing the social, economic, and political environment within which it is embedded, seeks to respond appropriately. Says Baltodano,

> Pastoral Care means both transforming the immediate situation of a family who must watch the death by hunger of their child and the transformation of society such that this tragedy no longer happens to any child. (Baltodano, p. 205)

A cardinal principle of Popular Pastoral Care is that the poor are agents of their own liberation not merely subjects of the pity and action of others. Following Clodovis and Leonardo Boff, Sara Baltonado presents the concept of the existence of only "one history" in which God is acting through the poor such that the poor are active subjects who participate in the process of their own liberation and are not merely passive objects. As such, Popular Pastoral Care travels with the poor as they seek their liberation. Rejecting a hierarchical, top-down approach to pastoral care, Latin American theologians and people have embraced Basic Christian Communities (BCCs) as the loci through which care is mediated. These small groups (approximately ten people) meeting in houses, chapels, or under trees, are made up of ordinary people who gather together to reflect on their faith and act caringly within their communities. In terms of pastoral care, BCCs try to fulfill two aspects, namely (1) to take care of individuals, families and small groups, and (2) to serve as agents of social change in the community. These coincide with the pastoral aims of Popular Pastoral Care—personal care and care of communities.

Pursuing these aims, Baltodano proposes a *liberating pastoral care* of the poor that joins the theological insights of liberation theology with a deep knowledge of the situation of the poor in Latin America. Such an approach takes into account the culture of the poor and recognizes the poor as active subjects who are able to change their own situation. Thus emerge forms of pastoral care and counseling that are indigenous, communal, socioeconomically informed, and relevant to the context. Liberating Pastoral Care is a hope-filled vision and struggle with the complex problems faced by poor families in Latin America.

The Widening European Context

The Society for Intercultural Pastoral Care and Counseling (SIPCC), based in Düsseldorf, Germany, represents a highly significant development in the practice of pastoral care on the global scene. Since the late-1970s, Helmut Weiss, German Parish minister and CPE supervisor, has been in the forefront of this movement for internationalization in pastoral care and counseling. In 1986 Weiss invited American pastoral theologian, Howard Clinebell, to stimulate international dialogue at a gathering of German practitioners addressing the theme "Hope and wholeness in a threatened world." Intercultural Seminars were held in Kaiserswerth, Germany. The aim was to enable German practitioners to develop and hone their practices through exposure to and encounter with practitioners from different cultures. These gatherings have allowed encounters between Western and Eastern Europeans in the face of the rapid socioeconomic change initiated with the collapse of the Berlin wall. These encounters of the "new expanded Europe" have been a very important feature of the SIPCC and of pastoral care and counseling in Europe.

The SIPCC invites practitioners and teachers in the fields of pastoral care, counseling, therapy, or other disciplines from all Christian denominations or other religions desiring to improve their helping skills to learn in an inter-cultural setting. In this approach,

> Participants **encounter** people from other cultures and exchange various cultural experiences. They give and receive new impulses for new **lifestyles.** They give and receive new impulses for their **spiritual and com-munal living.** They reflect on cultural, social, political, economical and religious **contexts of people.** They challenge their own cultural and reli-gious **assumptions and presuppositions.** They present their **practices in care and counselling** and reflect upon them from various perspectives. They extend their **professional knowledge** in dealing with the theme of the seminar. They enter into a process of **theory building** of Intercultural Pastoral Care and Counselling. (From the website www.sipcc.org; February 2003; emphasis in the original)

The emphasis is upon face-to-face encounter and exchange with people of different cultures and lately also religious traditions. There is an overt and clear ethos of learning to overcome racist, sexist, and other dehumanizing attitudes and behaviors. Moreover SIPCC "encourages exchange between and meeting humans of other cultures as neighbours and the creation of com-munity with them in an open and fearless atmosphere" (www.sipcc.org, Feb. 2003). There is an express aim of reducing violence, imperialistic imposi-tion, and cultural indifference. This process is described as "intercultural," and bears the hallmarks of the international model explained in this chapter.

From West German beginnings, SIPCC now has an international executive committee and between 80 and 120 participants at its annual gatherings including significant numbers from Poland, the Czech Republic, Switzerland, The Netherlands, France, Estonia, Romania, Hungary, and Great Britain. Each year there are also participants from Africa, Asia, and Latin America, most often as speakers and workshop leaders who enhance intercultural encounter, exchange, and learning. The SIPCC can genuinely be described as a European movement that has had a significant impact upon the develop-ment of models of practice and theory of pastoral care and counseling that take human diversity seriously within an internationalist framework.

Implications for Practice, Pastoral Identity, and Formation

This study of pastoral care and counseling across different contexts points toward several issues of concern for pastoral identity, formation, and practice.

Diversity

In the light of the diversity that exists in the world, initiated by the God of all creation, the assumption that needs to be made is that *diversity is the norm*. Instead of insisting that all pastoral caregivers across the world operate on the basis of what is desirable within European or American cultures, pastoral caregivers need to assume diversity as normative, true, and basic. The theories and practices of pastoral care and counseling differ across cultures, and these differences need to be respected. Instead of imposing culturally alien practices, pastoral caregivers need to become culturally sensitive and aware, able to utilize from their particular culture the norms and practices likely to be most effective in ministries of healing.

On the American scene there is ample opportunity to explore diversity. Ed Wimberly for example, in numerous books (1979, 1982, 1986, 1990, 1992, 1994, 1997, 1999, 2000, 2003), has consistently sought to articulate an African American voice based on experience, clinical practice, and theological reflection. He demonstrates that African American experience differs in particular ways from the European American. Carroll Watkins Ali (1999), among others, has similarly articulated an African American Womanist perspective. Asian American voices are also being heard and need the attention of all.

Formation

The normalcy of diversity has implications for the formation and self-understanding of pastoral caregivers. Processes of formation need to emphasize respect for varied personal and social identities. Formation also needs to encourage flexibility of thought and the ability to use a variety of approaches in caregiving activities. Making particular theories and practices normative for all is no longer appropriate or acceptable. American and other Western pastoral caregivers need to recognize their heritage and celebrate its usefulness in their own context. Similarly, they need to realize that the dominant approaches they cherish are not universally useful. All thoughts and feelings of superiority in matters therapeutic or interpersonal need also to be eschewed.

Sociocultural Analysis

In every context we have surveyed, the appropriateness of therapeutic and transformative interventions has been based on how well they fit cultural and social assumptions. Pastoral caregivers and counselors have to be conscious of social and cultural assumptions in particular communities. The widening of horizons implicit in U.S.-based works such as those by James Poling (2002), the edited work of Pam Couture and Rod Hunter (1995), and unpublished work of Judith Orr (1991) all bear testimony to a significant growing edge in the disciplines of pastoral care and counseling that pays closer attention to social, economic, and cultural factors. Pastoral care and counseling need to be premised on research that unearths and permits indigenous voices to be heard clearly. Because many are excluded from counseling and therapy on financial grounds there is a need for new forms of care to arise—as indeed is happening in Latin America, Africa, and other parts of the world—that work directly with the poor and underprivileged, enabling them to articulate their own agency and strategies of care. Such attention to the experience and wisdom of the poor needs to feature more prominently in American pastoral counseling. American pastoral counselors need to pay attention to the development of therapeutic practices and theories that are suited to the needs, finances, and abilities of the socioeconomically underprivileged here in American neighborhoods.

The Need to Hold Together Personal and Community Care

The person-to-person work of a pastoral counselor cannot be divorced from the social conditions prevalent in a community. As such, care for communal needs should be seen as a pastoral concern. Strategies of care that address persons-in-context, such as family systems approaches, need more positive recognition within pastoral counseling circles. Moreover, the concept advocated in Singapore, of "community as client" needs serious attention. This theme that takes careful account of the Judeo-Christian theological heritage of pastoral care is a much-needed corrective for the hyperindividualism prevalent in Western training and practice.

Pastoral Identity Needs to Be Seen in Multivalent and Corporate Terms

The pastor in this view is a facilitator of difference. She or he values difference and enables communities to respect and cohere in the midst of difference. Indeed the aim is for communities to cherish difference instead of being havens of neurotic ethnocentrism. In this way of thinking pastoral leadership is catalytic of processes of change that are communal. It is the whole community of faith that, with such leadership, begins to see itself as having a pastoral identity. The community itself is the locus and ecology of care. Entry into such communities brings one into a web shaped by love and care where one may be nurtured, strengthened, and challenged to a life of love and service to others.

Encounter Is Crucial for Growth

For intercultural practices of pastoral care and counseling to take place, caregivers need to encounter persons who differ from themselves in significant ways. These encounters need to be set within contexts where respect and genuine dialogue can take place. As such, programs of study need to be premised on intercultural encounter. The enriching diversity of cultures can only become available within settings where people shaped by different experiences can interact respectfully and truly.

CHAPTER 5

Ferment and Imagination
in Training in Clinical Ministry

Loren L. Townsend

The late-1980s and 1990s were a time of rapid change in the social and medical contexts in which pastoral care and counseling live and breathe. These changes have been a rich context for revision and have profound implications for training. They have shaped professional practice and the next generation of clinical ministers. They also frame the primary questions of this chapter: How have clinical education, approaches to training, and supervision changed in response to cultural shifts? What corresponding shifts in imagination emerge, and what do these suggest about possible futures? Are shifts in context and imagination driving particular forms of ferment in our theories, theologies, and practice? Are there particularly fertile areas for new constructive work in pastoral supervision and clinical education? These questions guide my observations and evaluation.

Guiding Assumptions

Metaanalysis requires a clear set of assumptions to anchor observation and facilitate discourse. My assumptions include the following:

Pastoral care and counseling reside in particular social locations. There is no universal, definitive "pastoral care," "pastoral counseling," "pastoral supervision," or "clinical training" apart from specific contexts. At best, this analysis can observe particular forms of training in a North American context with some descriptive reports from locations other than North American. Furthermore, this review will observe the dominant narrative of training in North America observed in published supervision literature, professional meetings, accrediting reports, and shared experience. Less dominant (and perhaps more creative) stories will be under-represented or missed altogether. These deserve their own attention and will enrich the field as they are articulated.

The location of the observer determines the outcome of evaluation. All research is purposeful and political—it is *for* someone and will act to benefit some and disenfranchise others. New realities are created in the interaction between observer and the phenomenon described.

I approach this essay from the position of a white male supervisor and seminary professor who has trained pastoral counselors and marriage and family therapists for more than twenty years. I have directed training programs in specific locations—California, Arizona, Georgia, and Kentucky. I presently teach pastoral care and counseling at a Presbyterian seminary that houses a marriage and family therapy degree program. I am a native of the American west and was educated in a specific place—Berkeley, California. My formation as a pastoral counselor took place in the intellectual and cultural milieu of the San Francisco Bay Area in a program that allowed me to steep in process thought, theologies of liberation, and postmodern psychotherapeutic innovations emerging from the Mental Research Institute.[1] These influences continue to inform my work and professional development. My professional journey reflects experiences that provide the lens through which I observe and evaluate supervision and training in the past twenty years. Those who are living the dominant story of accredited training and supervision are most likely to benefit from my observations and conclusions. Accounts such as this necessarily privilege the dominant story of accredited training and supervision and its literature.

It is possible within these limitations to observe, describe, and evaluate shifts in social context and how these impact pastoral care and counseling. For this study, observation and description will rely primarily on the pastoral supervision literature and information provided by professional associations.

Training is central to pastoral care and counseling's future. Training must ground students in the best of clinical tradition and encourage imagination to meet changing social circumstances. This requires supervisors to be conversant with new, emerging information from social, behavioral, and natural sciences and theology that continually redefine our realities.

Pastoral care and counseling is not a unified discipline. Describing and evaluating changes in clinical training presents a particular challenge. While claiming common roots in a clinical pastoral perspective, pastoral counselors and chaplains have worked to differentiate their methods and specialties since the mid-1960s. In this study I try to recognize similarities and point out differences in how changes in the past twenty years have affected the practice, identity, and training of chaplains and pastoral counselors. Other challenges are unique either to pastoral counselors or chaplains. When possible, I have maintained a conceptual link between the two. When necessary I mark distinctions between their respective methods, histories, and futures.

Definitions

AAPC: The American Association of Pastoral Counselors—the primary professional organization and certifying agency for pastoral counselors in the United States and Canada.

ACPE: Association for Clinical Pastoral Education—the primary accrediting agency for chaplaincy training programs in the United States. ACPE also has international affiliates.

APC: Association of Professional Chaplains—an interfaith association of professional pastoral care providers of pastoral care endorsed by faith groups throughout the world.

CAPPE: Canadian Association for Pastoral Practice and Education—accredits clinical pastoral training and practitioners in Canada.

NACC: National Association of Catholic Chaplains—a group of chaplains and CPE supervisors endorsed by the Catholic Church.

NAJC: National Association of Jewish Chaplains—an association of endorsed Jewish chaplains and CPE supervisors.

Chaplain: Historically refers to a clergyperson or layperson commissioned by a faith group to provide pastoral services in an institution or government entity. Chaplain services may include crisis ministry, supportive counseling, help in ethical decision making, community coordination, and sacraments. More recently, chaplains are understood to provide care for the spiritual dimension of persons in institutional contexts that is not limited to a religious understanding of ministry. Most chaplains are recognized by APC, NACC, NAJC, or a similar group.

Clinical ministry: Chaplaincy, pastoral counseling, and other ministries which require specialized training to integrate behavioral science, medical, and theological resources into acts of care.

CPE: Clinical Pastoral Education—a professional education program for ministry that provides supervised practice in pastoral care with a focus on pastoral identity, interpersonal competence, and developing chaplaincy skills. CPE programs are usually accredited by the Association for Clinical Pastoral Education or the Canadian Association for Pastoral Practice and Education. International CPE programs are often associated with one of these accrediting agencies.

Pastoral: Refers to care and counseling's historic roots in the ministry of the Christian church and is embodied through theological methods that hold counseling theories and procedures in critical conversation with religious tradition; by clear attention to the religious and spiritual meaning of acts of ministry in counseling; and by the therapist's formation as a minister.

Pastoral Care: Draws from the biblical image of shepherd and denotes care from the religious community for persons in time of need or distress. In its broadest sense, pastoral care is an attitude engendered within a faith community to nurture individuals, families, and the community as a whole through normal developmental processes and unforeseen crises. As such, preaching, teaching, administration, organizational programming and community development may include pastoral care. As a specialized ministry, pastoral care describes the activities of persons trained and set aside by a faith community to respond to individuals and families with appropriate emotional support, concrete help in life tasks, and religious guidance in times of critical need.

Pastoral Counseling: Historically, pastoral counseling refers to specialized care provided by clergy to individuals, families, and couples to deal with problems in living. Contemporary pastoral counseling is a ministry specialty that includes ordained and nonordained counselors with special training in counseling and theology and who are endorsed for ministry by their faith community. Most pastoral counselors in the United States are certified by the AAPC or the state in which they reside.

Spiritual: Reflects a broad range of popular, political, and religious meanings. Popular definitions refer to the natural human ability to explore the deepest dimensions of human experience and self-transcend toward causes, meanings, and realities greater than one's self. In this context, spirituality is seen as independent of specific religious expression. "Spiritual" is also used politically to codify a discrete and observable dimension of human life that transcends biophysical existence. This dimension is available for study, clinical definition, social or clinical intervention, and organization as a resource for living. Religious definitions articulate a specific faith community's vision of how individuals apprehend ultimate concerns (or the presence of God) and how this awareness enlivens belief, religious practice, moral decision making, and movement toward renewed possibilities.

Supervision: Occurs through a process of instruction and professional development in which experienced clinical ministers facilitate student growth and skill development through a process of action and reflection in real-life contexts of care and counseling.

Training: Describes a multidimensional context that brings clinical educators and students together in dynamic interaction. This is a broad term that includes academic preparation, supervised practice, personal/collegial formation, and socialization into professional identity.

Beginnings

In his history of pastoral care and counseling, McNeil (1951) concludes that several millennia of physicians of the soul "would be astonished if they could suddenly enter our world of today" (p. 319). Radical changes in late-nineteenth-century and early twentieth-century science, technology, philosophy, and theology had a profound effect on the way the church approached care. What was once a moral activity that returned lost souls to the fold and comforted those who suffered was altered by complex new information. Emerging medical and social sciences undercut anthropological assumptions of earlier centuries and gave new direction to care and counseling. A fledgling sociology and anthropology outlined how society influenced expectations and belief systems. Psychoanalysis asserted with power that everyday behavior—including moral behavior—was driven by motivations over which an individual had little conscious control. Psychology discovered childhood, adolescence, and developmental processes that defined individual volition, motivation, and cognition. Medical science anchored human problems in a metaphor of illness that assumed both a definable nonmoral cause and discrete treatment to eliminate symptoms, pain, and deviance. Pioneers in pastoral care and counseling attended to these developments. They embraced emerging clinical disciplines and interpreted them for religious care. Perhaps more important, they established pastoral care as a necessary presence in an increasingly complex and nonreligious health care environment.

As clinical ministry emerged in the first half of the twentieth century, it motivated a new approach to ministry education. Early pastoral clinicians expanded classical theological education to include case study methods borrowed from social work, law, and medicine. These methods were indispensable to teaching new skills. Equally important, they established a venue for supervisors to nurture pastoral formation in a clinical context and articulate a vision of the pastoral relationship in specialized ministry. New psychological information and a growing body of clinical experience proposed that all acts of care are expressed through the self of the minister. Training must do more than teach skills. It must also facilitate students' psychological development and their ability to manage a multidimensional self, relating to others through complex layers of unconscious motivation. Supervision using case study method and psychotherapeutic theory proved effective to teach skills, give attention to the pastoral relationship, and define clinical ministry. These innovations marked a significant departure from traditional education for ministry (Fuller, 2000). In clinical ministry, supervisors shifted away from classical "top down" theologies of revelation, God, and anthropology and revised theologies to include experiences of human brokenness and the place of empathic healing. This movement away from traditional theological authority was not a retreat from religious concern. Instead, it embodied a spiritual awakening that took seriously human experience and invested in uncovering those elements that motivate wholeness and vitality. By doing so, it "enabled the Christian ministry to address a range of modern spiritual needs and interests which lie beyond the purview of traditional, denominationally based seminary education" (Fuller, p. 32).

By the mid-1960s, chaplaincy and pastoral counseling took diverging paths. They shared a common ancestry, a common focus on pastoral identity, and a commitment to the centrality of the pastoral relationship. However, different methods and training trajectories crystallized into separate professional organizations, certifications, and purposes. Training foci and methods highlighted their differences. The mission of the ACPE and CAPPE was to train chaplains, teach foundational care skills to seminarians and parish pastors, and uphold high standards in supervision by focusing on supervisor training. Pastoral counselors, represented in the U.S. and Canada by AAPC, highlighted specific qualifications to practice pastoral counseling and defined the pastoral and psychotherapeutic training necessary for competence. Through the 1970s and 1980s both specialties consolidated standards for training and professional practice. Seminaries confirmed the strength of clinical training in ministry by revising curricula to include clinical study. By 1980, some denominations required CPE for ordination, and many churches had associations with pastoral counseling centers. Most religious communities recognized chaplains and pastoral counselors through ordination, endorsement, and support for training and supervision standards that assured competence.

Shifts, Ferment, and Imagination
Shaping a New Century

Clinical ministry was a visible and important specialty as the twentieth century drew to a close. Training possibilities were attractive to new students and formal programs flourished. This stability was challenged by cultural and contextual shifts in the 1990s.

Healthcare Reorganization

In the 1980s, clinical training programs were anchored to institutional healthcare, certification, and professional standards. Seminaries provided an educational foundation. Extensive hands-on training took place in hospitals, counseling centers, and other institutions with a commitment to clinical ministry. However, shifts in the American political, economic, and religious landscape late in the twentieth century destabilized more than 40 years of development. Carefully woven interactions between pastoral care, pastoral counseling, other clinical disciplines, and the medical context began to unravel in the chaotic reorganization of healthcare that marked the 1990s. CPE programs that had drifted almost exclusively toward hospital chaplaincy were no longer secure as hospitals cut back on all forms of education. In some institutions, the place of chaplaincy itself was questioned. Were pastoral specialists needed when parish pastors—though not always clinically trained—were available at a fraction of the cost? Furthermore, medicine, psychiatry, nursing, and other disciplines claimed to treat spiritual and religious problems. Did chaplains deliver any unique service another medical professional could not also provide? Chaplains and CPE supervisors worked hard to clarify their ministry, institutional identity, and unique contribution. Nevertheless, many hospitals eliminated CPE or declined to pay chaplains. Surviving programs found creative ways to finance training and were less reliant on hospital budgets.

New approaches to hospital administration and managed care forced chaplains and CPE supervisors to measure the outcome of ministry to demonstrate their value to patients and hospital budgets. DeVelder (2000) observed that regulatory trends pressed CPE toward "becoming a standardized course in pastoral skill instruction" (p. 137). Historic commitments to inductive learning and relational ministry were partly displaced by empirical and pragmatic tasks (Hilsman, 2000; Hemenway, 2000). The character of clinical education changed. Some supervisors questioned the future of CPE.

In the 1970s and 1980s, pastoral counseling emerged as a specialty that moved away from the historic congregational context of pastoral care and toward a model of therapeutic medicine. Most pastoral counselors in the 1980s worked in counseling centers or private practice. As healthcare reorganized, traditional psychotherapy practice was upended and fragmented. Managed care redefined psychotherapy practice and had a serious impact on pastoral counselors. It controlled which professional a client could see, what kind of therapy a client would receive, and how long therapy could continue. These policies were rarely generous toward pastoral counselors who lacked a viable political voice and did not hold a state license in a legislatively approved discipline. Furthermore, managed care and employee assistance programs required models of therapy inconsistent with most pastoral counselors' longer-term approach to therapy.

Severed from traditional connections to hospitals, mental health centers, and health insurance payments, pastoral counselors struggled against extinction. Training became less important than gaining competitive licenses and maintaining clinical practices. Strong training centers shifted energy away from training as funds and clients disappeared. AAPC records illustrate that the number of approved training programs nationwide dropped more than 10 percent—from 37 to 32 between 1987 and 2002. However, this description obscures a more complex reality: Fifteen historic training centers were lost. Supervisors who reorganized disbanded training programs, creatively raised funds for new programs, experimented with new models, or led seminaries toward accredited clinical training tempered this loss.

Healthcare reorganization changed how pastoral counselors are trained. Traditionally, supervisors taught clinical skills to theologically educated ministers, helped them reorient their pastoral identity to the practice of counseling, and shepherded them through AAPC certification. However, this training rarely satisfied managed care or met license requirements. Contextual economic and regulatory realities collided with historic educational and pastoral commitments and forced supervisors to reconsider the shape of training.

Ferment and Imagination in CPE

Healthcare reorganization resulted in crises of survival for CPE and opened several creative doors for supervisors to redefine clinical training. First, strong hospital-based programs began to experiment with models that capitalize on corporate structure. Several programs are now learning to demonstrate that chaplains and CPE improve patient treatment while still participating in corporate healthcare goals. Supervisors will need to evaluate carefully how corporate models change training priorities, affect theologies of ministry, and impact historic commitments to inductive learning and relational ministry. Risks related to this model highlighted by DeVelder (2000) and others may be worth the gains accrued by training a generation of chaplains able to survive in a corporate context. These chaplains will know how to attend to research, validate ministry outcomes, and articulate ministry's place in larger diverse structures. This emphasis is clearly demonstrated in a "White Paper" published in 2001 and funded by the Bristol-Myers Squibb Foundation. This landmark statement "describes the role and significance of spiritual care and is the first joint statement on this subject prepared by the five largest healthcare chaplaincy organizations in North America representing over 10,000 members" (Vandecreek & Burton, 2001, p. 81). It defines spiritual care, provides a rationale for chaplains as primary providers of spiritual care, outlines a chaplain's role and function in a healthcare environment, and documents clear benefits.

The White Paper defines an essential place for chaplains in healthcare and attends carefully to religious pluralism. It redefines chaplains as "spiritual caregivers" who may also offer pastoral care. As spiritual caregivers, chaplains attend to the spirit, that "natural dimension of every person" (p. 82) that is more than a mere physical body and requires more than mechanical care. The authors of the White Paper see "spirituality" as a contemporary bridge to renew a relationship between religion and medicine. Spirituality and spiritual care are general terms that may or may not include traditional religious communities, practices, beliefs, or values. Functionally, this redefinition de-emphasizes the specific religious formation of chaplains as *pastoral* representatives of caregiving communities and highlights instead the *specific dimension of a person* chaplains will treat as spiritual specialists in medical contexts. This definitive replacement of pastoral care with spiritual care is matched by recent changes in ACPE's mission statement.

According to Anderson (2001), this redefinition is no small matter. It "signals a fundamental shift in the pastoral care movement as it has been developing over the last decades" (p. 1). It appears to be part of a larger cultural revolution that recognizes mystery, a universal longing for meaning, and ancient connections between spiritual and physical health, while at the same time refusing to tie spiritual practices to identifiable communities of faith. Anderson suggests that redefining chaplaincy is an understandable accommodation to rekindled interest in spirituality and religious pluralism. However, this change has taken place without full consideration of long-term results. In particular, he suggests that "spiritual care" rests on a shaky foundation of popular spirituality with little grounding in tradition or community. It does not provide a metaphor rich enough to meet the depth of "the human and the divine story" (p. 3). He offers a theological challenge to consider whether this change serves the field well, and he invites chaplains carefully to evaluate whether such a rapid shift to metaphors of "spiritual care" is able to sustain the work of chaplains over the long term.

The White Paper provides a new directive for training. It insists that CPE programs take seriously cultural shifts, religious pluralism, and the contexts in which care is provided. By clearly listing ten functions of professional chaplains (pp. 86-88), it establishes competencies to be mastered by students. As stated, these de-emphasize CPE's historic focus on pastoral formation and highlight "specialized education to mobilize spiritual resources so that patients can cope more effectively" (p. 85). Theological and clinical training are required to prepare clergy and laypersons for certification as a professional chaplain and to manage a core set of competencies and values. However, CPE programs must necessarily focus on specific skills assigned to chaplain specialists—treating the spiritual life of patients—with less emphasis on pastoral grounding in specific religious symbols, traditions, or communities. On one hand, chaplain training is more available to non-Christians, is accessible to those without traditional connections to religious communities, and encourages increasing lay participation in CPE programs. On the other hand, supervisors must now reorganize training to manage increasing religious, cultural, gender, ethnic, and racial diversity and focus this training on spiritual competencies rather than pastoral formation. These emerging tensions are likely to provide a fertile area for professional discourse in the next decade.

Just as hospital chaplains have redefined themselves and are working to assure a place in health care, other supervisors are reorganizing to decentralize hospital chaplaincy. Some are returning to traditional nonhospital locations in prisons or other institutions. Others are highlighting congregational CPE and forming new alliances with business and industry. These programs have an opportunity to train a generation of clinical ministers who attend to community connections, envision human persons living in a web of relationships, and see their work as part of a continuum of care (Hemenway, 2000; DeVelder, 2000). This training will teach clinical ministers to intervene at different levels of systemic life and participate in rapidly changing cultural contexts. Parish pastors are uniquely positioned for this ministry. These new forms of CPE must be creative to fund training, discern what skills students will need, and articulate new frames for theological reflection.

Finally, contextual changes, funding problems, and a changing student population are pressing CPE supervisors to imagine part-time and lay models for training. These mark two areas of innovation. First, part-time CPE programs make training accessible for those unable to manage a full-time curriculum. More important, they embody a multiple-task orientation to ministry. Increasingly, ministers, chaplains, and pastoral counselors must anchor their vocational lives in more than one location and have multiple skills. These programs can teach a reflective foundation to hold several expressions of ministry together in a coherent whole.

Lay CPE is the fastest growing area of clinical training. ACPE records show that the number of students who are ordained, in seminary, or in a religious order has slowly declined since 1987. The number of nonordained, nonseminary students has doubled. By 2000, more than half of all CPE students were laypersons (T. Snorton, personal communication, November 11, 2002). This shift is paralleled by a similar dynamic in AAPC. In recent years most new members have entered through portals meant to include nontraditional, nonordained persons licensed in another discipline. These shifts in chaplaincy and pastoral counseling mirror cultural religious changes and interact with the impetus to redefine chaplains as spiritual rather than pastoral caregivers. However, this dramatic demographic change has not been observed, analyzed, critiqued, or discussed in the pastoral supervision literature. The fact of this lacuna is as important as the shift itself. Changes of this magnitude have profound implications for training and call for conversation and imagination. One starting point is Hilsman's (2000) observation that a "new breed" of spiritual clinicians is arising. Many of these are medical professionals who have completed one or more units of CPE. They are trained to offer appropriate spiritual care to individuals, but they are disconnected from denominational endorsement and traditional ecclesial authority and accountability.

Structural changes in pastoral care training are shaped by multiple, diverse voices among supervisors. While most have retained connections with ACPE and AAPC, a growing number of supervisors disagree with institutional directions their parent groups have taken. One group, the College of Pastoral Supervision and Psychotherapy, was established in 1990 as a response to ACPE and AAPC's increasing focus on certification, legislation, and organizational structure. Founding members of the College were motivated to focus on theology to ground pastoral care and counseling. They rejected a trajectory that institutionalized care and counseling hierarchically and relied on accreditation, legislative action, and nontheological theory. Now an established group with more than 300 members, the College asserts that pastoral care and counseling—including training and supervision—resides not in competency to provide spiritual care, but in covenantal relationships between spiritual pilgrims that focus on recovery of the soul. The College offers alternative training focused on personal formation and a "living experience that reflects life and faith with a milieu of a supportive and challenging community of fellow pilgrims" (CPSP, 2003).

Increased CPE training for lay and medical professionals, religious plurality, fewer students entering ordained ministry (Hough, 2001), and shifts toward generic spirituality as the locus of attention for chaplains propose a complex question: Who are we training and for what? Increased participation by nonordained caregivers enlarges pastoral care ministries in positive ways (Patton, 1993). However, supervisors and theologians have yet to wrestle with theological anchors such as authority and accountability for these ministries in a contemporary religious context.

This picture becomes more confusing when chaplains become "spiritual clinicians" who are specialists in the spiritual dimension of patients' lives. This position relieves narrow denominationalism, appears to embrace religious plurality, and gives chaplains an institutionally definable task. However, it also raises important epistemological and ecclesiological questions. Who defines the spiritual dimension of human experience? How is it identified, especially when distanced from specific religious expression or connections with traditional communities of faith? Chaplains redefined as spiritual caregivers appear to be one small part of a growing movement of psychologists, counselors, and social workers who claim expertise in responding to universal human spiritual needs. Summits on spirituality sponsored by nonpastoral organizations (Miller, 1999) highlight interdisciplinary concern for competency in spiritual care, most often seen as independent of religious life (Young et al., 2002, CACREP, 2001). These cross-disciplinary developments deserve serious conversation in the pastoral supervisory literature. CPE supervisors and theologians must evaluate carefully what future is imagined when spiritual competencies are shared by other disciplines and separated from the religious connections, commitments, and practices of the caregiver. Finally, new theologies of care, anthropology, ministry, and the activity of God in the world are implied in chaplains' redefined roles and identities. These require careful analysis and articulation.

Ferment and Imagination
in Pastoral Counselor Training

Pastoral counselors responded in two ways to healthcare changes that threatened to eliminate them from competitive practice. These options imagine very different futures and two discrete frames for training. Both deserve careful evaluation and critical dialogue.

Legislative Activism

As pastoral counselors' practice was restricted, lobbies pressed for new laws to recognize pastoral counseling as a mental health discipline. Two decades of hard work resulted in a license or certificate in six states (New Hampshire, North Carolina, Maine, Kentucky, Tennessee, and Arkansas). These laws acted to retain traditional practices, establish competitive equity with other licensed professionals, and offer consumers an alternative of religiously based care. Legislation was successful in more conservative states with populations of pastoral counselors large enough to form an effective lobby. Pastoral counselors in other states found the legislative process expensive, slow, unpredictable, and fraught with competing interests. Furthermore, as attractive as pastoral counseling licenses are, they have had a marginal impact. They grant legitimacy to pastoral counselors, but fail to guarantee competitive access to managed care panels dominated by stronger lobby groups.

New laws impact training by defining pastoral counseling legally, mandating formal standards for training, and determining how mastery of this discipline will be judged. These are by no means minor points. They recapitulate lively historic debates about the appropriate location of pastoral counseling. Seward Hiltner and Wayne Oates argued that pastoral counseling was defined by its location within church ministry (Holifield, 1990).

Specialization and regulation outside of the church—for instance by AAPC or state regulating agencies—erased the boundary between ministry and the work of psychologists or other professional counselors. Neither saw a place for private pastoral counseling, which Hiltner maintained was inconsistent with theologies of ministry. On the other hand, Howard Clinebell and Frederick Keuther supported the idea that pastoral counseling did not belong exclusively to the religious community. Clinebell believed that pastoral counselors were distinct because of their theological training and use of religious symbols to enhance spiritual growth in counselees (Holifield, 1983). In the 1990s these same issues were rekindled as lobby leaders pressed to regulate pastoral counseling and define it as one mental health option available to the general public.

As a result of regulation, pastoral theologians and supervisors are challenged to articulate a theology of ministry inclusive of pastoral counseling as a *mental health* discipline in contrast to a theological discipline. Pastoral counseling so defined is connected only circumstantially to specific religious communities and theologies of faith traditions. This shift changes the locus of authority and accountability for clinical ministry and requires careful evaluation.

New laws subtly redefine and recreate training and practice, but they do not necessarily encourage new generations to become pastoral therapists. Licensing statistics show that legislation has benefited those in the original lobby groups. However, a second generation appears stillborn. In seven years (1996–2002) fewer than 30 new pastoral counselors were certified nationwide. In 2002 the Pastoral Counselor Examination Board, which designed and maintained the standardized examination used by all states except North Carolina, disbanded because there were too few applicants to maintain board operations (PCEB, personal communication, 2002).

This trend raises the important question of what professional identity should define training. Legislation forced pastoral counselors to define a literature, tradition, and skills testable by a standard examination. This process had obvious benefits for training curricula and supervision. It was supported financially and conceptually by AAPC leadership, but rejected by AAPC membership as not representative of their pastoral counseling values. The question more at the heart of the matter may be, *is* pastoral counseling a discipline set apart with its own skill set and counseling methods? Emerging from this question are conversations that position pastoral counseling as a theological discipline capable of building bridges between borrowed counseling theories and religious/spiritual and theological traditions.

Pastoral Counseling as An Integrative Bridge Discipline
A second vision has gained strength in response to health care changes that has very different results for training. In most parts of the United States,

pastoral counselors lacked the lobby power to gain new licenses. If pastoral counselors were to practice, they had do so with a license in another discipline. Furthermore, many pastoral therapists philosophically and theologically rejected the restrictive visions of their discipline that were driving legislation. Others questioned whether state control of ministry was a realistic remedy for managed care problems and were motivated to redefine pastoral counseling itself more broadly. Their position implied that pastoral counseling embodies an integrative bridge discipline that is expert at holding ministry and behavioral sciences in creative tension.

Proponents of this position suggest that therapy skills and theories used by pastoral therapists are identical to those of other psychotherapeutic disciplines. "Pastoral" is defined by *theological* methods that hold counseling theories and procedures in critical conversation with religious tradition, by clear attention to the religious and spiritual meaning of acts of ministry in counseling, and by the therapist's formation as a minister. In effect, pastoral counselors do not "own" a set of skills or theories. Most are licensed and trained in a "borrowed" or "adopted" therapeutic discipline. Their pastoral identity resides in theological and ministry methods that bridge psychotherapeutic theory, personality theory, and therapeutic procedures on one hand, and religious meaning, ministry action, and theological understanding of humans and their context on the other. Pastoral counseling is the "holding environment" for multiple models of counseling and the interpretive frame for the motion of therapy. It is an informed dialogical position. Pastoral counselors are not united by a common license, but live in collaborative, conversational relationships with groups such as AAPC. This approach is highly inclusive, allows competitive practice, and affirms that a pastoral approach to therapy is unique. It also corresponds with recent changes in AAPC. Standards for membership have been rewritten to reduce reliance on ordination, establish minimum theological education requirements, and define a fundamental body of knowledge to support integrative functioning (AAPC Membership Manual, 2003). These changes downplay traditional clinical certification and invite diverse mental health professionals to join core conversations as pastoral counselors. They also have profound implications for training and supervision.

Traditional pastoral counselor training programs have declined or disappeared. However, creative dual-focus training programs that defocus clerical paradigms and teach pastoral counseling as a "bridge discipline" are flourishing. Several seminaries and religious graduate schools now offer degrees in pastoral counseling that qualify for marriage and family therapy, professional counseling, or psychology licenses. Some have redesigned D.Min. degrees to be license-eligible. Most attend to accreditation standards of both AAPC and another professional association. All require at least entry-level mastery of a clinical discipline and integrational theological studies. Ordination is not an expected outcome; licensing in a mental health discipline is. Unlike previous generations of pastoral counselors, graduates from these integrative programs are prepared to work in traditional pastoral counseling locations (agencies, parishes, and private practice) and in other locations historically closed to pastoral clinicians.

This approach requires programs to teach a variety of therapy models, establish a broad range of supervisory expertise, enhance interdisciplinary collaboration, and creatively teach theological engagement with clinical theory and ministry practice. For instance, faculty in a dual-focus pastoral counseling/marriage and family therapy program must teach emerging theory that is quite different from historic psychoanalytic commitments of pastoral counseling. Supervisors must be able to guide students experimenting with new models of therapy delivery—such as home-based therapy, school-based interventions, community therapy in rural and inner-city areas, and a variety of postmodern approaches to the human person and family context. They must also be creative theologians able to help students learn critical methods and evaluate the religious meanings of a diverse body of theory and clinical procedures. Perhaps most important, faculty and supervisors must model a new vision of pastoral counseling as a bridge discipline holding ministry and licensed psychotherapeutic practice in critical dialogical tension.

Most freestanding pastoral counseling training programs lack the resources to offer licensable degrees. This fact has shifted the weight of training to academic institutions and changed the focus of clinical training centers. Instead of teaching theologically educated ministers new clinical skills, centers now help clinically prepared students gain theological integration skills, solidify their pastoral identity, and gain experience required for a license. Traditional training programs now meet a different student than they have known in past generations. Most trainees do not have a foundation in CPE, parish ministry, or a strong endorsement as a minister from their faith tradition. Consequently, supervisors must shift their focus from teaching basic *clinical skills to ministers* and instead teach basic *ministry and theological reflection skills to clinicians*. For many supervisors this is a dramatic shift. However, it is necessary to an emerging bridge discipline. Supervisors must be able to identify the "bridge" and teach it to dual-focus students and seasoned clinicians who are now invited to identify with AAPC and pastoral counseling.

Interpretive conversations about training organized by a "bridge discipline" metaphor are just emerging in the pastoral literature (Hightower, 2002; Townsend, 2002; Ramsay, 1998). To develop this model, supervisors and pastoral theologians must engage AAPC and other pastoral counselors in active conversation to clarify directions, standards, and methods for teaching an integrative discipline that nonapologetically "borrows" clinical procedures. There are also important theological considerations that must not be short-circuited by enthusiasm for a new vision.

(1) *This model decentralizes professional Christian ministry.* Organic attachments through ordination are replaced by functional conceptions of ministry that have no formal standing with religious or governmental bodies. This dramatically increases the diversity of pastoral counselors, but also means that they are no longer identified with those who marry, bury, and sustain the symbols of religious community. This is a desired effect for AAPC and holds the potential to retrieve care as a ministry of the church not tied to clerical paradigms. However, without the ritual and symbol embedded in clerical function, pastoral identity becomes diffuse. Careful theological dialogue is needed to define "pastoral" for new non-clerical and religiously plural contexts of ministry. Joining chaplains as "spiritual clinicians" may be an appealing substitute for some. However, pastoral counselors now have a legislated identity and, unlike chaplains, are not forced to justify their institutional existence. Furthermore, pastoral counselors are close to other disciplines seeking to universalize spiritual care and so would reap little benefit in exchanging "pastoral" for "spiritual."

(2) *This model radically diversifies theories appropriated by pastoral therapists.* It rejects any unified theory of pastoral counseling that stands apart from other counseling theories. What makes counseling pastoral is the *context of meaning* in which it takes place and not a particular *form* of therapy, service delivery, or personality theory. This means that pastoral counselors are trained to maintain an integrative tension between the therapeutic cultures of "borrowed" counseling theories and critically examined religious and theological foundations. Through creative tension, pastoral counselors are informed by multiple theological and behavioral science sources and become constructive theologians as well as effective clinicians (Townsend, 1996; Ramsay, 1998; Browning, 1987). Without this tension, the line between pastoral counselor and "spiritually informed mental health professional" disappears.

This integrative approach sets pastoral counselors apart from Christian Counselors. The American Association of Christian Counselors is an evangelical alternative to AAPC bound together by a common statement of faith[2] and a mission "to equip professional, pastoral and lay caregivers with biblical, theological and psychological truth that ministers to the soul of a hurting person and helps them move to personal wholeness, interpersonal competence, mental stability, and spiritual maturity" (AACC, 2003). Christian counseling is "Christ-centered, biblically based, and oriented toward the eternal more than the immediate" (Crabb, 2003). In contrast, pastoral counselors learn a methodological frame through which a therapist manages tensions between psychological theory, ministry activity, and diverse religious belief systems.

As a "bridge discipline" pastoral counseling becomes a discipline able to celebrate plurality and call for conversation to describe particular social locations for pastoral counseling, a body of knowledge to guide training, and a set of therapeutic and theological skills to guide therapy. Specifically, pastoral supervisors must teach multiple counseling theories in critical theological ways, including how to distinguish pastoral contributions from generalized spiritual concern now expressed by most disciplines, and learn to socialize new generations of therapists into integrative and "bridging" methods. Articulating this position will help pastoral counselors form a public language to move from privatized ministry to public ministry and toward a theology appropriate to postmodernity. It will also give training centers and supervisors a conceptual frame to train "women and men who have a high tolerance for complexity and ambiguity" and "are also able to respect difference, celebrate diversity, live in questions that have no simple answers, and discover that most truth in life and in faith is paradoxical" (Anderson, 2000, p. 11).

(3) *This model decentralizes accountability for clinical and ministerial behavior.* Without ordination, ties to religious authority for ministry are no longer simple or clear. Clinical accountability now resides in state Boards that issue counseling licenses. Future conversations must address to whom pastoral counselors are accountable for their ministry and "bridging" work.

Ferment in Pastoral Counseling
Training—a Notable Hiatus

Since the mid-1960s, pastoral counseling has moved away from congregational ministry. "Pastoral counseling" no longer refers to parish ministers meeting the needs of a congregation. In fact, its literature often describes *non*congregational care and methods that discourage parish ministers from counseling. Stone (2001) asserts that despite specialization, most pastoral counseling continues to take place in congregations and is delivered by parish ministers. However, neither model described above includes parish pastors in its imagined future. Training programs rarely are accessible to parish pastors. Those who enter training rarely continue congregational leadership. Reviewing fifty years of pastoral literature, Stone found that many pastoral counseling theorists trained in the clinical paradigm obscure details about counseling and overtly discourage congregational ministers from using therapeutic methods. Meanwhile, methods appropriate to short-term parish intervention have grown prolifically in other disciplines. Pastoral theorists have largely rejected these in favor of "seemingly endless variations of early twentieth century therapeutic approaches" (p. 187) that fail to address the problems usually encountered by parish ministers.

Stone's critique is important. However, his research design illustrates a substantial problem. He limited his review to single-author books published before 1996 by major theorists in pastoral counseling which were widely accepted by pastoral counseling leaders and had a distinct pastoral counseling rather than pastoral care or pastoral theology focus. Perhaps most important, Stone excluded new authors "as it is too early to gauge their importance to the field. Unfortunately, this . . . had the effect of omitting most women and people of color from the study" (p. 183). Stone accomplished his purpose. He highlighted the limitations of dominant pastoral counseling theory. On the other hand, his study itself illustrates how voices not privileged by an easy "fit" with the dominant clinical pastoral paradigm are minimized by leaders in the field. To access these contributions (including methods for counseling in the parish), educators must attend to literature that has emerged especially in the last twenty years written by European American women and women and men of other racial and cultural heritages in single author, collaborative edited works, and books about pastoral care and pastoral theology. This emerging information will be more visible as these historically marginalized voices are included in the central dialogue of pastoral counseling.

It seems imperative that seminaries, training programs, and AAPC find ways to include congregational ministers and teach counseling methods relevant to parish life. While the AAPC encourages parish pastors to become members as Pastoral Care Specialists, AAPC policies restrict their work to "supportive pastoral care" and specifically exclude counseling.

Student Diversity and Cultural Complexity

Chaplain and pastoral counselor training programs changed to meet economic and health care challenges. Woven into these changes were dramatic shifts in the student population. Traditionally, clinical ministers have been white, male, ordained clergy with M.Div. degrees and denominational endorsement. This pattern was challenged in the late-1980s and 1990s. European American women and women and men of other racial and cultural heritages, as well as gay and lesbian persons, found voice and demanded that accrediting agencies attend to the fact they were excluded because they lacked access to seminary degrees and ordination. By the mid-1990s, both ACPE and AAPC had new policies allowing nonordained persons to be certified. These decisions by AAPC and ACPE paralleled a fundamental shift in theological education itself. Hough (2001) observed that at the turn of the century more women, non-Euro-American, gay, lesbian, and other nontraditional students are entering seminary. Many students are choosing M.A. degrees in ministry specialties rather than traditional M.Div. degrees. Increasingly, students are conceiving ministry in noncongregational, individually defined ways with marginal loyalty to a religious tradition or faith community. For clinical training, this means that traditional methods that were appropriate for white, male, heterosexual clergy now are inadequate for a more diverse student population. Supervisors are challenged to reinterpret training methods, standards, and the contexts in which students learn to reflect a changing environment and accelerating student diversity.

Ferment and Imagination

Anderson (2000) suggests that *"[B]eing more inclusive of diversity is not simply a matter of assimilating different voices: it means rethinking how we supervise, taking into account those contributions from different perspectives"* (p. 10, italics in original). Anything less than full re-evaluation of our supervisory assumptions and procedures is indifference.

Cultural and gender diversity arrived as an energetic issue for supervisors in the late-1980s. In 1990, the *Journal of Supervision and Training in Ministry* included an "International Section" which invited articles with a global perspective. This section disappeared in 1996, but later volumes included articles written by international authors. During this same period, gender concerns became a focus of publication. However, Lee's analysis of pastoral supervision (2000) observes that any genuine practice of supervision or training based on multicultural competencies is presently no more than a vision. Other fields, such as counseling psychology, began integrating these competencies into training more than twenty years ago. While he does not advocate uncritical imitation, his point is well taken. As a group, pastoral supervisors have not begun a "vigorous investigation of how multicultural reality impacts training content and process" (p. 117). Lee further contends that there has been little revision of training curriculum to respect how diagnosis, choice of treatment modality, client assignment, or treatment outcome interact with these realities.

Effective supervision will require revising historic theoretical and theological training methods that uncritically reproduce oppressive dimensions of the dominant culture embedded, for example, in models of authority in supervision and pedagogical practices developed for middle-class white men. Such reflection will allow supervisors to look beyond the limitations of their own cultural experience and critically revise training models to respect a diverse range of values, traditions, and needs. Inviting multicultural conversations to revision core training commitments will also require more collaborative power arrangements.

Student diversity, postmodernity, and multicultural awareness are instrumental in challenging theoretical hegemony in pastoral training. Historically, pastoral care and counseling has relied on individualistic models of personality to guide clinical ministry. Stone (2001) notes that after fifty years, dominant models of pastoral counseling remain tied to psychodynamic theory and Carl Rogers's relationship methods. While other clinical disciplines have changed to reflect new research and changing social contexts, pastoral counseling has not substantially diversified its psychological base. The result is a dated theological anthropology and understanding of human problems embedded in psychoanalysis—a model that is no longer dominant in either theology or psychology.[3] Lester (2000) argues that postmodern, contextual, and systemic frames are reshaping theological anthropology in a way that makes this position untenable. He highlights a tendency among CPE supervisors to "cling to a particular theory of personality and methodology as if it were Truth, in the same way that religious fundamentalists cling to a particular dogma, as if it were the life raft that keeps them afloat" (p. 151). Singular commitment to one theory is inconsistent with research that demonstrates no clear advantage of one theory over another. He proposes that AAPC and ACPE must now question training that is not theoretically multilingual.

Lester highlights the need for theoretical diversity in clinical training. This must include increased diversity in the pastoral literature to establish a theological and practical base to train new generations of clinical ministers. Chaplains and pastoral counselors have yet to discuss what it means to retain individualistic, psychodynamic models of personality in the face of changing theological anthropologies, multicultural realities, and research suggesting a more complex picture of human life.

Student self-identity also influences the direction of clinical training. "Students preparing for ministry today have a fluid identity, plenty of autonomy, an overactive sense of entitlement, a suspicion of institutions, a longing for authenticity, and very little commitment to traditional religious categories" (Anderson, 2000, p. 9). Consequently, training methods designed for previous generations are almost certain to miss or underestimate the needs of today's learner. Anderson suggests that supervisors need to focus less on traditional categories of learning and more on helping students discover religious and theological roots for a faith they already "own." We cannot expect wineskins of previous generations to hold new futures emerging in a postmodern context.

International Training

There are few descriptions of international training in the pastoral literature in the United States. However, several observations are possible. In Europe, pastoral care and counseling training has retained its traditional position within university curricula and associated hospitals. There is little evidence that programs have been as affected by health care changes and cultural shifts as those in the United States. Innovations include a training program for supervisors at Maudsley Hospital in London and the development of a German association of pastoral psychotherapy. New programs have emerged in Asia, Africa, and Latin America over the past fifteen years. Most are led by professors trained in Europe and North America (E. Lartey, personal communication, 2003). In some cases, clinical training follows Western paradigms. Notable examples include three ACPE affiliated chaplain training programs in Hong Kong and two in Kenya; an AAPC accredited pastoral counselor training program in Seoul, South Korea, and a developing African pastoral care training network based in Tanzania.

These programs are not simple copies of American or European models. Farris (2002) shows how training necessarily adapts to local contexts, concerns, and theologies. Emmanuel Lartey (this volume) develops concepts of globalization, internationalization, and indigenization to describe pastoral care and counseling across national, continental, and cultural boundaries. Emerging training programs increasingly reflect a reciprocity of learning across cultures that Lartey identifies as international in character. However, as Lartey notes, more of the programs emerging in non-Western settings are drawing from the loam of their indigenous cultures, meanings, and processes. One important agenda for the immediate future is to enrich the pastoral supervision literature with substantial description and theological discussion of these creative non-Western expressions of training.

Theology and Science

Pastoral care and counseling have lived in historical interaction with sciences, particularly behavioral sciences. However, pastoral scholars and clinicians have rarely been full partners in research or designing new approaches to care. This is a critical concern for the future of clinical training. For example, an extensive medical and behavioral science literature has developed around spirituality, religion, and health (Weaver, Flannelly, & Stone, 2002). Vandercreek (1999) rightly observes that chaplains and pastoral counselors are nearly absent in this important conversation—the area in which clinical ministers claim specific expertise. These researchers are not theologically educated, are not chaplains, and have no history with clinical ministry. Using established research methods, these authors are producing an important literature outside of a theological dialogical context. O'Conner and others. (2002) rightly challenge clinical ministers to learn research methods and integrate these with appropriate hermeneutical methods. Equally important, clinical ministers must learn to extend their publication to interdisciplinary journals. To develop competent dialogical partners, training programs will need to teach students how to integrate methods of science with theological methods. It seems critical for chaplains and pastoral counselors to learn a public theological language to interpret our own findings within an increasingly complex interdisciplinary community.

Professionalization of Supervision

Clinical education in ministry has always organized around supervised experience. Most approaches to pastoral supervision highlight relational dimensions of supervision, as understood by depth psychology, and defocus more pragmatic approaches to skills training and practice management. However, recent legal redefinitions of supervision and interdisciplinary research demand changes for pastoral care and counseling.

Liability for supervised practice. In the late-1990s supervisors in all clinical disciplines learned they were responsible for interactions with students (McCarthy et al. 1995; Guest and Dooley, 1999) and for the care students provided (Stone, 1994; Disney & Stevens, 1994). Likewise, educational institutions found themselves liable for their supervisors and sometimes their graduates (Remley, 1994; Tolman, 2001). As a result, seminaries, hospitals, clinics, and religious judicatories carefully reexamined commitments to clinical training. Some chose to eliminate supervisory liability by ending their training activities. Most reorganized supervision to monitor students' work more carefully. AAPC revised its supervisor certification process to minimize risks. Supervisor liability is a troubling issue and is part of an ongoing critical dialogue in the literature of other helping disciplines. However, there has been silence in the pastoral literature apart from past AAPC President Margaret Kornfeld (2000) naming the issue a determining factor in pastoral counseling's future. Supervisory practice is changing to minimize risk. It is important to evaluate what changes are necessary and how these will impact the future of training.

Pastoral supervisors can benefit from several important conversations. First, supervisors will need to find new ways to take student complaints, problems in learning, and "program fit" seriously. Difficulty in supervision can no longer be defined first or primarily as the student's problem, particularly in a multicultural context with layers of embedded meaning. Supervisors will also need to evaluate learning environments, multiple layers of circular processes within training systems, and power dynamics that reflect particular racial, cultural, and gender values. Second, supervisors can benefit from creating nonadversarial ways to manage conflict that balance student concerns with issues of program quality. Third, other disciplines' professional literature suggests several important conversations. Informed consent (McCarthy et al., 1995; Cobia & Boes, 2000) needs to be interpreted for pastoral practice at *every* level of a system that includes client, carer, supervisor, training program, and legal contexts. Pastoral supervisors may also benefit from learning not to overestimate what they can offer students or what students can offer patients, clients, or parishioners. Training programs must be modest about their resources and outcomes they promise trainees (Stevens, 2000; Guest & Dooley, 1999). Other disciplines also offer methods of supervision that may reduce liability. For instance, live supervision and videotapes give supervisors more opportunity directly to observe students' work. How these are integrated into pastoral supervision can be a fruitful area of discussion. Finally, pastoral supervisors may need to attend more carefully to students' readiness to begin clinical practice. Liability places clear boundaries on supervising students who are unprepared for practice or unlikely to resolve learning problems early in supervision.

Interdisciplinary Research

In the past twenty years, supervision in most disciplines has become an empirically focused area of study and practice. Instead of relying on psychotherapeutic theory to guide supervision, researchers are turning to non-psychotherapeutic models of adult learning and postmodern paradigms to guide clinical education. Critical discourse about new forms of supervision such as reflect teams and postmodern collaborative models can lead pastoral supervision toward theologically integrated innovations able to bridge gaps between traditional models and a changing student population. Careful appropriation of empirically validated methods—such as live supervision, use of supervision contracts, objective criteria for evaluation, and matching supervisory interventions with student developmental progress—can increase the credibility of pastoral supervision and help manage liability issues. Finally, pastoral supervision and clinical training for ministry can benefit from theory supported by its own research agendas and outcome validated by appropriate empirical study.

Conclusion

Over the past two decades training for clinical ministry has been reshaped as educators responded to cultural and sociopolitical contexts. The picture today is a complex mix of creative improvisation played toward anticipated futures and intense effort to stay centered in historic precedents. Contemporary medical economics along with religious and cultural plurality have pressed chaplaincy and pastoral counseling toward dramatic changes. Two shifts are remarkable and have profound implications for future training and practice. First, chaplains have revised their identity away from religious connections that define care as an extension of particular religious communities. Its replacement resembles a medical specialty—chaplains are those practitioners who treat the spiritual dimension of patients through a set of competencies independent of ordination, religious commitments, or faith community. This change, now an ACPE policy, assures a future for hospital chaplains. It also shifts training priorities away from pastoral formation and toward learned competencies for professional practice. While this change is important to survival, it is critical that chaplains and pastoral theologians maintain conversations to evaluate effects and interpret this new identity in a theological context.

Second, struggles with diversity and professional viability moved pastoral counseling away from traditional clerical models of ministry and toward practice legitimated through legislation. Legislative activism since 1990 sought to secure traditional pastoral counseling as an alternative mental health practice, which benefited some pastoral therapists. An alternative response was to conceive pastoral counseling as a bridge discipline capable of holding behavioral sciences in tension with religious community and theological sources through deliberate theological methodology. Pastoral counselors can be licensed in a variety of psychotherapeutic disciplines, but are expert also in pastoral reflective methods. This approach has emerged with some power in the past decade and has driven training toward dual-focus counseling/theology degrees and supervision to teach diverse therapists theological and ministry methods. Legislative activism requires ongoing analysis and conversation to evaluate its future viability and its ability to engage religious and cultural plurality. A "bridge discipline approach" responds well to plurality and easily allows pastoral counselors to practice with recognized licenses. However, ongoing conversation is required to highlight theological tensions inherent in diverse theoretical models of counseling, to interpret a new model of ministry, and to evaluate accountability for ministry.

Several additional issues emerge that are critical for clinical education in the immediate future. The theological significance of advances in medicine, social sciences, and physical sciences need to be integrated into training programs. These will help revise theological anthropologies and inform ministry methods. Clinical education in the future can also benefit from attending to supervision as an emerging discipline in its own right. This will include new approaches to supervisor-supervisee relationships, critical self-awareness and other-awareness regarding racial and cultural difference, training liability, and use of empirically validated approaches to supervision. Finally, cultural shifts and changes in training point out important gaps in the pastoral supervision literature. Ferment and imagination in training can be encouraged by critical evaluation and interpretive conversations designed to fill these important gaps.

Notes

1. The Mental Research Institute in Palo Alto, California was established in the late-1950s to study schizophrenia. Its multidisciplinary team approach was one of the first postmodern departures from traditional psychoanalytic psychotherapy.

2. Assent to an infinitely perfect Trinity, complete and inerrant biblical authority, human depravity, substitutionary atonement, and eternal salvation only for those born of the Holy Spirit through Christ (AACC, 2003).

3. As discussed above, Stone's research focuses on historically dominant literature addressed to mainline Protestant and Catholic clergy (Stone, 2001, 183). His method required that he exclude pastoral care and pastoral theology books, recently published authors, and most works by women and non-Euro-American authors. By not including these voices, his theoretical and theological conclusions may be overstated.

CHAPTER 6

Methods in Pastoral Theology, Care, and Counseling

Joretta L. Marshall

Methods related to pastoral theology, care, and counseling have shifted and changed over the last twenty years, even while continuities with the past retain the essential character of our work. As theological education has become increasingly aware of issues of diversity, of the global nature of our lives, and of the importance of having an impact on church and culture, methodological shifts have occurred that reflect these realities. The field of pastoral theology was enriched by the creation of the Society for Pastoral Theology (1985) and the complementary work of the *Journal of Pastoral Theology* (1991), while professional organizations such as the American Association of Pastoral Counselors and the Association for Clinical Pastoral Education continue to enhance education and training for persons practicing the art of care and counseling. Together these forces in the last twenty years have both built on the assumptions brought to methods for research, scholarship, and practice prior to 1985 and have created constructive possibilities for the future of pastoral theology, care, and counseling.

This essay examines the methods utilized in the training, practice, research, and scholarship of pastoral theology, care, and counseling. More specifically, the intent herein is to consider methodological continuities with the past and the changes apparent in present work, along with imagining some trajectories for the future. This chapter will attend to five things. First, as is important to many contemporary methodological claims, noting the context and social location out of which this essay is written is significant in placing it within a broader understanding of pastoral theology, care, and counseling. Second, historical antecedents that ground contemporary methodological trends are traced by examining the definition of method as articulated in the mid-1980s, particularly in the *Dictionary of Pastoral Care and Counseling*. Third, an examination of some of the challenges to method in the last twenty years will illuminate the impact of particular populations upon the field. Fourth, trajectories for the future are suggested, based on broader cultural, theoretical, and theological developments. Finally, this essay will note briefly the implications of method on issues related to formation, training, practice, research, scholarship, and education.

Before proceeding to define terms and to note the historical context in which we find ourselves as a field in relationship to method, it is important to locate this issue in broader and more significant ways. Questions of method are relevant to the larger issues addressed in this volume, globalization, public theology, the analysis of power and differences in postmodernity that educational movements in clinical training raise. Methodological concerns affect every aspect of work for practitioners and scholars in pastoral care and counseling. Whether one is a parish pastor engaging a parishioner in conversation, a clinician writing an article for the *Journal of Pastoral Care*, or a pastoral theologian asserting theological claims, attention to method is critical. The simple fact that particular questions are asked while others escape thought, that some disciplines are consulted and others are not, or that certain perspectives and concerns are given greater attention while others shift to the background reflect the impact of our methods upon the actual practice, research, scholarship, and writing of pastoral caregivers and counselors.

The commitment among the authors of this volume to note the particular social location for each of us suggests a shift in method from what one might have expected twenty or thirty years ago. The belief that social location, standpoint, and context are critical to the interpretation of the content is relatively new. My perspective and vantage point on issues of methods are related to factors about my personhood and my training. The fact that I am a Protestant, European American faculty member in a historically Germanic-based institution in the United States informs the vantage point I bring to the field and discipline of pastoral theology, care, and counseling. As a woman I sit both in the center and at the margins of my discipline and my denomination. My choice to partner with another woman adds a particular angle of vision for my work within both the academic guilds in which I participate and the denomination of which I am a part. As a member of a mainline denomination who has served local churches and who has passion for the church in the rural United States, I am eager to address particular concerns. All of these factors make a difference in the methods I use, and for the ones that I find most persuasive in the work of others.

My identification primarily as a pastoral theologian who participates in the activities of care and counseling is also essential for understanding the perspective of this chapter. I understand that the way practitioners and scholars make explicit the theological claims of their work is fundamental to methodologies related to pastoral care and counseling. Hence, as you read this chapter, you will note a desire to retain theological integrity through the various methods employed by practitioners, scholars, and teachers.

There is not one but many methods relevant to pastoral theology, care, and counseling. In the last few years the methods have expanded as we have become more aware of the complexities of the cultures and contexts in which we live. This essay suggests some of the methods utilized in contemporary pastoral theology, care, and counseling, particularly as they grow out of historical antecedents and as they have emerged in the last two decades. Trajectories for the future have their base in both our historical context and our current realities. Now, in turning to look at definitions, it is possible to trace some of the constitutive elements of methods central to pastoral theology, care, and counseling.

Definition and Historical Antecedents

The *Dictionary of Pastoral Care and Counseling* (1990) contains several entries related to method. These selections provide a starting place for this chapter both in defining terms and in looking at where the field located itself in the mid- to late-1980s. When used in the context of pastoral care and counseling, the term *method* usually refers to one of four aspects, all found in various entries in the *Dictionary*: (1) the techniques one employs in the practice of care and counseling; (2) the tools utilized in the teaching or training of pastoral theologians and caregivers (both for pastoral-generalists and for the care specialist); (3) the articulation of the relationship between particular fields and disciplines; and (4) the process of constructing a pastoral or practical theology and the various elements for consideration in such a construction. The *Dictionary* provides a way to ground our conversation and to arrive at common constitutive elements present in every method.

First, when method is linked more closely with the practice of pastoral care and counseling, it often refers to the techniques and/or the development of skills for practitioners in the parish or in the counseling center. Wayne Oates (1990) in "Pastoral Care Contemporary Methods, Perspectives, and Issues" categorizes methods for pastoral care into neotraditional methods, twentieth century influences, and emerging issues. Oates focuses upon the practice of the pastoral caregiver rather than upon the methods one uses to arrive at a particular practice. For example, in neotraditional methods Oates highlights the use of Scripture, prayer, preaching, and initiative. Twentieth century influences on the methods of pastoral care reflect the move toward psychotherapeutic interventions, new psychologies, and the development of retreat centers. Oates identifies the emerging issues as leadership, variety, and uniqueness in ministry, women specialists in pastoral care, spiritual balance, responsibilities and financial support, and pastoral identity. A similar entry on "Technique and Skill in Pastoral Care" by Bruce Hartung (1990) draws attention to the tools used in the practice of pastoral care.

Second, and in a related way, method refers to pedagogical approaches for training and teaching pastoral caregivers and specialists. James Ashbrook (1990) in an entry on "Teaching" alludes most directly to methods in a pedagogical fashion. The importance of teaching and education for generalists and pastoral care specialists such as chaplains or pastoral psychotherapists is also found in John Patton's (1990) entry on "Pastoral Counseling" and Edward Thornton's (1990) description of "Clinical Pastoral Education (CPE)." Concern for the development of practitioners, pastoral care specialists, and pastoral counselors has always been important in developing methods for the field. As we will note later in this essay, the centrality of formation is emerging once again as a significant factor in "methods" in many educational arenas.

A third aspect of method is the articulation of the relationship between discreet disciplines, particularly theology and psychology. "Theology and Psychology," written by James Loder (1990), articulates the way theology and psychology relate to one another "in the effort to lay a systematic interdisciplinary foundation for ministry" (p. 1267). Loder notes that there are six dominant methods and suggests more will appear. For Loder, the dominant methods are: Tillich's correlational method, Hiltner's perspectival method, transcendental neo-Thomism, phenomenology, hermeneutics, and structuralism. Loder suggests that a new method on the horizon put forward by Don Browning might become important for the field. Building upon David Tracy's notion of the revised correlational method, Browning outlined a method that continues to have incredible impact on the field. More will be said about this in the following section.

Other ways of relating the disciplines of psychology and theology can be seen in entries such as "Psychology in American Religion" (Holifield, 1990), "Psychology of Religion Empirical Studies, Methods, and Problems" (Beit-Hallahmi, 1990), and "Psychology of Religion Theories, Traditions, and Issues" (Spilka, 1990). This set of entries has in common a methodological concern for defining the relationship between psychology, theology, and religion. The manner in which disciplines are related and the correlate criteria that assist one in determining what carries authoritative weight are related to the method one uses in approaching the study and practice of pastoral theology, care, and counseling.

Finally, the question of how theology and the activities of pastoral care and counseling are connected is central to historical definitions of method. J. Russell Burck and Rodney Hunter (1990) in "Pastoral Theology, Protestant" note that,

> The question is whether pastoral theology will see its task primarily in traditional terms as one of applying theology to pastoral situations and developing theories of pastoral care—essentially regarding the discipline as a branch of ecclesiology or ethics—or that of doing theology itself, contextually, or of the pastoral situation, in a pastoral mode or perspective. The question is whether the discipline entails doing a theology *of* something, or doing theology *pastorally.* (pp. 871-872)

From my perspective, it is the latter constructive efforts of pastoral theology that will best serve pastoral care and counseling in the future. Theology needs to be retained, but not simply as a convenient conversation partner for application to situations and needs of communities and parishioners; rather theological inquiry and reflection must rest at the integral core of every constructive effort and every pastoral action.

Congruent with this approach, Theodore Jennings's (1990) contribution to the *Dictionary of Pastoral Care and Counseling*, "Pastoral Theological Methodology," notes that method refers to "the critical evaluation of the procedures for arriving at theological judgments, proposals or assertions" (p. 862). Here Jennings points to the importance of method in the construction of theological claims as he asserts a *pastoral* theological method that builds upon an understanding of three orders of reflection. First order religious language is the commonplace, everyday language we use to "give expression to the way in which a person or community's life is related to God. Second order religious language (theology) is the explication and critical evaluation or appropriation of their basic meaning" (p. 862). The result of this second order religious language is doctrine. Jennings notes that, "theological method, including pastoral theology, is a third order reflection upon the way in which such judgments are made and a critical evaluation of the appropriateness of such procedures. Thus theological method is concerned with an evaluation of sources, norms, and procedures of theological judgments" (p. 862). Much of the constructive work in pastoral theology has depended upon this critical development of the criteria we bring to our scholarship and practice.

These four aspects of method provide the strands of continuity that appear in the current literature in our field. However, more important, these four understandings about method suggest the critical importance of the epistemological assumptions that ground our work. It is, in part, through method that we come to know a field or a discipline or a practice. Methods provide the framework for thinking, reflecting, constructing, and functioning as pastoral theologians and caregivers.

What holds these various approaches together is their attention to five distinct constitutive elements that are present in every methodological position. For a method to have integrity, it must attend to and account for: (1) the explicit or implicit role of theology; (2) the relationship to various fields and disciplines outside of religion or theology, especially the social and behavioral sciences; (3) the awareness of the import of communities and context; (4) the integration of theory and praxis; and (5) the role of the experience of individuals and communities in the construction of theological and faith claims. Two dynamics undergird these constitutive elements and provide the integrative framework that brings cohesiveness to any particular method. First, the particularity of an individual and the faith community in which one is grounded reflect the central role of formation and identity in the establishment of one's methodological principle. Second, the development of authoritative criteria that assist the pastoral theologian and caregiver in the integration of theory and practice provide the basis for concrete responses to particular situations.

As one looks at the developments in methodological approaches for pastoral theology, care, and counseling in the last two decades it is possible to see how the five constitutive elements noted above vary over time. While each of the constitutive elements is always present, the emphasis changes contextually and is often dependent on the particularity of scholars, teachers, practitioners, students, and clients. The transition over the last twenty years illuminates the way in which these five elements vary in scope during any given period of history in pastoral care and counseling.

Transitional Times: Fermentation and Challenges

By the mid-1980s it was clear that the methods that shaped and formed the core of pastoral theology, care, and counseling were distinct from such things as the psychology of religion, the academic study of religion, or the simple correlation of psychology and theology. While there was considerable overlap with other areas of discourse and study, the field was moving clearly in the direction of critical engagement with theological issues that arose in the context of human reality. In addition the field of practical theology began to emerge as a separate, yet inter-related discipline. For some, practical theology is interchangeable with the nomenclature and method of pastoral theology and has a similar relationship to the art and practice of care and counseling, as does pastoral theology. For others, practical theology is a field that carries a distinct methodology, providing the ethical grounding and framework not only for acts of care, but also for various practices in ministry. In the latter case, pastoral care is understood as a subdiscipline of practical theology, with methods grounded in philosophical and theological ethics.

In a parallel process, by the mid-1980s more scholars and practitioners, students, and specialists asserted the need for methods to respond to various particularities in pastoral theology, care, and counseling. Increasing sensitivity to issues of social justice, community, and particularity pushed the field in new constructive directions. This section will identify ways traditional methods for the field were challenged and re-directed in the last two decades in light of the five constitutive elements noted in the conclusion of the last section.

The Explicit or Implicit Role of Theology

As suggested in Burck and Hunter's (1990) contribution to the *Dictionary*, the methodological role of theology in research, scholarship, and practice is central to determining whether one is engaging in applied theology or contextual and constructive pastoral theology. By the late-1980s and early 1990s several authors lamented that psychology had replaced the centrality of theology in the discourse of pastoral care and counseling.[1] The shift toward a more self-conscious articulation of theological criteria in developing pastoral practice and an increase in scholarship focusing on constructive pastoral theology represent some of the most significant methodological movements of the last two decades. In substantive ways, this shift reclaims concerns represented by earlier leaders in the field such as Seward Hiltner, James Lapsley, Liston Mills, Wayne Oates, Charles Gerkin, Peggy Way, and others.

This movement to make theology explicit in the methodological structures of pastoral theology, care, and counseling occurred alongside the parallel development among practical theologians to examine the theological, moral, and ethical underpinnings found in psychological theory. The influence of Browning's work, *Religious Thought and the Modern Psychologies: A Critical Conversation in the Theology of Culture* (1987), is particularly evident in these conversations. Browning's thesis is "that significant portions of the modern psychologies, and especially the clinical psychologies, are actually instances of religio-ethical thinking" (p. 8). Admonishing pastoral care specialists to examine the implicit religious and theological norms found in psychological theory opened the door for deeper, more mutual critical engagement with the behavioral sciences and with theological, ethical, and philosophical perspectives. Evangelical authors, on the other hand, responded to this critical engagement with psychological theory by reasserting the priority of Christian theological and biblical sources (Johnson, 1997).

More important, the revised critical correlational method used by Browning (1987, 1991) and others in practical theology focuses attention on the centrality of theology for the work of pastoral care and counseling. In an earlier era, pastoral care and counseling drew heavily upon the correlational method based in the work of theologians such as Tillich. The self-conscious move to a revised correlational method—where psychology and theology are more intricately engaged in a mutual process of forming and re-forming one another—allows pastoral theologians, caregivers, and counselors to attempt more constructive contributions in the field. The unfolding development of practical theology (Browning, 1983; Woodward & Pattison, 2000) and the parallel constructive efforts using revised critical correlational method allow for the integration of various disciplines and concerns, but always with an attention to the centrality of theology. Clearly, the particular theological and hermeneutical lens one brings to the revised correlational method affects the specific conversation partners and resulting content of one's pastoral or practical theology.

Illustrative of the general move to make theological discourse more central to the work of pastoral care and counseling is Ramsay's *Pastoral Diagnosis* (1998).[2] Her work compares the diagnostic criteria used in the bio-psychiatric model, the humanistic growth model, transgenerational family systems model, alongside the particular theological criteria of the Reformed Christian tradition. Again, Ramsay notes the central and explicit role of theology in the construction of theory and practice by focusing on an ecclesial paradigm. An explicit relationship with theology is evident, as well, among scholars who draw upon the sacred texts of Scripture in shaping and forming their pastoral method. For example, the work of Billman and Migliore (1999), Capps (1981), and Wimberly (1994) provide opportunities to think about how the sacred texts of communities guide pastoral theological reflection. Many scholars over the past twenty years have engaged in similar projects, shifting the primary lens from psychology back to theology, engaging a revised critical correlational model.

More conserving theological voices, such as Oden (1994) and Purves (2001), examine how classical theologians contribute to constructive efforts in pastoral theology and care in the present era. Mary Stewart Van Leeuwen (1988, 1996) has correlated classical theological understandings of maturity and family with contributions from contemporary feminism. Deborah van Deusen Hunsinger (1995) proposes a pastoral theological method indebted to Barthian perspectives and methodologically reliant on a Chalcedonian pattern that keeps theology and psychology distinct.

The ferment of the last twenty years created a methodological shift toward a more explicit and central role for theology in the constructive work of pastoral theologians and in the corresponding practices of care and counseling. In addition, new theological conversation partners emerged as the academic discipline of theology flourished and diversified, as is evident in the work of feminists, womanists, African and African Americans, Asian Americans, liberation theologians from Central America, and others.

The return to theology as integral in method could have resulted in narrower or more confining constructive efforts, or in diminishing the role of disciplines beyond theology. This has not been the case. Instead, what is gained in this theological turn is attention, once again, to the primary notion that methods in pastoral care and counseling are dependent upon the explicit articulation of theological claims and constructions.

Relationship with Fields and Disciplines
Outside of Religion and Theology

A somewhat related challenge during the last two decades has been a move away from a dependence upon psychoanalytic and Rogerian theory to a consideration of other psychological theories. In addition, some scholars have turned to disciplines and fields outside of psychology, such as anthropology, sociology, cultural critique, and other critical theories to expand their methodological inquiry.

The desire to draw upon various therapeutic approaches beyond the traditional models has resulted in a reconceptualization of pastoral care and counseling. No longer is the field concerned only with the care of individuals.

Instead, there is an increasing focus on the systems and structures out of which particular needs arise. An illustration of such broader systemic analysis can be seen in the work of Archie Smith (1982) who integrates Mead's relational theory with ethical-therapeutic norms to arrive at a particular "Black Church perspective." Similarly, Larry Graham, in *Care of Persons, Care of Worlds: A Psychosystems Approach to Care and Counseling* (1992), builds a convincing argument for a psychosystemic approach to care as

> the reciprocal interplay between the psyche of individuals and the social, cultural, and natural orders. This interplay is not neutral or static; it is value-laden and teeming with possibilities. The character of persons and their worlds come into being by the mutual influences of each upon the other. (p. 13)

The case studies analyzed by Graham include psychosystemic analysis in new ways. This, combined with Graham's use of process theology, brings new methodological approaches to care and counseling, moving the field to consider the broader systemic contexts in which people live.

In a similar way, using conversation partners outside of traditional psychology is well illustrated in *Pastoral Care and Social Conflict* (1995), a collection of essays in honor of Charles Gerkin. The editors, Pamela Couture and Rodney Hunter, note in the preface that their goal is "to develop pastoral care and counseling in dialogue with its social environment and to deepen its self-understanding sociologically and theologically as well as psychologically" (p. 10). The contributors to this volume draw upon fields such as economics, gender studies, cultural and political analysis, multicultural and racial studies, and other disciplines not heretofore instrumental in the methods of pastoral care.

Others, such as David Hogue (2003), move toward science by drawing more clearly on brain research, following up on the earlier work of his colleague, James Ashbrook. Andrew Lester (2003) also explores neuroscience sources to deepen our understanding of emotions. Expanding into fields beyond the behavioral or natural sciences, still others draw upon literature, plays, and novels in their constructive methodological efforts (Wimberly, 2003; Doehring, 1995, 2004).

The last two decades witnessed a rebirth in making theology central in pastoral method while retaining the importance of diverse psychological theories as significant conversation partners. At the same time the field broadened to consider theories outside of theology, enhancing the significant cognate disciplines in contemporary pastoral method. Together this expansion provides for greater multidimensional understandings of the contexts in which we live.[3] Of concern in the next decade for pastoral caregivers will be the ability to maintain a genuinely integrative and interdisciplinary approach without collapsing fields and disciplines into one another.

Awareness of the Impact
of Communities and Context

Expanding our methodological conversation partners and examining the systemic nature of pastoral care and counseling challenges a long-held assumption that universal and normative claims can be made that are applicable to all individuals and communities in all contexts. Increased awareness of diversity and particularity has had a deep impact on the methods related to pastoral theology, care, and counseling. The voices of more diverse populations in professional pastoral care and in the academy, along with a stronger sense of the role of communities of faith in the context of care, have allowed for a shift to what John Patton (1993) calls a "communal contextual paradigm for pastoral care" (pp. 3-4).

This major shift is central to the ongoing work of many pastoral theologians, particularly those who move toward engaging public theology. Indicative of this move are those whose pastoral methods introduce communal and systemic interventions into the work of pastoral care and counseling. Prophetic pastoral caregivers understand not only the significance of work with individuals, but they also interpret their care to extend to interventions in the systems that perpetuate suffering within communities.[4]

With an emphasis on community and context, earlier theories and theological claims that focused only on individual care gave way to multifaceted social and systemic analyses. The methodological work of assessment, diagnosis, and intervention now examines the reality of power and social structures upon the lives of individuals. Understanding and critiquing the systemic realities that lead to oppression around such issues as race, gender, economics, and orientation are central aspects of our common work. This emphasis appears again in the fifth constitutive element when we examine the role of experience in method.

The Integration of Theory and Praxis

The fourth shift evident in the last twenty years is a strong desire to move toward deeper theological integration by overcoming the split between practice and theory. Rather than maintaining an antithetical posture between those who write and teach and those who practice the art of care and counseling, scholars and practitioners are working together to construct integrative methods for pastoral theology and care. For example, editorials and articles in the *Journal of Pastoral Theology* in 1995 and 2000 encourage those reading the journal to stay connected to practitioners and to learn from those who are engaged in the daily work of caring and counseling (Neuger & Graham, 1995, pp. ix-x; Patton & Ramsay, 2000, pp. viii-ix; Graham, 2000).

A sign of this increased effort to integrate practice and theology/theory is evident in two recent book series from different presses. The *Counseling and Pastoral Theology* series, edited by Andrew Lester, provides a constructive pastoral theological clinical perspective to issues such as troubled adolescents (Dykstra, 1997), depressed women (Dunlap, 1997), lesbian partnerships (Marshall, 1997), adult adoptees (Nydham, 1999), and African American couples (Wimberly, 1997). The second series is the *Creative Pastoral Care and Counseling Series,* coedited by Howard Stone and Howard Clinebell, and builds on a series originating in the late-1970s. Again, the texts are written for pastoral care specialists who deal with issues such as woman-battering (Adams, 1994), counseling men (Culbertson, 1994), counseling adolescent girls (Davis, 1996), working with family systems theory and congregations (Richardson, 1996), cross-cultural counseling (van Beek, 1996), pastoral visitation (Gorsuch, 1999), and caring for gays, lesbians, and their families (Switzer, 1999).

As suggested earlier, the development of methods related to practical theology also strengthen the conversation between theory and practice. Browning's intent in *A Fundamental Practical Theology: Descriptive and Strategic Proposals* (1991) is to provide a reasoned, systematic, and practical philosophical approach to issues related to concrete acts of care. A number of scholars, following Browning's lead, are integrating theory and practice at fundamental levels and in ways that methodologically move us toward new systems and approaches. While some draw upon more traditional and classical understandings of theology, others are looking toward process, liberation, and various other contemporary theologians. Practical and pastoral theologians are looking not simply at the application of theology to situations of care and counseling, but are genuinely seeking methodological advances toward integration as well.

The integration of theory and practice has had an impact on method as more practitioners and scholars construct pastoral and practical theology in ways that move beyond applied theology or correlating theology with psychology. The ongoing development of the professional organizations for pastoral care and corresponding growth within the academic guilds has strengthened the impetus toward integration. Practitioners and academicians continue to find ways to work constructively from the expertise and vantage point of each.[5]

The Role of Experience in the Construction of Theological Claims

Perhaps what is most significant in the last two decades is the critical role experience has come to play in the methodological construction of pastoral care and counseling. Experience, and in particular the privileging of experiences of those who have often been under-represented in the literature of the field, in the academy, in the church, and in the culture of the United States, has challenged traditional methods. While there has always been a significant weight given to experience in pastoral care and counseling, the difference is that now those who either self-identify, or who are named by the broader culture as oppressed or under-represented are central to methodological developments.

What is true of many disciplines related to religion is also true for the field of pastoral theology, care, and counseling. Linked with broader cultural shifts, more persons from under-represented populations in the United States entered the field after the mid-1980s. Individuals taking leadership in the next generations of pastoral care and counseling as scholars, teachers, and practitioners embody some of these under-represented populations in greater numbers. In particular, there are four categories of persons who were under-represented in earlier historical periods but who are now actively changing the methods used in pastoral theology, care, and counseling: European American women, women and men of diverse racial and cultural heritages, international scholars, and lesbians, gays, and other persons whose experiences of sexuality are more diverse. Together these groups have introduced greater methodological diversity by broadening the conversation partners and the disciplines necessary for adequate scholarship and practice. Each of the four groups has had an impact in specific ways.

First, as is true with every major theological discipline, women have entered the field in critical mass in the last twenty years as pastoral caregivers, pastoral counselors and care specialists, and pastoral and practical theologians. As practitioners and scholars women have had a strong impact upon the methods utilized in the field. In an edited volume by Bonnie Miller-McLemore and Brita Gill-Austern (1999), Kathleen Greider, Gloria Johnson, and Kristen Leslie (1999) trace the writings of women in the field over three decades, from 1963 to 1993, suggesting in part that women have contributed significantly to the shift toward more "communal contextual paradigms" (p. 22). In the same volume, Carrie Doehring (1999) notes there is something particular about the criteria feminists bring to constructive efforts in pastoral theology, while Miller-McLemore (1999) articulates how feminist theology and theory have an impact on methodological and epistemological perspectives in the field.

Maxine Glaz and Jeanne Stevenson-Moessner (1991) adopted a collaborative method that represents a particular feminist approach to working on an edited text. The writers, all of whom were women, were invited not only to write about women's issues, but also to meet together, read and comment on one another's work, and develop their common text. The original work led to two other volumes of collected work edited by Stevenson-Moessner (1996, 2000).

The impact of women in the field is seen in multiple ways, including through the value given to first-person narrative accounts of women in the construction of pastoral theology and in the practice of care and counseling. James Poling (1991) includes the written journey of a woman survivor in his treatment of the abuse of power. The woman's voice becomes essential to his method. Most recently Christie Neuger (2001) draws on narrative and feminist theory to build a solid foundation for pastoral method. As more women are involved in the practice of care and counseling as well as the development of pastoral theology, theoretical and theological conversation partners broaden to include not only traditional theology, but feminist, womanist, and other perspectives identified with postmodernity. Critical analysis of social structures, power issues present in gender, and systemic realities are essential to feminist methods.[6]

A second population contributing to new methodological approaches in pastoral theology, care, and counseling is found in the scholarship and presence of women and men of diverse racial and cultural heritages. In particular, as African American scholars engage the academy and as more practitioners focus attention on the lived experiences of women and men of diverse racial and cultural heritages, methods expand to analyze systemic and racial oppression from theological, psychological, social, and ethnographic perspectives. Scholars such as Carroll Watkins Ali (1999), Homer Ashby (1996, 2000, 2003), Lee Butler (2000, 2001), Archie Smith (1982, 1997), Anne Streaty Wimberly (2002, 2003), and Edward Wimberly (1997, 2000, 2003) engage critical issues related to racism and culture in the context of constructive pastoral theology, care, and counseling. In addition, more Asian American scholars and practitioners are bringing additional conversation partners to their methodological work (Kim, 1992). Women and men of diverse racial and cultural heritage are involved in the professional life of ACPE, AAPC, and other organizations, developing strong and liberative approaches to care and counseling.

Drawing upon theologies from African, African American, Asian and Asian American perspectives encourages Euro-American colleagues to take seriously the contributions of persons outside of the mainstream, as well as to confront the racism present in pastoral theology, care, and counseling (Bohn, 1995; Boyd & Bohler, 1999; Eugene & Poling, 1998; Poling, 1996; Ramsay, 2002). Asking questions about the presence of racism in theory and practice with an eye toward liberation results in deeper attention to context and justice. The methodological integration of diverse theologies, literature from ethnic, cultural, and race studies, and the fields of ethnography and anthropology are creating new constructive efforts in pastoral methods.

The third population that has become increasingly involved in the field of pastoral theology, care, and counseling is international in scope. The role of international practical theology and issues related to globalization has been discussed at length in another essay in this volume, so I will only mention it briefly at this point. Emmanuel Lartey (1997, 2002) and Tapiwa Mucherera (2001) represent two African voices within the broader field of pastoral care and counseling. Others from the international community are rapidly having an influence upon the conversation partners and the methodological directions within the field of pastoral care and counseling (Farris, 2002; Wilson et al., 1996; Woodard & Pattison, 2000).

The impact on method by international scholars is at two points. First, international perspectives, particularly from the non-Western world utilize rich and diverse theological understandings in their constructive work. Drawing upon indigenous theologies, communities, and experiences enhances our common work as pastoral caregivers. Second, international scholars bring unique angles of vision to Western concepts found in narrative theory, family systems theory, critical race theory, and cultural theory by analyzing power and culture from the perspective of postcolonial discourse.

Finally, another literature that is changing the methodological landscape is written for and by lesbians, gay men, transgendered, and bisexual individuals. While sexual orientation issues are still approached somewhat hesitantly in some contexts, they are central to the developing work of pastoral theology, care, and counseling. One of the most helpful and significant methodological shifts has come as more heterosexual men and women in the field address issues of sexuality. For example, David Switzer addresses the needs related to parents and families whose relatives are gay or lesbian (1980, 1999). Switzer's method includes careful attention to such things as developmental theory, biblical traditions, and scientific inquiry. Larry Graham (1997) draws upon qualitative interviews for his work in addressing the "narratives of care among lesbians and gays." Graham's work promotes not only the activities of pastoral care for gays and lesbians, but also raises a constructive pastoral theological approach to the concept of the "image of God" through those narratives (Graham, 1997).

In the last two decades more lesbians and gay men have written from our own experience, drawing upon narratives, sexual theology, and feminist theory to construct pastoral theology, care, and counseling. For example, the earliest editions of the *Journal of Pastoral Theology* often included work by and for lesbians and gay men (Griffin, 1993; Marshall, 1994, 1996, 1999). Randle Mixon's (1997) contribution to *The Care of Men* focuses specifically on pastoral care for gay men while *Through the Eyes of Women* includes an article on identity formation for lesbians (Marshall, 1996).

The experiences of this population has an impact on method as it introduces another set of broad conversation partners for the field based in studies related to gender, sexuality, queer theory, and sexual identity development. The movement has yet to produce significant literature related to bisexual and transgendered theory, although there has been a mild start in this area (Marshall, 2001; Tanis, 2003).[7] The social construction of gender and orientation has become integral to broader pastoral theological claims about orientation. Realizing the role of sexuality in spirituality, psychosocial development, and ultimately pastoral theological construction lends new options for ongoing work in this field of study.

Each of the four groups named in this section contributes to the larger fermentation and change apparent in constructive methodologies in pastoral theology, care, and counseling. By looking at the five constitutive elements important in methods, it is clear that the integration of the elements shift as each component takes on different nuances at a particular time or in a specific manner. Over the last twenty years theology has become more explicit, conversation partners are broader and more diverse, and more attention to integration invites us toward new methodological approaches.

Trajectories for the Future

While it is difficult to project the future of a field, it is clear that there are some directions that have evolved during the last two decades that will continue to demand our attention. Broader movements in theology and in the culture will have an impact on the development of methods related to pastoral theology, care, and counseling. Four significant emerging trends in the coming years are apparent in the methods related to pastoral theology, care, and counseling.

First, pastoral methods will continue to attend to the particularities and diversity of the United States, while developing broader, more global understandings and pastoral theological methods. The last two decades have prompted increased awareness of the importance of particularity and experience. Alongside pastoral theological work that encompasses the four communities identified in the previous section, issues of religious pluralism will continue to come to the forefront in our conversations. On the one hand we find emerging strategies from within Christian communities for providing care across faith traditions (Lartey, 2003) as well as proposals that provide for dialogue between mainline and evangelical positions (Scalise, 1998). The goal for the coming years will be to continue to draw upon the particularities of experience in constructive pastoral theological work without dismissing the ability to generate more universal claims.

In relationship to this sense of particularity is a deep appreciation for hermeneutical methods, the role of suspicion in the development of theology and theory, and our ability to think about texts in new ways. Growing and expanding understandings of liberation theologies, Afro-centric and African-American theologies, feminist theologies, political theologies, and indigenous theologies all will contribute to the work of pastoral theologians and caregivers. Texts are understood, of course, to be not only biblical or historical theological works, but they also include the lived realities of individuals and the broader human communities of which we are a part. As new insights are brought forward methods will continue to reflect the authenticity of multiple contexts and perspectives alongside an ongoing analysis of power dynamics as experienced in the postcolonial context and within multiple cultures of care. Deeper engagement with diverse theologies from various perspectives must remain at the core of what we do.

Second, pastoral methods will continue to reflect interdisciplinary conversation partners. Postmodernity requires that pastoral theologians attend to epistemological formations that have not traditionally been a part of the field of pastoral care. Anthropology, ethnography, sociology, feminist epistemological theories, and contributions from a wealth of resources will make a difference in our discipline. In addition, more research in our field will have to undertake sophisticated qualitative work, while at the same time maintaining quantitative research and attending to concomitant developments in the sciences. Our understandings of the mind and of the brain will be profoundly enhanced by what science will discover in the future. As practitioners and pastoral theologians it will be important to provide frameworks for interpreting these new discoveries from theological perspectives.

Discerning how best to draw upon external disciplines with a sense of integrity will be important for the future. In particular, the temptation simply to collapse disciplines and realms of understanding into one metatheory or metanarrative must be avoided. In the process, pastoral theologians and caregivers will have to find ways to work with a pluralism of authorities and resources rather than attempt to find one single authority. Epistemological diversity will ultimately enhance our common work.

Third, pastoral theology has experienced a deepened commitment to participate in and lead the discourse now understood to be public theology (Ashby, 2000; Graham, 2000). This broader movement in theology represents the struggle among academicians and pastoral leaders to engage the culture in ways that bring our collective religious voices to the broader concerns of the world. In other words, public theologians want to be certain that the theological enterprise remains conversant with the larger challenges of the culture. Bringing various theological perspectives to bear upon issues of the broader culture will continue to be a significant trend in pastoral care and counseling (Browning et al., 2000; Couture, 2000). Participation in public theology is important not only to the practice and art of pastoral theology, care, and counseling, but it is essential as well within the churches and congregations we serve.

Fourth, pastoral methods must reflect broader definitions of care, including welcoming partners that reflect scopes of practice beyond those related to mental health. Attention to issues of spirituality will continue to be in the center of conversations about therapy, care, and counseling (McCarthy, 2002). Spiritual directors along with clinicians who research the role of spirituality must be partners in our pastoral theological work and in the practices of care we adopt. Other new partners in the caregiving network are becoming prominent in ecclesial structures. The presence of parish nurses, for example, is positively enhancing a large number of individuals and communities of faith around the country. Their research methods and work parallel and center on issues relevant to pastoral care and counseling.

Again, while it is impossible to note how the future of pastoral theology will take shape, it is possible to assume that these four trends will continue in the methodological work of pastoral care and counseling.

Pastoral Formation, Practice, Research, and Pedagogy

As noted earlier in this essay and as articulated in the *Dictionary,* methods are defined by four inter-related, yet distinct aspects within the field: the practice of pastoral care and counseling; the training of pastoral theologians and caregivers; the relationship between various disciplines related to pastoral theology; and the construction of pastoral and practical theological claims. These various aspects share five common constitutive elements related to the methodological perspectives for pastoral theology, care, and counseling:

(1) the explicit or implicit role of theology;

(2) the relationship to various fields and disciplines outside of religion or theology, especially the social and behavioral sciences;

(3) the awareness of the import of communities and context;

(4) the integration of theory and praxis; and

(5) the role of experience in the construction of theological and faith claims.

Two dynamics undergird these constitutive elements and provide the integrative framework that brings cohesiveness to any particular method: identity formation and the concomitant development of authoritative criteria within pastoral methods. It is to these dynamics that we will now turn, for they set the direction for assessing the integrative quality of one's pastoral method.

The last twenty years have witnessed significant challenges to traditional methods and their respective content, represented not necessarily by changes in the constitutive elements they share in common, but rather by changes in the dynamics brought to the five elements. Throughout history the identity of the pastoral caregiver has been central in determining how the five elements are integrated and what carries greater authoritative weight at any given moment. For example, immediately prior to the last decade, pastoral methods were guided more by disciplines outside of theology (psychological theories in particular). These latter theories were often granted more authoritative weight in the development of methods for pastoral care and counseling. The desire of pastoral caregivers and pastoral care specialists to identify closely with mental health practitioners guided the integration of the elements. However, during earlier historic periods in pastoral care and counseling the academic discipline of theology was central in setting the direction of practice, research, and scholarship. Here the identity of the pastoral caregiver was guided by theological concepts and one's connection to a faith tradition. What determines, in large part, what is most important in pastoral method at any particular moment in time has been the identity of that generation of teachers, scholars, and practitioners. Pastoral identity continues to hold one of the critical keys for shaping how the five constitutive elements are integrated.[8] The process of formation is significant at precisely this point.

There are few concepts in contemporary theological education that carry as much weight or freight as that of formation. Use of the word *formation,* has come to symbolize the breadth and depth of an essential component of education, whether that training be directed toward the preparation of ministers and care specialists, and/or the development of scholars, researchers, and teachers. To form something implies that there is a particular goal in mind, providing an overarching vision for a particular process. The heart of formation in educational venues is not in the achievement of a goal; rather the significance of formation is found in the development of disciplines that are attentive to the methods that ground one's practice and scholarship.

While each particular institution, denomination, judicatory, and discipline brings unique content and theological perspectives appropriate to the specific context, the process of teaching and learning must always be focused on our ability to engender appropriate angles of vision and tools for the practice of pastoral theology, care, and counseling. Toward this end, then, we engage educationally in three specific tasks of formation. First, individuals are shaped and formed within a particular context and faith community. Pastoral care belongs to the community and is not an activity of concern only to a pastor, a caregiver, a counselor, or an academician. Students, pastors, and academicians must remain connected to those communities of faith in order to resist both individualism and isolation and to maintain conversation with others who are invested in theological integrity.

Second, in order to participate in the pastoral nature of their work caregivers, scholars, and teachers must retain the art of theological reflection as the core of their identity no matter what the specific nature of the vocation to which they are called. The formation of pastoral leaders who are adept at theological reflection is essential for every educational task. Such pastoral theological formation provides the normative guide for caregivers, teachers, specialists, and scholars in various contexts. Theological sophistication is, indeed, one of the unique gifts of the vocation of pastoral care and counseling.

Third, specific practices and methods in care and counseling, research and scholarship must be congruent with the particular context of one's work. Developing skills in counseling may be more important for those engaged in the concrete practice of being a pastoral care specialist, while tools of research may be central for scholars and researchers. What holds all of these various skills together is attention to a method that is genuinely pastoral theological in nature and aimed at developing practitioners and scholars in pastoral theology, care, and counseling.

The five constitutive elements are held together and integrated in methods appropriately reflective of the pastoral identity of the caregiver, scholar, teacher, or researcher. With the overarching goal of developing practitioners and scholars who maintain a pastoral or practical theological perspective as central to such an identity, the development of authoritative criteria for the pastoral caregiver flows from one's identity and from one's connection to a faith community. Each of the five constitutive elements identified above must be in critical and mutual conversation with one another, and each pastoral caregiver must remain connected to a broader community of discourse to discern how to hold the elements in an integrative fashion. There are times and contexts when one element holds an authoritative center or where one perspective within an element becomes a critical component, but such discernments must occur within a broader context. Pastoral methods are not developed individually irrespective of the larger context of one's faith tradition, the particular context in which one works, or the conversation partners found within academic guilds and professional associations. It is in the milieu of these broader contexts that the authoritativeness of criteria becomes clearest. The coherence provided by these five elements and the integrative function of faith communities and their authoritative sources are equally apparent among mainline and more conserving caregivers.

Given this understanding of formation and integration, it is helpful now to look at the implications of method on teachers, practitioners, scholars, and researchers. Again, what is important to note is that while the particular training processes may be different for practitioners-scholars than for scholar-teachers, all persons in the field need to hold a pastoral theological perspective as part of their core identity. Turning, once again, to the five constitutive elements inherent to method can illuminate some of the implications for method in teaching, research, and scholarship.

First, theology and theological discourse must remain at the center of our work as pastoral theologians, whether we are faculty members in seminaries, Clinical Pastoral Education supervisors, pastors in local churches, pastoral counselors, or researchers and scholars. In order for pastoral care to avoid being merely the application of theological or biblical mandates, it is essential that training in pastoral theological reflection be at the core of every teaching and research activity related to pastoral care and counseling. Programs that train pastoral counselors must engage students in the critical examination of Scripture, history, ethics, and theology.

Pastoral theological reflection is more than sensitivity to religious and spiritual concerns. While such understanding about the nature of our spiritual lives is important, it does not adequately provide the theological depth required of pastoral caregivers. We cannot afford to confuse spirituality with theological depth. The gift of pastoral theologians who practice the art of care and counseling is not simply that they are sensitive to the importance of religious life; rather the gift is in the theological sophistication brought to that sensitivity.

Specifically, master's programs need to train generalists and specialists whose depth of understanding about Scripture, tradition, and theological discourse provides grounding for theological reflection in the context of caregiving. More work among the disciplines related to theological education will lead to a more profound integration of the sort that will provide appropriate pastoral care. In a similar way, doctoral programs (whether in professional or academic tracks) must continue to develop pastoral theologians whose primary task is not the application of theology or the simple correlation of psychological theory with theology. Doctoral programs must provide the kind of sophisticated theological reflection at their core that will lead to constructive methodological efforts in pastoral theology, care, and counseling.

Second, academic programs and clinical programs must continue to engage fields and disciplines outside of theology in ways that provide critical, thoughtful, and reflective work. The cognate sciences have always been important in our field. What is new, perhaps, is the broadening of cognate disciplines both within and outside of psychological theory. Engaging in broader fields in social sciences will result in multidisciplinary approaches that can lead to more complex understandings of human beings and communities. Research in the sciences related to physiology, brain chemistry, and genetics will continue to provide new opportunities for theological reflection. Again, what is needed most are genuinely interdisciplinary conversations where we do not move toward a melding of one field into another or to the sublimation of theology to the disciplines of the behavioral, social, or natural sciences. Developing methodologies that work to continue the task of integration will be critical in the future.

Third, attention to communities and contexts will continue to be important in the teaching and formation of pastoral caregivers, researchers, scholars, and teachers. Providing tools that allow students, pastors, and pastoral care specialists to analyze the contexts of which we are a part will remain essential. Insights from social analysis, including economics, gender, power, class, sexuality, ethnography, anthropology, sociology, rural/urban cultures, and more will provide more meaningful pastoral theological reflections and responses. Not all pastors, clinicians, and teachers need to be equally adept at every form of analysis, but all must be diligent in recognizing and theologically assessing some of the cultural and social contexts in which we live. In addition, pastoral caregivers and specialists must tend to the larger networks of care around them. Understanding the multiple options available to people in need of care whether referring people to other appropriate counselors whose modalities for treatment are different or connecting people to community-based resources are essential to our work. Pastoral theological scholarship and research that addresses the multiplicity of communities of care can assist caregivers and others in reflecting on appropriate responses in their own particular contexts.

Fourth, the relationship between theory and practice must continue to be an integral part of our common work. Again, we do not need more applied theology nor do we need greater attention only to clinical aspects of pastoral care. Instead, theoreticians and practitioners must be engaged in conversation with one another in such a way as to provide for more thoughtful theological integration and more complex understandings of human beings, communities, and contexts. Programs that train professional pastoral caregivers at masters, doctoral, and professional levels need to be in dialogue with the constructive work of pastoral theologians. In similar ways, those who do research and teaching in academic settings cannot proceed without deeper and more engaged conversations with those who are involved in the direct practice of ministry. We are at risk of isolating practice from theory, and pastoral theology from practice if we do not attend to these more meaningful dialogues between clinicians and academics.

Fifth, pastoral care generalists and specialists have always understood that the experience of individuals, students, clients, parishioners, and churches is important, including attention to spirituality. Experience of one's own community and of others often acts as the initial impetus for engaging theological questions and exploration. What is important in postmodernity is not to move too quickly into assuming that one's own story or vantage point is the single most important guiding principle in the development of pastoral theology, care, and counseling. Instead, it seems wiser to move into a process of allowing a larger diversity of stories to shape and form our theological reflections.

In addition to attention to our own experiences, pastoral theologians, caregivers, and specialists need to be trained in understanding and engaging multicultural complexities of the world. It is not enough to appreciate multicultural competencies; rather, pastoral caregivers must carry a deeper awareness of the epistemological differences of our experiences. In so doing we will arrive at more profound understandings of the complexity of God and of one another.

Teaching, learning, research, scholarship, and practice around these five constitutive elements provide significant opportunities for developing pastoral theological methods that enhance the practice of pastoral care and counseling.

Conclusion

Developing pastoral methods in the context of care and counseling is essential to the work of practitioners, scholars, and teachers. Without attention to method we are lost in the complex reality of pulling from different sources without providing an integrative framework for the activities of care and counseling. The field is also at a critical juncture as it expands and broadens the various conversation partners who are represented in the five constitutive elements of pastoral method. The critical strategies of crafting a pastoral identity and developing authoritative criteria for our work are essential in shaping the future of our field.

Notes

1. The historical dance of the twentieth century around the relationship of psychology and theology is played out in many texts. Charles Gerkin, in *An Introduction to Pastoral Care* (1997), briefly describes the tension in his second chapter, "Pastoral Care in the Twentieth Century." (pp. 53-77). Others who note the centrality of theological reflection for pastoral and practical method include contributors to the edited volume by Mudge and Poling (1987). See also Patton (1990) and Stone and Duke (1996).

2. In the limitations of this chapter it is impossible to note all of the texts and scholars in pastoral theology, care, and counseling who contribute to

conversations of method. Those mentioned in this chapter are attempts to be illustrative, not exhaustive. For an example of work that makes theological claims central to pastoral method in care and counseling see Grant (2001); Howe (1995); Lester (1995); Pattison (1994); Poling (1991); Stone (1996); Thornton (2002). Each of these authors approaches method from a distinct theological perspective.

3. There are many illustrations of the use of diverse conversation partners in the creation of pastoral method, including those found in the works of Couture (1991, 2000) who examines issues of children, poverty and theology; Furniss (1994) who reminds readers of the importance of sociology; E. Graham (1995, 1996) who draws upon gender studies and critical cultural theory of postmodernity; Moschella (2002), who utilizes anthropology in her method; and Poling (1991, 1996, 2002) who examines broader issues connected to class, economics, gender, and race.

4. Illustrative of public theology that moves toward communal and systemic interventions on the part of pastoral caregivers are the following: for example, Couture (1991, 2000); Gerkin (1991); Greider (1997); Kornfeld (1998); Marshall (1997); Neuger (2001), Pattison (2000); Poling (1996, 2002). Many authors in this category draw upon liberative theological themes and often identify with methodologies of practical or pastoral theology. What makes Browning's hermeneutical method distinct from these latter pastoral theologians is largely the theological lens they bring to the task of pastoral care.

5. There are many authors that work intentionally to overcome the praxis/theory split, including: Anderson, Hogue, and McCarthy (1995); Anderson and Foley (1998); Capps (2001); Capps and Fowler (2001); Doehring (1995); Leslie (2002); Neuger (1996); Townsend (2000); Wicks, Parsons, and Capps (1985).

6. Again, there are multiple works by women that present various methodologies. What many of them have in common, however, is attention to the experience and voice of women. See, for example: Bons-Storm (1996); DeMarinis (1993); Gorsuch (2001); Miller-McLemore (1994); Saussy (1991). In addition, the edited volumes by Neuger and Poling (1997, 2003), while dealing with issues related to men, explicity approach these issues methodologically from feminist perspectives.

7. The persons named thus far all represent a proactive and constructive approach around lesbian, gay, bisexual, and transgendered issues. However, it is also true that conversion therapy and other approaches to these issues are present in the literature. See, for example, selections in Maloney (2001).

8. Note here that I am aware of the complexity of talking about identity in a postmodern culture; yet, it is through the concept of identity that we have the best hope of claiming the particularity of our perspective in pastoral theology, care, and counseling. Without the concept of identity we are left with an obtuse understanding of who we are to be in relationship with others.

CHAPTER 7

Contemporary Pastoral Theology:
A Wider Vision for the Practice of Love

Nancy J. Ramsay

This essay investigates the current state of pastoral theology in light of the dynamic shifts and developments since the publication of the *Dictionary of Pastoral Care and Counseling* in 1990. The *Dictionary* well articulates an understanding of the field of care, counseling, and theology that prevailed from the 1940s until the 1980s often described as the clinical pastoral paradigm. During these years the field was deeply shaped by therapeutic theoretical sources and practices on which it drew to inform the theory and practice of care. Within this paradigm pastoral theology was often confined to providing theological insights for the practice of care as a theology of various aspects of care. By the latter half of the 1970s, there was a decided shift toward recovering a self-conscious, theological integrity for both pastoral theological reflection and the practice of care and counseling. In retrospect, with this shift, pastoral theology too began more often to demonstrate not only resources to support the practice of care but also the constructive theological possibilities envisioned by persons such as Seward Hiltner who first articulated the shape and goals of contemporary pastoral theology. Our focus will lie with the transitions in pastoral theology over the past 15 to 20 years and trajectories discernible in contemporary literature and practice. Necessarily this will also involve attention to the larger intellectual and social context of the United States during this time as well as changes in the larger field of theology as a whole.

Contemporary pastoral care and counseling are now frequently described as in transition. Certainly this is true for pastoral theology as the conceptual energy for these theological practices. Indeed, we will find major changes in the way pastoral theology itself is understood and authorized as well as changes in its aims and functions. We will trace these changes principally from within the context of the United States though the work of colleagues in other parts of the world will be considered, because in fact, it contributes to the transitions we will explore.

Certainly an analysis of such a highly dynamic and emerging story depends significantly on the perspective of the interpreter. I am an ordained,

European American, Christian woman in the Reformed tradition. I have taught pastoral theology and care in a seminary for more than twenty years. I also teach students preparing to serve as pastoral counselors, and I am active in the Association of Pastoral Counselors. I have deep commitments to assuring the theological integrity of pastoral care and counseling and the constructive theological possibilities of pastoral theology.

In the pages that follow I will offer definitions for three key terms. I will then move to trace briefly critical developments in the way pastoral theology has functioned over the past 15 to 20 years. I will explore the way several theological themes are developed in current literature in the field in order to illustrate dynamic transitions underway. These will include theological anthropology, difference, spiritual formation in a religiously plural context, and norms and authority. We will also consider several emerging trajectories that are currently identifiable in pastoral theology. Finally, we will consider the implications of the transitions and continuities addressed in the essay for the formation and professional identities of those who practice pastoral theology.

Definitions

Pastoral Theology

Contemporary pastoral theology emerged in the middle of the twentieth century when the influence of the therapeutic tradition was especially strong in ministry. Initially, as Liston Mills (1990) observed, it was principally to deepen understanding of the needs of persons seeking care and strategies for responding. However, Hiltner's (1959) publication of *Preface to Pastoral Theology* provided a vision for a constructive, contextual theology done from a "shepherding" perspective. Hiltner proposed that a pastor's practice was a source for theological insight, an idea that obviously is indebted to the work of Anton Boisen. Subsequently, the *Dictionary* (Burck & Hunter, 1990, p. 867) described three definitions of pastoral theology current in contemporary Christianity in the United States.

- Pastoral theology refers to the theological foundations for the principles and practices for all the functions of ministry. This definition functions especially in the Roman Catholic tradition and among some Lutherans and Episcopalians.
- In some largely Protestant contexts pastoral theology refers to "the practical theological discipline concerned with the theory and practice of pastoral care and counseling" as well as the study of supporting methods and theories.

- Among some Protestants and Roman Catholics pastoral theology is understood as a contextual theology done from a pastoral perspective that provides for not only resources for the practice of care but also, "critical development of basic theological understanding."

In contrast to systematic theology or ethics, pastoral theology in any of the forms above begins with the concrete particularity of experience and intends a useful response for that situation. It also articulates normative dimensions of the context of care. Methodologically, a revised critical correlation model has served pastoral theologians in Roman Catholic and more liberal Protestant denominations. Among many evangelical Protestants, Tillich's earlier correlation model that presumes Christian answers to human problems or questions is evident. Here biblical and theological resources have priority over the use of psychological resources rather than there being reciprocity between religious and secular sources in the revised critical correlation model.

In this chapter, we will trace the further development of pastoral theology as contextual theology that now includes not only the clinical paradigm's concern for individuals, but also the wider public horizon for care. As is more fully developed in Miller-McLemore's chapter on public theology in this volume, this wider horizon has meant that pastoral theologians now find themselves developing normative proposals for public policy debates on issues affecting care in our common life such as welfare and family policies. Further, we will consider ways epistemological shifts accompanying postmodernity have emphasized the performative character of pastoral theology in which knowledge and agency are joined. Practices of care themselves carry and give rise to new theological knowledge (Bourdieu, 1992). Various emancipatory movements and accompanying critical theories have also underscored the transformative or liberative intention of pastoral theology. Thus, the theological understanding described in the third definition above is now often less about existential meaning and more about the transformative possibilities inherent in practices of care.

Critical Postmodernity

The dynamic transitions in pastoral theology simply mirror larger ones in theological disciplines more generally that arise from what many agree is a paradigm shift from modernity that was shaped by Enlightenment thought to what is thus far described as postmodernity. Modernity gives primacy to rationality, autonomous selves, positivism, and uncritical "grand narratives" (Tracy, 1995) that sanction teleological notions about Western social and historical progress and authorize assumptions about knowledge and power at political and metaphysical levels. Critiques of modernity represented by postmodernity are especially associated with epistemology and the self, ethics, and redistributions of power to groups previously subjugated by grand narratives that authorized patterns of dominance (Lakeland, 1997). Epistemology, informed by postmodernity, is clearly visible in contemporary pastoral theology where we find an embrace of knowing that is shaped by socially and relationally situated persons whose knowing is inevitably perspectival albeit truthful. This essentially relational self is thus "de-centered" from the pretense of rational objective knowing in which the influences of context, power, and embodiment remained unacknowledged. The relation of power and knowledge now regularly informs the goals of pastoral theology. Such an epistemology immediately revalues difference and privileges particularity. Knowing is recognized as provisional. Recognizing and valuing the fact of multiple perspectives and irreducible difference in human experience of course poses ethical dilemmas regarding the authority of various perspectives that grand narratives uncritically reproduced and reauthorized as universally true. Pastoral theology increasingly reflects this struggle with criteria for authorizing normative claims and particular strategies especially in an increasingly plural religious and civil context.

Many pastoral theologians are critically embracing the influence of postmodernity. Although, for example, the intention of liberative or transformative praxis for pastoral theology and care still reflects a modernist sensibility and value for the rights of individuals apart from the extreme of individualism. Similarly, the field continues to value the significance of history for human thought and experience—a modernist perspective. As Christie Neuger observes in this volume, contemporary pastoral theology reflects that we are living in between these two paradigms.

Practices

While pastoral theologians begin their work in the context of situations requiring care, we have only recently begun to appreciate the capacity of certain shared practices arising within communities such as worship and patterns of care to provide identity and meaning and an orientation to shared values and hopes that shape action. Practices carry and disclose new theological understanding that is woven into the patterns of daily life that reproduce and carry that community forward. As British pastoral theologian, Elaine Graham (1996) observes, action and values inform each other. In other words, "faithful and purposeful practice springs from participation in a value- and vision-directed tradition" (p. 140). Pastoral theology as practice involves an epistemological shift that considers knowledge as discursive practices that carry transformative potential. Practical wisdom is measured heuristically rather than by pre-existing criteria in Tradition (Graham, 1996). Faithfulness is less an outgrowth of prior theological and ethical teaching and more a shared, lived engagement that enacts an identity, values, and knowledge that sustain such a theological and ethical vision. Change then is carried in the practices of individuals and communities at least as much as in more abstract ideas (Chopp, 1995).

Historical Context

When the *Dictionary* was published pastoral theology was described as including several functions: interrelating normative vision, engaging the particularity of human beings and behavior, and practical wisdom about care (Burck & Hunter, 1990). As our definitions have already suggested, these categories would now be enlarged. Competing normative visions complicate discerning what care requires. The focus of pastoral theology now includes not only particular human beings, but the larger public "web" of structures, systems, and policies that shape and are shaped by human communities. Further, understandings of practical wisdom have grown more complex with epistemologies informed by postmodernity.

The modernist assumptions in intellectual thought that prevailed during that time and the therapeutic traditions informing the clinical pastoral paradigm shaped the ways in which pastoral theology was understood and practiced as well as the sources that authorized it and the criteria that shaped its goals. For example, there was little if any critique of a grand narrative in which dominant values and norms operated uncritically. On the other hand, normative expectations informing the context of care were often subordinated to the needs of the individual seeking care, presented incarnationally through the relationship rather than directly addressed. In fact the therapeutic relationship was central so that persons were often understood apart from their social location and from the institutions and systems that impinged on their lives (Hunter, 1995). The norm of relational humanness (Patton, 1983) suggests this priority for individuals. Pastoral theology was largely in the service of pastoral care and counseling at this time, and it reflected a more narrow focus on the well-being of individuals that included increasing their capacities for autonomous action. Anthropologically, a priority was placed on understanding so called universal aspects of human experience that transcend embodied, social, cultural, and historical differences and the political factors that are associated with social location. The goal of theological understanding was enhanced meaning about the existential needs or problems such as suffering or loss. These interpretations guided the interventions developed by practical wisdom. Pastoral theologians ordinarily did not critically reflect on the effect of their own social location or privilege in the therapeutic relationship. Self-reflection on relevant therapeutic issues that could complicate effective care for others was the primary goal of self-critical awareness.

Several major intellectual, political, and cultural forces contributed to the demise of the clinical pastoral paradigm and this current period of continuing ferment and redefinition in the field of pastoral theology. The most encompassing of these forces seems to be a major shift in intellectual thought described earlier in this essay as postmodernity. It has contributed to four significant shifts in emerging new paradigms:

- The self-understanding of pastoral theologians is far more self-conscious regarding a wide range of our social identities such as gender, embodiment, age, race, sexual orientation, and religious worldviews as well as a recognition of the dynamics of privilege woven into aspects of that social identity.
- Principal among the changes in pastoral theology is a recognition of the essential relationality of human beings. Gone is the separate self developing in splendid isolation toward increasing autonomy. Now there is a realization that relationality better describes the developmental pathway. The experience of others also now includes priority for the fact and effects of radical difference in categories of social identity. Rather than emphasizing apparent universal human experiences, pastoral theologians encourage moving from particularity to build an empathic bridge to others in order to appreciate their situated, dynamic, politically shaped identity.
- This shift in self and other understanding is accompanied by an epistemology that no longer aspires to or trusts rational objectivity. Knowledge is provisional, contextual, and particular. Multiple perspectives are available and needed regarding situations requiring care, and conversations respectful of the value in those differing perspectives are necessary for an adequate response.
- The revaluing of difference suggested by the image of mutually respectful conversation above, points to major ethical shifts because issues of authority once obscured by assumed patterns of dominance regarding such aspects as race, culture, religion, gender, and class now must be renegotiated. On this point pastoral theologians embrace postmodernity critically asserting approximations of justice and truthfulness and a value for human rights. However, the criteria for such values now must be heuristic rather than an assertion of a particular tradition.
- Postmodernity includes not only a revaluing of difference, but also an insistence that asymmetries of power that have so long accompanied these differences as subordination, marginalization, and oppression be corrected. Power is no longer imaged as a zero-sum, quantifiable possession. Rather, more often it is now understood intersubjectively as existing in relationships as a bi-polar, expansive possibility.

As this last dimension of postmodernity suggests, this intellectual paradigm shift overlaps with the explosion of emancipatory movements around the world and in the United States that have significantly informed pastoral theology especially since the publication of the *Dictionary*. Feminist, Womanist, African American, and other forms of liberation theologies have been primary media for the current redefinition in paradigms in the field. In the pages that follow we will also review ways in which post-colonial political movements around the world have contributed to significant theological ferment among pastoral theologians on other continents. The fact of dramatically increasing racial, cultural, and religious pluralism in the United States also contributes significantly to current ferment and redefinition in the field.

Even these brief descriptions of intellectual, political, and cultural changes suggest the dramatic transitions underway in pastoral theology since the *Dictionary* was being readied for publication in the late-1980s. If we begin with the several categories used in the *Dictionary* to describe necessary elements of pastoral theology, interrelation of normative vision, attention to concrete behavior, and practical wisdom, it is easier to trace the level and kinds of change. Immediately important to observe is a marked shift in the normative visions that inform the field. Relational justice is regularly named as normative in contemporary pastoral theology (Graham, 1995). The inclusion of justice enlarges and revises the earlier clinical pastoral norm of relational humanness. The separation of love from justice and the loss of attention to justice in the clinical paradigm helps describe the consequences of pastoral theology's psychological captivity in that paradigm. The transformative energy of love was obscured by confining it to an individual and existential focus. Relational justice also bespeaks the effects of postmodernity and emancipatory movements that disclose asymmetries of power and their consequences for privileged and marginalized people. This norm also provides for a more adequate self-understanding for pastoral theologians who recognize the ethical implications that a relational anthropology creates. Adequate care now requires attention to the political implications of care concerns whether they arise at individual, group, institutional, or cultural levels.

The ecological image of living human web (Smith, 1982; Miller-McLemore, 1993; Gill-Austern, 1995) helps to capture the revaluing of interdependence and the ethical obligations of relationality intended by relational justice. This web image is used in two ways currently in the field. On the one hand, as Patton (1993) and Gill-Austern describe it, web refers to care that strengthens and supports communities of faith. As Miller-McLemore describes it, web refers to the public context of care, the interdependent network of systems, structures, policies, and symbols that are also locations for engaging issues of care alongside the needs of individuals. This normative image then bespeaks the wider horizons of care explored by Miller-McLemore in her chapter on pastoral theology as public theology in this volume.

Normative visions of relational justice and web also articulate the much more complex task of care in the racially, culturally, and religiously plural context that the United States is now recognized to be. Pastoral theologians now regularly acknowledge their particular social location and religious worldview because postmodernity has created a more de-centered self- and other-awareness and a keen appreciation for the fact that all knowledge is situated. Even among Christians values and perspectives vary widely as contemporary public debates about sexual orientation and family values illustrate.

Especially at public levels issues of care must be negotiated with persons whose normative images arise from other religious or spiritual perspectives or secular and political points of view. Even values such as justice may require negotiation in such diverse settings. Certainly in the public sphere pastoral theologians find the criteria for authority lie in the heuristic value of their proposals rather than a particular faith tradition.

The image of a web also discloses the highly ecological anthropology that informs contemporary pastoral theology. The particularity of person's lives, highlighted in the clinical paradigm, is important in new ways. Attention now is given to the particularity of experience shaped by differences previously obscured by, for example, gender, race, and class as well as by wider relational, group, systemic, religious, and cultural contexts.

Practical wisdom describes the awareness that pastoral theology arises in relation to theory-laden practices of care that address complex, moral concerns such as suffering, parenting, justice, or resisting oppression (Hunter, 1990). It arises from Aristotle's term *phronesis,* and signals a rejection of more reductive rational-technical approaches to practice. Since the publication of the *Dictionary* this appreciation for the theoretical and transformative dimensions of practice has only deepened. The epistemologies associated with postmodernity emphasize more deeply the linkage of agency and knowledge and create a significant shift for some contemporary pastoral theologians who now would locate the sources of wisdom in the practices of communities of faith or in the practices of faithful persons more than in prior historical theological criteria retrieved for reflection on such situations (E. Graham, 1992). This shift is particularly evident when we contrast the work of pastoral theologians such as Browning and Gerkin who draw on critical hermeneutical methods with the publications of pastoral theologians such as Couture, Miller-McLemore, L. Graham, Poling, and Marshall who draw particularly on liberation theology in their work. We see the early evidence of this epistemological shift in Poling's (1988) critique of the goal of meaning in pastoral theology in contrast to more liberative criteria now suggested by the norm of relational justice. British pastoral theologian, Elaine Graham, describes pastoral theology as "not an abstract series of philosophical propositions, but a performative discipline, where knowledge and truth are only realizable in the pursuit of practical strategies and social relations" (1992, p. 204). From this perspective, pastoral theology is "saving work" (Chopp, 1995), a critical and imaginative practice that discloses and articulates the transformative possibilities of the faith a people inhabit.

A recent illustration of pastoral theology as performative discipline is Pamela Couture's *Seeing Children, Seeing God* (2000) in which she focuses on ways care for the most vulnerable among us—poor children—invites us into deeper lived experience of creation in God's image, grace, sin and evil, mercy, and the mutuality of care. Couture also describes the emerging sensibility to the ecological connections between caring for particular persons and the public dimensions care. She writes:

As we do the work of care and learn about the gifts, the needs, and the care of the most vulnerable children among us, we will deepen our understanding of care for less vulnerable persons and the environments in which they live. We will find new connections between caring for children and caring for families, communities, nations, the world, and the earth. We will hold ourselves accountable to a criterion of care; as long as the most vulnerable persons among us—poor children—are sacrificed as means to lesser ends, as they presently are, we have more work to do, in practice and in theory. We will also be reminded that such care is the practice of theology. Caring with vulnerable children is a means of grace, a vehicle through which God makes God's self known to us and to them. (p. 13)

We have explored aspects of the significant transitions underway in pastoral theology since the publication of the *Dictionary*, in areas such as a widely adopted normative vision of relational justice, a shift to a relational anthropology, a recognition of the interconnections between persons and the systems, structures, and public policies that interweave particular experience widening the horizons of care, a revaluing of difference with the goal of mutuality, and a recognition of the linkage between theological knowledge and agency.

These transitions currently are giving shape to two new interrelated forms of pastoral theology. On the one hand there is a cluster of quite generative pastoral theological literature that represents the foci of what Patton (1993) described as the communal contextual paradigm. This is especially representative of work arising within the United States. The communal side of the paradigm addresses care within communities of faith. Here web is used to articulate a de-clericalized sensibility for care that strengthens and nurtures communities of faith. The pastoral theology arising from this communal perspective often draws at least implicitly from the perspective of theology as discursive practice though critical hermeneutic approaches are also used. The contextual side of the paradigm explicitly embraces the norm of relational justice and the ecological consciousness that links care for particular persons with care that engages systemic, public policy dimensions of well-being as illustrated in Couture's work noted above. Contemporary contextual pastoral theology largely arises from one of two methodological approaches, either as a critical personal and cultural correlation of theology and the social sciences with a transformative intent (Miller-McLemore, 1998) or as critical hermeneutics (Browning, 1987). Critical theory regarding gender, sexual orientation, economics, and violence is often a resource for contextual analysis. Both the communal and contextual aspects of this paradigm have largely shifted from earlier Neo-orthodox theologies to draw from liberation, narrative, and process theologies.

Another emerging paradigm has been generated especially by international partners and pastoral theologians in the United States who are addressing the challenges presented by racial, cultural, and religious pluralism. There are certainly affinities with the public dimensions of the contextual perspective in the United States. Liberation theology is a primary theological approach with a reliance on critical theory that lifts up the ecological consciousness linking the pain of individuals with the systemic, political distortions that interweave their particular distress. This intercultural or multicultural paradigm has generated promising pastoral theological work in areas such as anthropology, image of God, resistance, and sin. Early indications of pastoral theological resources for responding to religious pluralism are also evident from within this perspective while they are largely absent from the work of those otherwise working within the communal contextual paradigm.

Arising from these emerging paradigms we find significant generativity among pastoral theologians. New theological themes are being addressed by pastoral theologians such as embodiment, justice, power, violence, theodicy not reliant on substitutionary atonement, forgiveness, and spirituality. Also evident are significant revisions to more familiar themes such as theological anthropology, creation in the image of God, hope, and love.

Several factors account for this productivity in addition to the cultural, intellectual, and demographic changes that require contextual analysis and response. Particularly important have been three organizations: the Society for Pastoral Theology (SPT), the International Association for Practical Theology (IAPT), and the International Council on Pastoral Care and Counselling (ICPCC). The Society for Pastoral Theology, founded in 1985, has provided a context for U.S. based pastoral theologians to be in conversation. It also generated *The Journal of Pastoral Theology* that has provided a locus for further intellectual exchange. SPT also arose just as European American women and African American women and men, whose experience and insights were previously marginalized, were recognized as they entered the field in greater numbers. Their work especially drew on theological and theoretical resources informed by postmodern and emancipatory perspectives and became a medium for introducing these ideas. These demographic trends also informed the membership of the American Association of Pastoral Counselors and the Association of Clinical Pastoral Education so that their literature also began to reflect insights that offered a critique of the dominant perspective voiced by more privileged European American middle-class to upper-middle-class heterosexual men.

The IAPT has functioned to provide a context for intellectual exchange across cultures. Founded in 1991, it too has felt the generative energy of postmodern and emancipatory perspectives as well as increasing participation by women of various racial and cultural heritages and men whose heritage is other than northern European. Like SPT, it too has generated a journal, *The International Journal of Practical Theology*. Membership has been restricted to help avoid an imbalance of U.S. and northern European participants, but travel costs also limit the participation of those from developing countries so a Western influence often is still dominant. Nonetheless, here too, we find literature emerging from previously marginalized perspectives (Ackermann & Bons-Storm, 1998; Bons-Storm, 1996; Graham, 1992) as well as international reflection on shared concerns (Ballard & Couture, 1999, 2001). Also, pastoral theologians from the U.S. describe the de-centering effect on their self-understanding of intellectual engagement with scholars who embody real difference in their experience and articulate different concerns and methodologies in their work. Since pastoral theology, care, and counseling in the U.S. have long reflected an insular quality, this secondary effect at the personal level may be particularly significant.

The International Council of Pastoral Care and Counselling, more fully described in Emmanuel Lartey's essay in this volume, has also generated cross-cultural exchanges of intellectual and clinical reflection. It has also spawned geographical clusters for pastoral theologians and practitioners around the world, such as the African Association for Pastoral Studies and Counseling that now are developing indigenous constructive pastoral theological proposals as suggested in James Farris's recent edited volume, *International Perspectives on Pastoral Counseling* (2002).

Together these organizations are contributing to a remarkable ferment in pastoral theology that has significant promise for increasingly generative results in method, theory, and practice. The groundswell of new participants in an increasingly mutually respectful conversation across cultures still shaking off the consequences of colonial asymmetries is especially encouraging. Of course genuine intellectual, methodological, and practical challenges are also emerging, but it is difficult to imagine they will eclipse the gains of such energy and insight.

Given the scope of this chapter, we will explore only one category of theological reflection in order to observe ways pastoral theologians have been engaged in their work. However, by attending to the broad theme of theological anthropology, we can discern a number of the crucial shifts that have come especially through the intellectual, cultural, and theological changes that have characterized the field since the publication of the *Dictionary*. The influence of postmodernity described earlier in this chapter is immediately apparent in these changes. These shifts include attention to a relational connected self that includes a more ecological understanding of the context of human experience, issues of power and agency, multiple dimensions of socially constructed identities, sin as privilege, the vulnerability of human beings to sin as the abuse of power, and the need for addressing a pervasive spiritual hunger felt by many persons in this culture. Running through these categories are the influence especially of liberation, narrative, and process theologies, systems theory, self-psychologies, narrative theory, and critical theories of gender, sexual orientation, race, and class. While illustrations for changes in each category are numerous, I will draw from representative sources.

It is difficult to differentiate attention to relationality and the ecological or connected dimensions of human experience in social, cultural, and political context; however, it is useful first to describe a decided shift toward a self-in-relation that is informed by systems theories, narrative theories, Kohutian self-psychology, and Stone Center theories particularly. Archie Smith, Jr. (1982) and Graham (1992) used systems approaches to articulate a contrast to the prevailing existentialist anthropology that underscored individualistic psychological and theological sources. In these representative works we find relationality as the developmental pathway rather than separation. Attention to individuals now includes a wider lens that begins with family and immediate relational circles but extends to contextual factors such as cultural, historical, racial, and political dimensions of experience. Human beings are at once creatively responding to and engaging their world and necessarily shaped as social selves by the contextual setting in which they live including their embodied experience. Both Graham and Smith observe how this anthropological shift necessitates theological/ethical, theoretical, and social science changes. Freedom, for example, is now disciplined by social ties and commitments rather than being defined as autonomy. Love requires the corollary of justice because of the complexity of the interconnections this ecological view discloses. Care is no longer merely consolation at the individual level. Now its political dimensions are clearer. Reconnecting love with justice allows both terms to modify the other so that compassion is not restricted to individual care, nor is justice limited to a structural abstraction. Individual fulfillment and its corollary of ethical egoism are now qualified by the negotiated needs of the larger human and ecological community. Mutuality and reciprocity become the more prominent ethical criteria for pastoral theologians. Change is now understood as far more complex and arising in highly circular processes that reflect the organicity and simultaneity of interlocking systems (Graham, p. 46). Relationality clearly points to ways knowledge is inevitably social and therefore perspectival and relative.

Relationality also underscores the now widely recognized fact that identity is socially constructed. Self-understanding is inevitably shaped by the warp and woof of the threads that represent the particular narrative of an individual's experience and its social context. Narrative theology and theory have proven particularly helpful in elaborating this insight. Lester (1995) and Neuger (2001) have provided initial explorations of the ways enhancing self-awareness of participation in a larger familial and cultural story provides avenues for increased agency and transformation. Lester, in particular, has enlarged our understanding of temporality and the self so that pastoral theologians now recognize the importance of person's future narratives for their capacity for hope and a positive sense of agency.

This reorientation to a connected self also immediately widens the work of love and healing to attend, for example, to the implications of public policy as well as the more familiar concern for the dynamics of a particular family's experience. Both Smith (1982, p. 57) and Bonnie Miller-McLemore (1993) use the image of web to pick up this wider definition of care to include its public dimensions. Personal and social transformation are now often linked as goals for care in pastoral theology. Couture (1995), for example, links single parents and their children to the values embedded in contemporary family policy debates. British pastoral theologian, Stephen Pattison (1994), articulates the way in which liberation theologies have informed this widened focus of care to include social, economic, and political dimensions of human experience as equally relevant to psychological insights in devising strategies for care. In fact, he argues that if pastoral care and theology avoid attending to these political, economic, and social dimensions of human experience, they are complicit in reproducing injustice (p. 67).

"Underneath" these shifts are two increasingly prominent and revised theological themes in contemporary theological anthropology: creation in God's image and love. In his work on practices of care among gay and lesbian persons, Graham (1997) drew from contemporary theological resources such as Douglas John Hall (1986) that emphasize the quality of love in relationships to define creation in God's image rather than essential traits such as rationality or freedom. This theological shift is ethically important because authentic humanity becomes defined by the quality of communion, and relationality is ontologically primary. Love is the criterion for assessing fulfillment, but it is now grounded in relationality that requires the order justice provides (Williams, 1968). Now one finds among pastoral theologians recognition that care and healing find fulfillment as persons recover or claim their capacity for love that has transformative intention. Ramsay (1998), for example, explores how love as a relational ethic critiques norms of fulfillment that accompany images of separative selves embedded in psychological models in which maturity is defined as differentiation and autonomy. This relational ethic better supports freedom disciplined by commitments to love.

Love is also revised in contemporary pastoral theology by the insights of feminist pastoral theologians whose work recovers the threefold character of the love command that includes love of self that was obscured particularly by more patriarchal interpretations of scripture (McCarthy, 1985; Gill-Austern, 1996). Gill-Austern, for example, carefully describes the destructive consequences of an uncritical embrace of self-sacrifice and self-denial that are so often encouraged as important Christian virtues especially for women. She draws on contemporary theological reflection on the Trinity (Johnson, 1993) to construct a more adequate theology of love that values mutuality and reciprocity.

As might be expected with a shift from a separate to a connected or relational self, notions of human agency and normative aspects of power have evolved significantly in pastoral theology since the publication of the *Dictionary*. The intrinsic relationality of human experience now readily accepted underscores the bipolar character of power as both agential and receptive (Graham, 1993). This begins to correct the emphasis on agency in more individual anthropologies that focuses more singularly on expressions of power as influence over. However, process theology also helped pastoral theologians discern the inherent agency in each person that locates agency as the desire and capacity to be in relationships with others (Poling, 1991). Poling in particular helpfully explored the ways relationality shapes our agency and in fact is the context for power that exists as the energy of the relational web (p. 25). Both Graham and Poling draw on process theory and theology to articulate the personal and social dimensions of power. They replace hierarchical images of unilateral power with power that is intended for each and all as the energy for mutually respectful care and creativity. In their constructions, enlarging love for God and love and justice for our neighbors are the normative goals of agency. Feminist and womanist pastoral theologians have further developed these themes of agency and relational power to critique oppressive patriarchal and racist constructions of power in culture and offer strategies for resistance and empowerment that assist women in reclaiming their agency (DeMarinis, 1993; Neuger, 1996; Watkins Ali, 1999). They have helped to analyze the linkage of oppressive culturally pervasive ideological perspectives such as partriarchy, racism, and classism and the internalization of oppression that plague women and distort men's experience as well (Neuger & Poling, 1997).

A particularly rich theme for pastoral theology and anthropology since the publication of the *Dictionary* has been a recognition of the multiple social identities that persons inhabit. This concept significantly enlarges the theological theme of embodiment. Clearly an elaboration on the dynamics of power within relational webs and the social construction of the self discussed above, social identity describes the largely postmodern appreciation for the asymmetries of power that accompany different socially constructed aspects of identity such as gender, sexual orientation, socioeconomic class, and racial and cultural difference. Liberation theology and various critical theories especially inform this work.

Particularly significant in this attention to embodiment as social identity has been the extensive work around gender authored initially by women attending to the distinctive experiences and contributions of women and more recently including attention to masculinity. Neuger's recent *Counseling Women* (2001) is a helpful example of current reflections on care arising from a correlation of feminist theory and theology with narrative theory. Clearly informed by postmodern perspectives, Neuger explicitly addresses the social construction of gender and notes that her focus lies with those structures that create and maintain gender distinctions in culture that often are shaped by the asymmetries of patriarchal power structures. In addition to cultural critique her work reflects the move among feminist and womanist pastoral theologians to consider how gender shapes ways of knowing and criteria for valuing differing perspectives. For example, feminist theory and theology have proven particularly generative for constructing new insights in areas such as creation in God's image, atonement and suffering, and sin and evil. Neuger's work is also representative in her attention to the dynamics of power symbolized through the metaphor of voice woven through women's lives in relational, economic, and political spheres. Womanist pastoral theologians have helpfully contributed careful explorations on the interactions of race, class, and gender informing the practice of care and theological insights constructed from resisting multiple forms of oppression (Hollies, 1991; Snorton, 1996, 2000; Boyd & Bohler, 1999; and Watkins Ali, 1999).

Masculinity has more recently emerged as a focus of critical reflection among pastoral theologians. Currently their work attends to the structures that shape and reinforce gender rules and roles for heterosexual European American and African American men (Dittes, 1996; Neuger & Poling, 1997; Anderson, 1997; Wimberly, 1997). Theological themes such as hope, creation in God's image, atonement and suffering, love, and vocation are also being reconstructed as critical reflections on the social construction of gender and the distortions sexism creates for masculinity are probed. Wimberly's work, as those of womanist theologians mentioned above, explores the oppression interwoven through the intersections of race, class, and gender in men's social identity.

Sexual orientation is an aspect of social identity that has been explored more directly by pastoral theologians since the publication of the *Dictionary*. Joretta Marshall (1994, 1996, 1997) has given particularly careful attention to the consequences of stigma in the formation of identity and the processes entailed in healing that includes reclaiming a positive and empowered sense of self. Larry Graham's (1997) research regarding patterns of care among gay and lesbian persons further discloses distinctive dimensions of gay and lesbian social identity. Randle Mixon (1997), like Marshall, helpfully explores the particular effects of stigma and oppression for the experiences of gay men while also noting resources that promote healing and empowered resistance.

Shortly after the publication of the *Dictionary* socioeconomic class emerged as an aspect of social identity that pastoral theologians and caregivers identified as requiring attention. The late Judith Orr made especially important contributions to pastoral theological work in the intersections of gender and class with her essays regarding care for working-class women and men (Orr, 1994, 1997, 2000). She was able to clarify significant differences between middle class and working class regarding family and individual developmental patterns as well as gender rules and roles, and experiences in relation to the exercise of power. She also noted the implications of these differences for relevant theological themes and patterns of care with working-class women and men. Jim Poling (2002) takes the issue of class into the arena of public theology as he pursues economic policy and the effects of economic vulnerability particularly as it intersects with experiences of vulnerability in domestic violence and racial and sexist oppression. Together these two resources are especially helpful in better understanding the complexity of socioeconomic class and the distinctive ways it marks human experience.

Difference as an essential feature of humanity has emerged since the publication of the *Dictionary*. Difference signifies a self-awareness that de-centers the experience of any person or group from normative status. Especially illustrative anthropologically are racial and cultural difference. Certainly the *Dictionary* contains multiple entries describing the fact of racial and cultural difference and ways those differences manifest themselves in the United States in the behaviors and experiences of persons whose heritage is other than northern European. Entries also describe ways care is practiced differently in other parts of the world. But difference is located in these others. What is not evident in the *Dictionary* that would be necessary now is a discussion of ways racial and ethnic identity shape members of the European American or white dominant culture in the United States. Difference, as a category, is descriptive for all.

Increasingly, in the clinical and pastoral theological literature of the field we find persons in the dominant culture acknowledging a "de-centered" self in which there is a greater awareness that previously unquestioned norms and practices emerging from European intellectual and historical values no longer have normative status. Rather there is an emerging recognition of the reciprocity of difference that requires of those in the dominant culture a new self-understanding about how being White shapes them profoundly (Ramsay, 2002; Ballard & Couture, 1999). Emerging from this cultural embeddedness also revalues racial and cultural difference and ways of understanding the Other (Anderson, 1999). As this valuation for difference changes in the United States, pastoral theologians are also helpfully pursuing a nuanced interculturality that sustains the tensive balance between cultural/racial/national aspects of identity and more particular ways individuals embody a plurality of social identities (Greider, 2002; Lartey, 2003).

In postcolonial cultures this re-evaluation of difference is reflected in a determination to articulate pastoral theological priorities that arise from valuing indigenous experience and needs. This contrasts with an earlier dependence on Western models and practices often presented as if universally applicable (Lartey, 2003; Farris, 2002). Pastoral theologians in the United States whose heritage is not European American have begun to write in ways that articulate and celebrate culture specific wisdom and practices noting that they may also be useful for those of other heritages (A. Wimberly, 1997; A. Wimberly & Parker, 2002; Ashby, 2003).

Sin, evil, and suffering are long-standing foci of pastoral theology. Since the publication of the *Dictionary* significant developments in this area have emerged. Edward Farley (1990) described the distortions that crept into understandings of sin through the field's undue reliance on psychological paradigms whose worldviews regarding distortions in human experience and relationality that displaced sin and redemption as guiding symbols. One instance of this psychologization of sin is the equation of sin and sickness (Grant, 1990). On the one hand this recognition of the cumulative effects of pre-critical violations of human being was a helpful corrective to theological anthropologies that failed to incorporate a developmental understanding of the vulnerability of human freedom. However, it also participated in an individualistic anthropology that failed to account for the ethical dimensions of sin that are absent in the medical model of sickness (Ramsay, 1998b). In his dictionary article, Farley called on pastoral theologians to revise and enlarge our understanding of sin and redemption.

We do see remarkable energy in exploring the concepts of sin and evil in pastoral theology over that past 15 to 20 years. Especially important has been the exploration of sin in its structural and systemic forms and the shape of care found particularly in the work of pastoral theologians engaging public theological issues such as violence, poverty and public policy, patriarchy, heterosexism, and racism (Poling, 1991, 1996; Eugene & Poling, 1998; Ramsay, 1991; Couture, 1991, 2000; Saussy, 1991; Bons-Storm, 1996; E. Graham, 1995; Miller-McLemore, 1994; Neuger, 2001; L. Graham, 1997; Marshall, 1997; E. Wimberly, 2000; Watkins Ali, 2000). We find in these authors and many others a description of sin that not only incorporates the pre-critical developmental vulnerability of human beings to intimate violence, but also describes structural and systemic dimensions of sin as evil in the abuse of power visible in the violence of poverty, and oppressive ideologies such as sexism, heterosexism, and racism that are also readily internalized. This more complex exploration of sin corresponds to the relational and ecological character of human beings in community discussed earlier.

One of the effects of exploring the evil of violence and oppression has meant that pastoral theologians have begun to explore suffering that does not rely on the atonement. Rather, they have differentiated the sin of those who abuse power and the suffering of those who experience victimization. Now we find more often recognition of the complexity of care for those who have perpetrated violence and oppression as well as for those who have suffered unnecessarily (Billman & Migliore, 1999; Ramsay, 1998a; Poling, 1991, 2003).

In the case of oppressive ideologies sin has also been disclosed as privilege. Racism, for example, is not merely a system of disadvantage based on race. Rather, the systemic advantages of white privilege have become a significant factor in the revaluing of racial and cultural difference. Such privilege is also acknowledged in other forms of oppression such as sexism and heterosexism.

An area of particular ferment and creativity in theological anthropology and contemporary pastoral theology lies in the spiritual dimensions of human experience and relationality. As the hegemony of therapeutic models recedes, pastoral theologians are increasingly attentive to the linkage of healing and soul care. One particular evidence of this lies in the work of those addressing the consequences of violence and violation who are careful to name the spiritual losses for those affected by clergy sexual misconduct, child sexual abuse and domestic violence, and rape (Doehring, 1995; Ramsay, 1998a, 1999; Leslie, 2003).

Womanist and feminist pastoral theologians have articulated a spirituality of resistance to the oppression of racism and sexism and constructive spiritual practices and theological proposals for women in such a context. Snorton (1996, 2000), for example, describes the consequences of double oppression in the lives of African American women and strategies that develop more adequate spiritual and emotional practices of care. Carroll Saussy (1991) named the alienating consequences of patriarchy for self-esteem and spirituality for women and proposed alternative approaches.

A number of African American and European American pastoral theologians have addressed the consequences of modernity's separative self who prizes autonomy. McCarthy (2000) describes the dislocating effects of moving from modernity's clarity about norms and myth of progress to the more ambiguous and de-centered experience of postmodernity that requires more intentional spiritual practice. Many observe the deep spiritual hunger that has arisen in the U.S. and make remarkably similar proposals for responding (McCarthy, 2000, 2002; Van den Blink, 1995; Gill-Austern, 1997; Wimberly, 2000, 2003; Smith, 1997).

Brita Gill-Austern articulates a shared sense of the seriousness of this spiritual need when she describes Americans as "ravenous" for spiritual nourishment and trying to satisfy themselves with "spirituality lite." Such thin gruel fails to restore them to traditions and faith communities that will truly nourish the hunger created by the consequences of disconnected, disembodied, privatized, commodified, purposeless, and anxious lives. Her four essential elements for soul food that satisfies articulate the themes others also raised. An adequate spirituality will:

- Substantively address the fact of sin and evil;
- Give "sustained and vigorous attention to practices of the Christian faith";
- Prioritize communities as a locus of relationships and healing and networks of care; and
- Practice the commandment to love as active attention to the other's well- being through empathic connection and hospitality (pp. 69-72).

Edward Wimberly and Archie Smith, Jr. deepen the analysis of this culture's pervasive soul sickness by noting the further alienation of the chronic unemployment, violence, and poverty of racism. Both Wimberly and Smith propose that the life-giving spiritual traditions of African American faith communities offer restorative experiences for "relational and spiritual refugees" that live in every community in the U.S. Wimberly proposes that faith communities practice mentoring those who are alienated in order to "apprentice" them into the practice of love. He summarizes the sense of other pastoral theologians addressing spiritual alienation when he describes the work of care as nurturing a "sacred identity" that will empower persons to resist the negative identities in culture and choose to live guided by God's love (2003).

This review of developments in theological anthropology by pastoral theologians over the past 15 to 20 suggests a remarkable level of ferment and creativity. The influence on the field of a critical postmodernity is apparent alongside emancipatory modern values of justice and love. Particularly evident is the way in which restoring the interdependence of love and justice in pastoral theology modifies both theological themes and provides dynamic, ethical, and spiritual direction for pastoral theological reflection.

Trajectories

Given the scope of this brief chapter, I can only name a few of the emerging themes and issues prompted by the ferment of these times. I will draw out issues suggested in this chapter related to the implications of the communal contextual paradigm and the related but distinct issues posed in the U.S. and internationally by racial, cultural, and religious difference. I will also note the implications of emerging research in the value of neuroscience and neuropsychology for pastoral theology.

In considering the issue of spirituality that has gained more prominence in pastoral theology, we noted a considerable unanimity in the need for deepening persons' sense of belonging in communities of care and nurture as well as encouraging intentional formation in a theological worldview through practices that help persons inhabit what Wimberly calls a sacred identity. We have also noted that a shift from modernity toward a critical postmodernity heightens our appreciation of the need to honor the particularity of each person's perspective or context. Pastoral theologians in the United States have only begun to engage the pressing need to sort out what McCarthy (2002) describes as, "the simultaneous need for some form of public language and criteria for judging the relative adequacy of various understandings and expressions of spirituality" (p. 9). Chaplains in hospitals and other institutions are already confronting this dilemma as they offer spiritual care to persons of various faiths as well as those who claim no faith tradition as a ground for their spirituality. Christians are notoriously and publicly recognized as having little consensus on these issues as recent debates on family policy and sexuality demonstrate. The increasing religious pluralism in the United States and the need for pastoral theological reflection that honors such pluralism here and around the world poses a remarkable challenge for scholarship and teaching, pastoral leadership, and specialized ministries. Exploring care and counseling in interfaith contexts offers an opportunity for collaboration between practitioners and pastoral theologians.

David Hogue (2003) and Andrew Lester (2003) have each contributed important research on the role that neuroscience and neuropsychology will offer to pastoral theology. The late James Ashbrook (1996) pioneered in this effort, and these new resources significantly enlarge our appreciation for the contributions that brain research will make to ministries of transformation with persons and communities. For example, the relational anthropology discussed earlier in this chapter appears more adequately to mirror the structures of the brain that allow us to connect and empathize. Both Lester and Hogue note that neuroscience will significantly inform our work in theological anthropology as we understand more deeply human physiological capacities for emotion, perception, imagination, and memory.

While this chapter focused on theological anthropology, the communal contextual paradigm is encouraging renewed attention to ecclesiology as we consider how to address the distortions in spirituality noted above and how to strengthen the abilities of faith communities to practice effective care. Pastoral theologians need to draw on the strength of our acquaintance with communities of faith to develop and refine ecclesiologies that will be adequate for the anthropological and contextual complexities of these postmodern times (Scheib, 2002). This provides an opportunity for conversation among colleagues of diverse racial heritages to hear ways those heritages have contributed to communal patterns and practices (A. Wimberly, 2002). Ecumenical and interfaith conversations are also necessary.

Postmodernity has brought with it a growing recognition among European American pastoral theologians and practitioners that while we ordinarily address the asymmetries of power that accompany sexism, we regularly fail to appreciate how our work reproduces the inequities associated with racism and classism. This recognition of privilege, or the advantages that accrue to those groups that benefit from asymmetries of power at group, institutional, and cultural levels is prompting a heightened self-awareness on the part of European American pastoral theologians who now need to understand ways racial and class identity shape our scholarship and teaching and resist their destruction aspects.

The emerging intercultural paradigm poses a similar challenge to pastoral theologians in the U.S. whose scholarship and teaching currently are only rarely informed by the work of colleagues in other cultures. The political and cultural dominance of the U.S. allows us to write and teach without mindfulness of the ways in which our perspectives are insular and often unwittingly reproduce levels of indifference to the wisdom and experience in practices of care of those beyond our borders. Budget constraints mean that a relatively small number of pastoral theologians in the United States and an even smaller number in other nations are able to travel to international conferences.

However, in the context of such international conferences and through better attention to publications by colleagues outside the U.S., especially in post-colonial settings, pastoral theology in the U.S. will better reflect an international awareness.

Formation and Professional Identity

We began this chapter by describing pastoral theology as contextual theology done from a pastoral perspective to fund practices of care and to develop theological understanding. The epistemological shifts brought about through postmodernity have disclosed the way practices of care are theory laden and give rise to new theological understanding. Pastoral theology is a performative discipline whether done by chaplains, pastoral counselors, pastors, or pastoral theologians in seminary classrooms.

Formation for pastoral theological reflection requires attention to several competencies: the self-understanding and values of the person; a priority for the practical wisdom yielded by pastoral theological reflection; and the practices and methods appropriate for the particular context(s) in which the person will collaboratively work whether as a pastor, chaplain or scholar/teacher. (See Marshall's chapter in this volume for discussion of formation and theological methods.) Each of these competencies has become more complex since the publication of the *Dicionary* due to the epistemological shifts introduced by postmodernity and the wider contexts of care that also require a larger circle of theoretical conversation partners. The deconstruction of the "grand narratives" of modernity have also altered assumptions regarding the way authority functions in the faith communities in which pastoral theology is anchored and whether authority is granted to the fruits of pastoral theological reflection by the larger public. This means that those who engage in pastoral theological reflection must become more intentional in claiming their identification in a particular faith tradition and their accountability for ways they are shaped by its practices and values. Knowing now is recognized as perspectival or partial albeit truthful so that those engaged in pastoral theology learn to value the particularity of their insight and build from it to engage and learn from difference. The capacity to bridge empathically from one's particular experience to engage difference in another is an increasingly important skill (Huffaker, 1998; McCarthy, 1993).

Forming persons for the effective practice of pastoral theological reflection necessarily builds on their self-awareness as one shaped in community by the commitments and practices of a particular tradition. To the extent that pastoral theologians look for the transformative, redemptive potential of practices within and beyond communities of faith, they need to learn that knowledge lies not only within the historical tradition that they must know, but also in the lived experience of those who practice that faith. This means that pastoral theologians learn to discern practical wisdom in the lived enactment of a community's faith and vision. The ecological metaphor of a web that now guides pastoral theology also requires that pastoral theologians come to value the urgency of claiming the wisdom of their community's vision for public dimensions of care in issues such as violence and health policies as well as in the more familiar context of faith communities. Relational justice provides a helpful ethical norm for shaping the goals of pastoral theological reflection in public as well as ecclesial contexts.

Conclusion

Pastoral theology finds itself in a time of considerable redefinition and ferment with new contributors, new interdisciplinary sources, and new definitions of the context and breadth of care. New paradigms are emerging, and new norms to guide theological reflection are apparent now. The psychological captivity of the field is clearly over. Constructive theological contributions are being proposed as our review of current reflection on anthropology disclosed. The changes just beginning to unfold particularly in the area of intercultural perspectives and the public horizons of care will be even more far reaching. In every case the test of this ferment and change lies in our faithfulness to enlarge the love of God and loving care for neighbor, self, and creation.

AACC (2003). American Association of Christian Counselors, Mission and Statement of Faith. http://www.AACC.net

Ackermann, D., & Bons-Storm, R. (Eds.). (1998). *Liberating faith practices: Feminist practical theologies.* Bondgenotenlaan, the Netherlands: Peeters.

ACPE. (2001). A white paper: Professional chaplaincy: Its role and importance in healthcare. *Journal of Pastoral Care, 55*(1), 81-98.

Adams, C. (1994). *Woman-battering.* Minneapolis, MN: Fortress Press.

Adams, C. J., & Fortune, M. M. (Eds.) (1995). *Violence against women and children: A Christian theological sourcebook.* New York: Continuum.

Alves, R. (1977). Personal wholeness and political creativity: The theology of liberation and pastoral care. *Pastoral Psychology, 26*(2), 124-136.

American Association of Christian Counselors (www.AACC.net).

American Association of Pastoral Counselors (www.AAPC.org).

Anderson, H. (1997). Men and grief: The hidden sea of tears without outlet. In C. Neuger & J. Poling (Eds.), *The care of men* (pp. 203-226). Nashville, TN: Abingdon Press.

Anderson, H. (1999). Seeing the other whole: A habitus for globalisation. In P. Ballard & P. Couture (Eds.), *Globalisation and difference* (pp. 3-18). Cardiff, UK: Cardiff Academic Press.

Anderson, H. (2000). Pastoral supervision at the crossroads. *Journal of Supervision and Training in Ministry, 20*, 8-12.

Anderson, H. (2001). Spiritual care: The power of an adjective. *Journal of Pastoral Care, 55*(3), 1-5, 233-237.

Anderson, H., & Foley, E. (1998). *Mighty stories, dangerous rituals: Weaving together the human and the divine.* San Francisco: Jossey Bass.

Anderson, H., Hogue, D., & McCarthy, M. (1995). *Promising again.* Louisville, KY: Westminster John Knox Press.

Anderson, V. (1996). The search for public theology in the United States. In T. G. Long & E. Farley (Eds.), *Preaching as a theological task: World, gospel, scripture.* Louisville, KY: Westminster John Knox Press.

Ashbrook, J. (1990). Teaching. In R. Hunter (Ed.), *Dictionary of pastoral care and counseling* (pp. 1252-1255). Nashville, TN: Abingdon Press.

Ashbrook, J. (1996). *Minding the soul: Pastoral counseling as remembering.* Minneapolis, MN: Fortress Press.

Ashby, H. (1996). Is it time for a black pastoral theology? *Journal of Pastoral Theology, 6,* 1-16.

Ashby, H. (2000). Pastoral theology as public theology: Participating in the healing of damaged and damaging cultures and institutions. *Journal of Pastoral Theology, 10,* 18-27.

Ashby, H. (2003). *Our home is over Jordan: A black pastoral theology.* St. Louis, MO: Chalice Press.

Augsburger, D. (1986). *Pastoral counseling across cultures.* Philadelphia: Westminster Press.

Augsburger, D. (1992a). *Conflict mediation across cultures: Pathways and patterns.* Louisville, KY: Westminster/John Knox Press.

Augsburger, D. (1992b). Multicultural pastoral care and counseling. *Journal of Pastoral Care, 46*(2), 97-99.

Ballard, P., & Couture, P. (Eds.). (1999). *Globalisation and difference: Practical theology in a world context.* Cardiff, UK: Cardiff Academic Press.

Ballard, P., & Couture, P. (Eds.). (2001). *Creativity, imagination and criticism: The expressive dimension in practical theology.* Cardiff, UK: Cardiff Academic Press.

Ballou, M., & Gabalac, N. (1987). *A feminist position on mental health.* Springfield, IL: C.C. Thomas Press.

Baltodano, S. (2002). Pastoral care in Latin America. In J. Farris (Ed.), *International perspectives on pastoral counseling* (pp. 191-224). Binghamton, NY: Haworth Press.

Becher, W., Campbell, A. V., & Parker, G. K. (Eds). (1993). *The risks of freedom*. Manila, Philippines: The Pastoral Care Foundation Inc.

Beit-Hallahmi, B. (1990). Psychology of religion (Empirical studies, methods, and problems). In R. Hunter (Ed.), *Dictionary of pastoral care and counseling* (pp. 1005-1007). Nashville, TN: Abingdon Press.

Becker, T. (2002). Individualism and the invisibility of monoculturalism/ whiteness: Limits to effective clinical pastoral education supervision. *Journal of Supervision and Training in Ministry, 12*, 4-20.

Bell, C. R. (2000). Pastoral supervision and cultural issues. *Journal of Supervision and Training in Ministry, 20*, 124-131.

Berg, I. K., & Jaya, A. (1993). Different and same: Family therapy with Asian American families. *Journal of Marital and Family Therapy, 19*(1), 31-38.

Berinyuu, A. A. (1988). *Pastoral care to the sick in Africa: An approach to transcultural pastoral theology*. Frankfurt/New York: Peter Lang.

Berinyuu, A. A. (1989). *Towards theory and practice of pastoral counseling in Africa*. Frankfurt-am-Main/Bern/New York: Peter Lang.

Billman, K., & Migliore, D. (1999). *Rachel's cry: Prayer of lament and rebirth of hope*. Cleveland, OH: United Church Press.

Boff, L., & Boff, C. (1987). *Introducing liberation theology*. Maryknoll, NY: Orbis Books.

Bohn, C. (Ed.). (1995). *Therapeutic practice in a cross-cultural world: Theological, psychological, and ethical issues*. Decatur, GA: Journal of Pastoral Care Publications.

Bohn, C., & Brown, J. (1989). *Christianity, patriarchy, and abuse: A feminist critique*. Cleveland, OH: Pilgrim Press.

Boisen, A. (1936). *The exploration of the inner world: A study of mental disorder and religious experience*. New York: Willett.

Bons-Storm, R. (1996). *The incredible woman: Listening to women's silences in pastoral care and counseling*. Nashville, TN: Abingdon Press.

Bourdieu, P. (1992). *The logic of practice*. Cambridge, UK: Polity Press.

Boyd, M., & Bohler, C. (1999). Womanist-feminist alliances: Meeting on the bridge. In B. Miller-McLemore & B. Gill-Austern (Eds.), *Feminist and womanist pastoral theology* (pp. 189-210). Nashville: Abingdon Press.

Brennan, M., O'Reilly, J., Bronersky, L., Burbank, B., McCabe, J., & McWilliams, F. (1988). Gathering at the threshold. *Journal of Pastoral Care, 42*(3), 273-279.

Browning, D. S. (1968). Religion, revelation, and the strengths of the poor. *Journal of Pastoral Psychology, 19*(4), 37-49.

Browning, D. S (1976). *The moral context of pastoral care*. Philadelphia: The Westminster Press.

Browning, D. S. (1983a). *Religious ethics and pastoral care*. Philadelphia: Fortress Press.

Browning, D. S. (1983b). Pastoral theology in a pluralistic age. In D. S. Browning (Ed.), *Practical theology: The emerging field in theology, church, and world* (pp. 187-202). San Francisco: Harper & Row.

Browning, D. S. (Ed.). (1983c). *Practical theology: The emerging field in theology, church, and world*. San Francisco: Harper & Row.

Browning, D. S. (1987a). *Religious thought and the modern psychologies: A critical conversation in the theory of culture*. Philadelphia: Fortress Press.

Browning, D. S. (1987b). Mapping the terrain of pastoral theology: Toward a practical theology of care. *Pastoral Psychology 36*(1), 10-28.

Browning, D. S. (1988). Pastoral care and the study of the congregation. In J. C. Hough, Jr. & B. Wheeler, *Beyond clericalism: The congregation as a focus for theological education* (pp. 103-118). Atlanta, GA: Scholars Press.

Browning, D. S. (1991). *A fundamental practical theology: Descriptive and strategic proposals*. Minneapolis, MN: Fortress Press.

Browning, D. S., Miller-McLemore, B. J., Couture, P. D., Lyon, K. B., & Franklin, R. M. (1997, 2000). *From culture wars to common ground: Religion and the American family debate*. Louisville, KY: Westminster John Knox Press.

Bruce, C. (1976). Nurturing the souls of black folk. *Journal of Pastoral Care, 30*(4), 259-263.

Bryant, C. (1995). Pastoral care and counseling in a cross-cultural context: The issue of authority. *Journal of Pastoral Care, 49*(3), 329-337.

Burck, J. R., & Hunter, R. (1990). Pastoral theology, protestant. In R. Hunter (Ed.), *Dictionary of pastoral care and counseling* (pp. 867-872). Nashville, TN: Abingdon Press.

Butler, L. (2000). *Loving home: Caring for African-American marriage and family.* Cleveland, OH: Pilgrim Press.

Butler, L. (2001). The unpopular experience of popular culture: Cultural resistance as identity formation. *Journal of Pastoral Theology, 11*(1), 40-52.

CACREP. (2001). *Council on accreditation of counseling and related education programs accreditation manual.* Alexandria, VA: Council on Accreditation of Counseling and Related Education Programs.

Cady, L. E. (1993). *Religion, theology, and American public life.* Albany: State University of New York Press.

Cady, L. E. (1997). Identity, feminist theory, and theology. In R. Chopp & S. G. Devaney (Eds.), *Horizons in feminist theology: Identity, tradition, and norms* (pp. 17-32). Minneapolis, MN: Fortress Press.

Capps, D. (1981). *Biblical approaches to pastoral counseling.* Philadelphia: The Westminster Press.

Capps, D. (1993). Sex in the parish: Social scientific explanations for why it occurs. *Journal of Pastoral Care, 47*(2), 350-361.

Capps, D. (2001). *Giving counsel: A minister's guidebook.* St. Louis, MO: Chalice Press.

Capps, D., & Fowler, G. (2001). *The pastoral care case: Learning about care in congregations.* St. Louis, MO: Chalice Press.

Carter, Stephen L. (1994). *The culture of disbelief: How American law and politics trivialize religious devotion.* New York: Anchor Press.

Chopp, R. S. (1987). Practical theology and liberation. In L. S. Mudge & J. N. Poling, *Formation and reflection: The promise of practical theology* (pp. 120-138). Philadelphia: Fortress Press.

Chopp, R. S. (1995). *Saving work*. Louisville, KY: Westminster John Knox Press.

Clarke, K. (1994). Lessons from feminist therapy for ministerial ethics. *Journal of Pastoral Care, 48*(3), 233-244.

Clarke, R. L. (1986). *Pastoral care of battered women*. Louisville, KY: Westminster/John Knox Press.

Clebsch, W., & Charles, J. (1983). *Pastoral care in historical perspective,* 2d. ed. New York: Aronson.

Clebsch, W. A., & Jaekle, C. R. (1967). *Pastoral care in historical perspective*. New York: Harper.

Cobia, D. C., & Boes, S. R. (2000). Professional disclosure statements and formal plans for supervision. *Journal of Counseling and Development, 78,* 293-296.

Cooper-White, P. (1995). *The cry of Tamar: Violence against women and the church's response*. Minneapolis, MN: Augsburg Fortress Press.

Cooper-White, P. (2000). Opening the eyes: Understanding the impact of trauma on development. In J. Stevenson-Moessner (Ed.), *In her own time: Women and developmental issues in pastoral care* (pp. 87-102). Minneapolis, MN: Fortress Press.

Couture, P. (1991). *Blessed are the poor? Women's poverty, family policy, and practical theology*. Nashville, TN: Abingdon Press.

Couture, P. (1993). The family policy debate: A feminist theologian's response. *Journal of Pastoral Theology, 3,* 76-87.

Couture, P. (1996a). Rethinking private and public patriarchy. In A. Carr & M. S. Van Leeuwen (Eds.), *Religion, feminism, and the family* (pp. 249-274). Louisville, KY: Westminster John Knox Press.

Couture, P. (1996b). Weaving the web: Pastoral care in an individualistic society. In J. Stevenson-Moessner (Ed.), *Through the eyes of women: Insights for pastoral care* (pp. 94-106). Minneapolis, MN: Fortress Press.

Couture, P. (1998). Feminist, Wesleyan, practical theology and the practice of pastoral care. In D. Ackermann & R. Bons-Storm (Eds.), *Liberating faith practices: Feminist practical theologies in context* (pp. 27-50). Leuven, Belgium: Peeters.

Couture, P. (2000). *Seeing children, seeing God: A practical theology of children and poverty*. Nashville, TN: Abingdon Press.

Couture, P. (2001). Pastoral care and the social gospel. In C. H. Evans (Ed.), *The social gospel today* (pp. 160-169). Louisville, KY: Westminster John Knox Press.

Couture, P. D., & Hunter, R. J. (Eds.). (1995). *Pastoral care and social conflict*. Nashville, TN: Abingdon Press.

CPSP (2003). http://www.cpsp.org.

Crabb, L. (2003). American Association of Christian Counselors, homepage. http://www.aacc.net.

Culbertson, P. (1994). *Counseling men*. Minneapolis: Fortress Press.

Culbertson, P. (2000). *Caring for God's people: Counseling and Christian wholeness*. Minneapolis, MN: Fortress Press.

Culbertson, P. L., & Shippee, A. B. (Eds.). (1990). *The pastor: Readings from the patristic period*. Minneapolis, MN: Fortress Press.

Davis, P. (1996). *Counseling adolescent girls*. Minneapolis, MN: Fortress Press.

DeMarinis, V. (1993). *Critical caring: A feminist model for pastoral psychology*. Louisville, KY: Westminster/John Knox Press.

DeVelder, J. R. (2000). Clinical pastoral education in the future. *Journal of supervision and training in ministry, 20,* 136-148.

Disney, M. J., & Stephens, A. M. (1994). Legal issues in clinical supervision: *The ACA legal series, Vol. 10.* American Counseling Association, Alexandria, VA.

Dittes, J. (1996). *Driven by hope: Men and meaning*. Louisville, KY: Westminster John Knox Press.

Doehring, C. (1992). Developing models of feminist pastoral counseling. *Journal of Pastoral Care, 46*(1), 23-31.

Doerhing, C. (1995). *Taking care: Monitoring power dynamics and relational boundaries in pastoral care and counseling*. Nashville, TN: Abingdon Press.

Doehring, C. (1999). A method of feminist pastoral theology. In B. Miller-McLemore & B. Gill-Austern (Eds.), *Feminist and womanist pastoral theology* (pp. 95-111). Nashville, TN: Abingdon Press.

Doehring, C. (2004). *Theologically based care: a postmodern approach.* Louisville: Westminster John Knox.

Dumalagan, N., Becher, W., & Taniguchi, T. (Eds.). (1983). *Pastoral care and counseling in Asia: Its needs and concerns.* Manila, Philippines: Clinical Pastoral Care Association of the Philippines.

Dunlap, S. (1997). *Counseling depressed women.* Louisville, KY: Westminster John Knox Press.

Dykstra, R. (1997). *Counseling troubled youth.* Louisville, KY: Westminster John Knox Press.

Eiseland, N. (1994). *The disabled god: Toward a liberatory theology of disability.* Nashville, TN: Abingdon Press.

Ellen, C. (1990). Feminist therapy. In R. Hunter (Ed.), *Dictionary of pastoral care and counseling* (pp. 435-437). Nashville, TN: Abingdon Press.

Enriquez, V. (1989, 1994). *Indigenous psychology and national consciousness: The Philippine experience.* Tokyo: Institute for the Study of Languages and Cultures of Asia and Africa.

Eugene, T. (1995). "If you get there before I do": A womanist ethical response to sexual violence and abuse. In J. Grant (Ed.), *Perspectives on womanist theology* (pp. 91-113). Atlanta, GA: ITC Press.

Eugene, T., & Poling, J. (1998). *Balm for Gilead: Pastoral care for African American families experiencing abuse.* Nashville, TN: Abingdon Press.

Faber, H. (1990). International pastoral care movement. In R. Hunter (Ed.), *Dictionary of pastoral care and counseling* (pp. 589-590). Nashville, TN: Abingdon Press.

Farley, E. (1983a). Theology and practice outside the clerical paradigm. In D. S. Browning (Ed.), *Practical theology: The emerging field in theology, church, and world* (pp. 21-41). San Francisco: Harper & Row.

Farley, E. (1983b). *Theologia.* Philadelphia: Fortress Press.

Farley, E. (1990). Sin/sins. In R. Hunter (Ed.), *Dictionary of pastoral care and counseling* (pp. 1173-1176). Nashville, TN: Abingdon Press.

Farris, J. (2002). *Pastoral perspectives on pastoral counseling*. New York: Haworth.

Farris, J. (Ed.). (2002a). *International perspectives on pastoral counseling*. Binghamton, NY: Haworth Pastoral Press and *American Journal of Pastoral Counseling, 5*, (1/2,3/4).

Fitchett, G. (1993). *Assessing spiritual needs*. Minneapolis, MN: Augsburg Press.

Fortune, M. (1987). *Keeping the faith: Questions and answers for the abused woman*. San Francisco: HarperSanFrancisco Press.

Fortune, M. (1989). *Is Nothing Sacred? When sex invades the pastoral relationship*. Cleveland, OH: Pilgrim Press.

Fortune, M. (1993). The nature of abuse. *Pastoral Psychology, 41*(5), 275-288.

Fortune, M. M., & Poling, J. N. (1994). *Sexual abuse by clergy: A crisis for the church*. Decatur, GA: Journal of Pastoral Care Publications.

Foskett, J. (1988). Playing with one another: Some reflections on a visit down under. *CONTACT, 96*, No. 2.

Foster-Boyd, M., & Bohler, C. (1999). Womanist-feminist alliances: Meeting on the bridge. In B. Miller McLemore & B. Gill-Austern (Eds.), *Feminist and womanist pastoral theology* (pp. 189-210). Nashville, TN: Abingdon Press.

Fuller, R. (2000). Rediscovering the laws of spiritual life: The last twenty years of supervision and training in ministry. *Journal of Supervision and Training in Ministry, 20*, 13-39.

Furniss, G. M. (1992). The forest and the trees: The value of sociology for pastoral care. *Journal of Pastoral Care, 46*(4), 349-359.

Furniss, G. M. (1994). *The social context of pastoral care: Defining the life situation*. Louisville, KY: Westminster John Knox Press.

Garma, J. M. (1991). A cry of anguish: The battered woman. In M. Glaz and J. S. Moessner (Eds.), *Women in travail and transition: A new pastoral care* (pp. 126-145). Minneapolis, MN: Fortress Press.

Gerkin, C. (1979). *Crisis experience in modern life*. Nashville, TN: Abingdon Press.

Gerkin, C. (1984). *The living human document: Revisioning pastoral counseling in a hermeneutical mode*. Nashville, TN: Abingdon Press.

Gerkin, C. (1986). *Widening the horizons*. Philadelphia: Westminster Press.

Gerkin, C. (1991). *Prophetic pastoral practice: A Christian vision of life together*. Nashville, TN: Abingdon Press.

Gerkin, C. (1997). *An introduction to pastoral care*. Nashville, TN: Abingdon Press.

Gill-Austern, B. (1995). Rediscovering hidden treasures for pastoral care. *Pastoral Psychology, 43*(4), 233-253.

Gill-Austern, B. (1996). Love understood as self-sacrifice and self-denial: What does it do to women? In J. Stevenson-Moessner (Ed.), *Through the eyes of women: Insights for pastoral care* (pp. 304-321). Minneapolis, MN: Fortress Press.

Gill-Austern, B. (1997). Responding to a culture ravenous for soul food. *Journal of Pastoral Theology, 7*, 63-79.

Gilpin, W. C. (Ed.). (1990). *Public faith: Reflections on the political role of American churches*. St. Louis, MO: CBP Press.

Gilpin, W. C. (1996). *A preface to theology*. Chicago: University of Chicago Press.

Gingrich, F. C. (2002). Pastoral counseling in the Philippines: A perspective from the west. In James Farris (Ed.), *International perspectives on pastoral counseling* (pp. 5-55). New York/London/Oxford: The Haworth Press.

Glaz, M. (1990). Gender issues in pastoral theology. *Journal of Pastoral Theology, 1*(1), 93-115.

Glaz, M., & Stevenson-Moessner, J. (1991). *Women in travail and transition: A new pastoral care*. Minneapolis, MN: Fortress Press.

Goldstein, V.S. (1960). The human situation: A feminine viewpoint. *Journal of Religion, 40*(2), 100-112.

Gorsuch, N. (1999). *Pastoral visitation.* Minneapolis, MN: Fortress Press.

Gorsuch, N. (2001). *Introducing feminist pastoral care and counseling.* Cleveland, OH: Pilgrim Press.

Govig, S. (1989). *Strong at the broken places: Persons with disabilities and the church.* Louisville, KY: Westminster John Knox Press.

Grace, M. (2002). Thinking through pastoral education with culturally diverse peer groups. *Journal of Supervision and Training in Ministry, 22,* 21-39.

Graham, E. (1995). *Making the difference: Gender, personhood and theology.* Minneapolis, MN: Fortress Press.

Graham, E. (1996). *Transforming practice: Pastoral theology in an age of uncertainty.* London: Mowbray.

Graham, E., & Halsey, M. (1993). *Life cycles: Women and pastoral care.* London: SPCK Press.

Graham, L. K. (1992). *Care of persons, care of worlds: A psychosystems approach to pastoral care and counseling.* Nashville, TN: Abingdon Press.

Graham, L. K. (1995). From relational humanness to relational justice: Reconceiving pastoral care and counseling. In P. Couture & R. Hunter (Eds.), *Pastoral care and social conflict* (pp. 220-234). Nashville, TN: Abingdon Press.

Graham, L. K. (1996). From impasse to innovation in pastoral theology and counseling. *Journal of Pastoral Theology, 6,* 17-36.

Graham, L. K. (1997). *Discovering images of God: Narratives of care among lesbians and gays.* Louisville, KY: Westminster John Knox Press.

Graham, L. K. (2000). Pastoral theology as public theology in relation to the clinic. *Journal of Pastoral Theology 10,* 1-17.

Grant, B. (1990). Sin and sickness. In R. Hunter (Ed.), *Dictionary of pastoral care and counseling* (pp. 1176-1178). Nashville, TN: Abingdon Press.

Grant, B. (2001). *A theology for pastoral psychotherapy: God's play in sacred spaces.* New York: Haworth Press.

Greenberg Quinlin Research. (2000). http://www.aapc.org/survey.htm.

Greider, K. (1997). *Reckoning with aggression: Theology, violence, and vitality.* Louisville, KY: Westminster John Knox Press.

Greider, K. (2002). From multiculturalism to interculturality: Demilitarizing the border between personal and social dynamics through spiritual receptivity. *Journal of Supervision and Training in Ministry, 22,* 40-58.

Greider, K., Johnson, G., & Leslie, K. (1999). Three decades of women writing for our lives. In B. Miller-McLemore & B. Gill-Austern (Eds.), *Feminist and womanist pastoral theology* (pp. 21-50). Nashville, TN: Abingdon Press.

Griffin, H. (1993). Giving new birth: Lesbians, gays, and "the family." *Journal of Pastoral Theology, 3,* 88-98.

Guest, C. L. Jr., & Dooley, K. (1999). Supervisor malpractice: Liability to the supervisee in clinical supervision. *Counselor Education and Supervision, 38*(4), 69-279.

Gustafson, J. M. (1970). *The church as moral decision maker.* Philadelphia: Pilgrim Press.

Gutiérrez, G. (1973). *A theology of liberation: History, politics, and salvation* (C. Inda & J. Eagleson, Eds. & Trans.). Maryknoll, NY: Orbis Books.

Hall, D. J. (1986). *Imaging God: Dominion as stewardship.* Grand Rapids, MI: Eerdmans.

Halmos, P. (1965). *Faith of the counsellors.* London: Constable.

Hartung, B. (1990). Technique and skill in pastoral care. In R. Hunter (Ed.), *Dictionary of pastoral care and counseling* (pp. 1255-1256). Nashville, TN: Abingdon Press.

Hemenway, J. E. (2000). The shifting of the foundations: Ten questions concerning the future of pastoral supervision and the pastoral care movement. *Journal of Supervision and Training in Ministry, 20,* 59-68.

Hightower, J. (2002). Pastoral counseling training: Training goals in a changing environment. *Journal of Pastoral Care and Counseling, 56,* 3.

Hilsman, G. J. (2000). Windows into the future of the pastoral care and counseling movement. *Journal of Supervision and Training in Ministry, 20,* 69-79.

Hiltner, S. (1958). *Preface to pastoral theology.* New York: Abingdon Press.

Hogue, D. (2003). *Remembering the future imagining the past: Story, ritual, and the human brain.* Cleveland, OH: Pilgrim Press.

Holifield, E. B. (1983). *A history of pastoral care in America: From salvation to self-realization.* Nashville, TN: Abingdon Press.

Holifield, E. B. (1990a). Pastoral care movement. In R. Hunter (Ed.), *Dictionary of pastoral care and counseling* (pp. 845-849). Nashville, TN: Abingdon Press.

Holifield, B. (1990b). Psychology in American religion. In R. Hunter (Ed.), *Dictionary of pastoral care and counseling* (pp. 1001-1005). Nashville, TN: Abingdon Press.

Hollenweger, W. J. (1978). Intercultural theology. *Theological Renewal, 10,* 2-14.

Hollies, L. (Ed.). (1992). *Womanistcare.* (Vol. 1.) Joliet, IL: Woman to Woman Ministries, Inc.

Hopkins, P. (1987). On being a compassionate oppressor. *Journal of Pastoral Psychology, 34*(3), 204-213.

Hough, J. C. (2001). Reading the signs. *Theological Education, 37*(2), 101-107.

Houts, D. (1991). *Clergy sexual ethics: A workshop guide.* Decatur, GA: Journal of Pastoral Care Publishing.

Howe, L. (1995). *The image of God: A theology for pastoral care and counseling.* Nashville, TN: Abingdon Press.

Huffaker, L. (1998). *Creative indwelling: Empathy and clarity in God and self.* Atlanta, GA: Scholars Press.

Hunsinger, D. (1995). *Theology and pastoral counseling: A new inter-disciplinary approach.* Grand Rapids, MI: Eerdmans.

Hunter, R. (Ed.). (1990a). *Dictionary of pastoral care and counseling.* Nashville, TN: Abingdon Press.

Hunter, R. (1990b). The personal, concept of, in pastoral care. In R. Hunter (Ed.), *Dictionary of pastoral care and counseling* (p. 893). Nashville, TN: Abingdon Press.

Hunter, R. (1990c). Wisdom and practical knowledge in pastoral care. In. R. Hunter (Ed.), *Dictionary of pastoral care and counseling* (pp. 1325-1326). Nashville, TN: Abingdon Press.

Hunter, R. (1991). What is pastoral about pastoral theology? Insights from eight years shepherding the dictionary of pastoral care and counseling. *Journal of Pastoral Theology, 1*, 35-52.

Hunter, R. (1995). The therapeutic tradition of pastoral care and counseling. In P. D. Couture and R. Hunter (Eds.), *Pastoral care and social conflict* (pp. 17-31). Nashville, TN: Abingdon Press.

Hunter, R. (2001, October). Spiritual counsel: An art in transition. *Christian Century*, pp. 20-25.

Imbens, A., & Jonker, I. (1992). *Christianity and incest*. Minneapolis, MN: Fortress Press.

Jackson, B., & Holvino, E. (1988). Developing multicultural organizations: Creative change. *The Journal of Religion and Applied Behavioral Sciences, 9*(2), 14-19.

Jennings, T. (1990). Pastoral theological methodology. In R. Hunter (Ed.), *Dictionary of pastoral care and counseling* (pp. 862-864). Nashville: Abingdon Press.

Jernigan, H. (2000). Clinical pastoral education with students from other cultures: The role of the supervisor. *Journal of Pastoral Care, 54*(2), 135-145.

Johnson, E. (1993). *She who is: The mystery of God in feminist discourse*. New York: Crossroads.

Jones, S. (1997). Women's experience between a rock and a hard place: Feminist, and mujerista theologies in North America. In R. Chopp & S. G. Davaney (Eds.), *Horizons in feminist theology* (pp. 33-53). Minneapolis, MN: Augsburg Fortress Press.

Justes, E. (1971). The church—for men only. *Spectrum, 47*.

Justes, E. (1978). Theological reflections on the role of women in church and society. *Journal of Pastoral Care, 32*(1), 42-54.

Justes, E. (1979). Role perceptions and the pastoral care of women. *Journal of Pastoral Counseling, 14*.

Justes, E. (1996). Crossing bridges of no return. *Journal of Pastoral Theology, 6*(1), 119-126.

Karaban, R. (1990). Cross-cultural counseling: Is it possible? Some personal reflections. *Pastoral Psychology, 38*(6), 219-224.

Kelsey, D. (1990). Church discourse and public realm. In B. D. Marshall, (Ed.), *Theology and dialogue: Essays in conversation with George Lindbeck*. Notre Dame, IN: University of Notre Dame Press.

Kim, Y. (Ed.). (1992). *Knowledge, attitude, and experience: Ministry in the cross-cultural context*. Nashville, TN: Abingdon Press.

Kluckholn, C., & Murray, H. (1948). *Personality in nature, society and culture*. New York: Knoff.

Kornfeld, M. (1998). *Cultivating wholeness: A guide to care and counseling in faith communities*. New York: Continuum.

Kornfeld, M. (2000). Back to the future: Thoughts about the supervision of pastoral counseling. *Journal of Supervision and Training in Ministry, 20*, 80-89.

Lago, C., & Thompson, J. (1996). *Race, culture, and counselling*. Buckingham, UK: Open University Press.

Lakeland, P. (1997). *Postmodernity*. Minneapolis, MN: Fortress Press.

Lambourne, R. A. (1974). Religion, medicine and politics. *Contact 44*, 1-40.

Lartey, E., (1987). *Pastoral counseling in inter-cultural perspective*. Frankfurt, Germany: Peter Lang.

Lartey, E. (1997a). *Pastoral counseling in intercultural perspective*. London: Cassell.

Lartey, E. (1997b). *In living colour: An intercultural approach to pastoral care and counseling*. Herndon, VA: Cassell.

Lartey, E. (2002). Embracing the collage: Pastoral theology in an era of post-henomena. *Journal of Pastoral Theology, 12*(2), 1-10.

Lartey, E., J. N. Poling, G. Y. Bri-wnant-Jones (2003). *In living color: An intercultural approach to pastoral care and counseling* (Revised 2nd. Ed.). London: Jessica Kingsley.

Lartey, E., Nwachuku, D., & wa Kasonga, K. (Eds.). (1994). *The church and healing: Echoes from Africa.* Frankfurt/Bern/New York: Peter Lang.

Lebacqz, K., & Barton, R. G. (1991). *Sex in the parish.* Louisville, KY: Westminster John Knox Press.

Lebacqz, K., & Driskill, J. (2000). *Ethics and spiritual care.* Nashville, TN: Abingdon Press.

Lee, K. S. (2000). A multicultural vision for the practice of pastoral supervision and training. *Journal of Supervision and Training in Ministry, 20,* 111-123.

Lee, K. S. (2001). Becoming multicultural dancers: The pastoral practitioner in a multicultural society. *Journal of Pastoral Care, 55*(4), 389-396.

Lee, K. S. (2002). The teacher-student in multicultural theological education: Pedagogy of collaborative inquiry. *Journal of Supervision and Training in Ministry, 22,* 81-99.

Lee, S. Y. C. (2002). Pastoral counseling in Chinese cultural contexts: Philosophical, historical, sociological, spiritual, and psychological considerations. In J. Farris (Ed.), *International perspectives on pastoral counseling* (pp. 119-149). Binghamton, NY: Haworth Pastoral Press.

Leslie, K. (2002). *When violence is no stranger: Pastoral counseling with survivors of acquaintance rape.* Minneapolis, MN: Fortress Press.

Lester, A. (1995). *Hope in pastoral care and counseling.* Louisville, KY: Westminster John Knox Press.

Lester, A. (2000). In search of ideal: Future stories for pastoral supervision. *Journal of Supervision and Training in Ministry, 20,* 149-157.

Lester, A. (2003). *The angry Christian: A theology for care and counseling.* Louisville, KY: Westminster John Knox Press.

Loder, J. (1990). Theology and psychology. In R. Hunter (Ed.), *Dictionary of pastoral care and counseling* (pp. 1267-1270). Nashville, TN: Abingdon Press.

Lovin, R. (Ed.). (1986). *Religion and American public life.* New York: Paulist Press.

Louw, D. J. (2002). Pastoral hermeneutics and the challenge of a global economy: Care to the living human web. *Journal of Pastoral Care and Counseling, 56*(4), 339-350.

Maloney, H. N. (Ed). (2001). *Pastoral care and counseling in sexual diversity.* New York: Haworth Press.

ma Mpolo, J. M., & Nwachuku, D. (Eds.). (1991). *Pastoral care and counselling in Africa today.* Frankfurt/Bern/New York/Paris: Peter Lang Publishing.

Marchesani, L., & Adams, M. (1992). Dynamics of diversity in the teaching-learning process: A faculty development model for analysis and action. *New Directions for Teaching and Learning, 52* (winter), 9-19.

Marshall, J. (1994). Pastoral theology and lesbian/gay/bisexual experiences. *Journal of Pastoral Theology, 4*, 73-79.

Marshall, J. (1995). Covenants and partnerships: Pastoral counseling with women in lesbian relationships. *Journal of Pastoral Theology, 5*(1), 81-93.

Marshall, J. (1996a). Pedagogy and pastoral theology in dialogue with lesbian/bisexual/gay concerns. *Journal of Pastoral Theology, 6*, 55-69.

Marshall, J. (1996b). Sexual identity and pastoral concerns: Caring with women who are developing lesbian identities. In J. Moessner (Ed.), *Through the eyes of women: Insights for pastoral care* (pp. 143-166). Minneapolis, MN: Fortress Press.

Marshall, J. (1997). *Counseling lesbian partners.* Louisville, KY: Westminster John Knox Press.

Marshall, J. (1999). Communal dimensions of forgiveness: Learning from the life and death of Matthew Shepard. *Journal of Pastoral Theology, 9*, 49-63.

Marshall, J. (2001). Pastoral care and the formation of sexual identity: Lesbian, gay, bisexual, and transgendered. In H. N. Maloney (Ed.), *Pastoral care and counseling in sexual diversity* (101-112). New York: Haworth Press.

Marty, M. E. (1981). *The public church: Mainline, evangelical, catholic.* New York: Crossroad.

McCarthy, M. (1985). *The role of mutuality in family structure and relationships: A critical examination of select systems of family therapy from the perspective of selected options in contemporary theological ethics* (Doctoral dissertation, University of Chicago, 1985).

McCarthy, M. (1992). Empathy: A bridge between. *Journal of Pastoral Care, 46*(2), 119-130.

McCarthy, M. (1992-1993). Growing into a professional self: A theory of pastoral supervision as a formational process. *Journal of Supervision and Training in Ministry, 14*, 109-124.

McCarthy, M. (1993). Empathy amid diversity: Problems and possibilities. *Journal of Pastoral Theology, 3*, 15-28.

McCarthy, M. (2000). Spirituality in a postmodern era. In J. Woodward & S. Pattison with J. Patton (Eds.), *The Blackwell reader in pastoral and practical theology* (pp. 192-206). Oxford, England: Blackwell Publishers.

McCarthy, M. (2002). Spirituality, pastoral theology, and the pastoral theologian. *Journal of Pastoral Theology, 12*(1), 1-18.

McCarthy, P., Sugden, S., Koker, M., Lamendola, F., et al. (1995). A practical guide to informed consent in clinical supervision. *Counselor Education and Supervision, 35*(2), 130-138.

McCrary, C., & Wimberly, E. P. (Eds.). (1998). Introduction: Personhood in African American pastoral care. *The Journal of the Interdenominational Theological Center, 25*(3), 5-7.

McNeill, J. T. (1951/1977). *A history of the cure of souls.* New York: Harper & Row.

McWilliams, F. C. (1996). Pushing against the boundaries of pastoral care: Clinical pastoral education in urban ministry settings. *Journal of Pastoral Care, 50,* 2, 151-160.

Mental Health, United States, 2002. U.S. Department of Health and Human Services (see http://www.mentalhealth.org/cmhs/MentalHealthStatistics/default.asp).

Mercado, L. N. (Ed.). (1977). *Filipino religious psychology.* Tacloban City, Philippines: Divine Word Publications.

Miller, G. (1999). The development of the spiritual focus in counseling and counselor education. *Journal of Counseling and Development, 77*, 498-501.

Miller-McLemore, B. (1993). The human web: Reflections on the state of pastoral theology. *Christian Century, April 7*, 366-369.

Miller-McLemore, B. (1994). *Also a mother: Work and family as theological dilemma.* Nashville, TN: Abingdon Press.

Miller-McLemore, B. (1996a). Family and work: Can anyone "have it all?" In A. Carr & M. S. Van Leeuwen (Eds.), *Religion, feminism, and the family* (pp. 275-293). Louisville, KY: Westminster John Knox Press.

Miller-McLemore, B. (1996b). The living human web: Pastoral theology at the turn of the century. In J. Stevenson-Moessner (Ed.). *Through the eyes of women: Insights for pastoral care* (pp. 9-26). Minneapolis, MN: Fortress Press.

Miller-McLemore, B. (1998). The subject and practice of pastoral theology as a practical theological discipline: Pushing past the nagging identity crisis to the poetics of resistance. In D. Ackermann & R. Bons-Storm (Eds.), *Liberating faith practices: Feminist practical theologies in context* (pp. 175-198). The Netherlands: Peeters.

Miller-McLemore, B. (1999). Feminist theory in pastoral theology. In B. Miller-McLemore & B. Gill-Austern (Eds.), *Feminist and womanist pastoral theology* (pp. 77-94). Nashville, TN: Abingdon Press.

Miller-McLemore, B. (2000). The public character of the university-related divinity school. *Theological Education, 37*(1), 49-61.

Miller-McLemore, B. (2003). *Let the children come: Revisioning childhood from a Christian perspective.* Nashville, TN: Abingdon Press.

Miller-McLemore, B., & Gill-Austern, B. (Eds.). (1999). *Feminist and womanist pastoral theology.* Nashville, TN: Abingdon Press.

Miller-McLemore, B. (2004). Pastoral therapy and public theology developments in the U. S. In E. Graham & A. Rosslands, (Eds.), *Pathways to the public: practical theology as public theology.* Xlibris.

Mills, L. O. (1990). Pastoral theology, graduate education in. In R. Hunter (Ed.), *Dictionary of pastoral care and counseling* (pp. 865-867). Nashville, TN: Abingdon Press.

Mixon, R. (1997). Pastoral care of gay men. In C. Neuger & J. Poling (Eds.), *The care of men* (pp. 163-182). Nashville, TN: Abingdon Press.

Moody, J. (1994). A half decade of learning: Cross-cultural ministry education at interfaith ministries of Hawaii. *Journal of Supervision and Training in Ministry, 15*, 23-32.

Moschella, M. (2002). Food, faith, and formation: A case study on the use of ethnography in pastoral theology and care. *Journal of Pastoral Theology, 12*(1), 75-87.

Moseley, R. M. (1990). Liberation theology and pastoral care. In R. Hunter (Ed.), *Dictionary of pastoral care and counseling* (pp. 645-646). Nashville, TN: Abingdon Press.

Mucherera, T. (2001). *Pastoral care from a third world perspective: A pastoral theology of care for the urban contemporary Shona in Zimbabwe.* New York: Peter Lang.

Mudge, L., & Poling, J. (Eds.). (1987). *Formation and reflection: The promise of practical theology.* Philadelphia: Fortress Press.

Neuger, C. (1991). Women's depression: Lives at risk. In M. Glaz & J. S. Moessner (Eds.). *Women in travail and transition: A new pastoral care* (pp. 146-161). Minneapolis, MN: Fortress Press.

Neuger, C. (1993). Feminist pastoral counseling and pastoral theology. *Journal of Pastoral Theology, 3*(1), 35-57.

Neuger, C. (Ed.). (1996). *The arts of ministry: Feminist-womanist approaches.* Louisville, KY: Westminster John Knox Press.

Neuger, C. (1998). Religious belief in a postmodern era: Framing the issues. *Journal of Pastoral Theology, 8*, 1-14.

Neuger, C. (1999). Establishing boundaries for clergy well-being. In J. Cobble & D. Houts (Eds.), *Well-being in ministry: A guide for pastors, staff members, and congregational leaders* (pp. 25-36). Matthews, NC, Christian Ministry Resources.

Neuger, C. (2000). Narratives of harm: Setting the developmental context for intimate violence. In J. Stevenson-Moessner (Ed.), *In her own time: Women and developmental issues in pastoral care* (pp. 65-86). Minneapolis, MN: Fortress Press.

Neuger, C. (2001). *Counseling women: A narrative, pastoral approach.* Minneapolis, MN: Fortress Press.

Neuger, C., & Graham, L. (1995). Editorial. *Journal of Pastoral Theology, 5,* vi-xii.

Neuger, C., & Poling, J. (1997). *The care of men.* Nashville, TN: Abingdon Press.

Neuger, C., & Poling, J. (Eds.). (2003). *Men's work in preventing violence against women.* New York: Haworth Press.

North, William A. (1988). The American association of pastoral counselors. *Journal of Pastoral Care, 42*(3), 197-202.

Nydham. R. (1999). *Adoptees come of age: Living within two families.* Louisville, KY: Westminster John Knox Press.

Oates, W. (1974). *Pastoral counseling.* Philadelphia: Westminster.

Oates, W. (1990). Pastoral care (Contemporary methods, perspectives, and issues). In R. Hunter (Ed.), *Dictionary of pastoral care and counseling* (pp. 832-836). Nashville, TN: Abingdon Press.

O'Conner, T. S., McCarroll-Butler, P., Meakes, E., Davis, A., & Jadad, A. (2002). Review of quantity and types of spirituality research in three health care databases (1962-1999): Implications for health care ministry. *Journal of Pastoral Care and Counseling, 56*(3).

Oden, T. (1994). *Care of souls in the classic tradition.* Philadelphia: Fortress Press.

Orr, J. L. (1991a). *A dialectical understanding of the psychological and moral development of working-class women with implications for pastoral counseling.* Unpublished doctoral dissertation, University of Michigan, Ann Arbor.

Orr, J. (1991b). Ministry with working-class women. *Journal of Pastoral Care, 45*(4), 343-353.

Orr, J. (1997). Hard work, hard lovin', hard times, hardly worth it: Care of working-class men. In C. Neuger & J. Poling (Eds.), *The care of men* (pp. 70-91). Nashville, TN: Abingdon Press.

Orr, J. (2000). Socioeconomic class and the life span development of women. In J. Stevenson-Moessner (Ed.), *In her own time: Women and developmental issues in pastoral care* (pp. 45-64). Minneapolis, MN: Fortress Press.

Pasewark, K. A., & Paul, G. E. (1999). *The emphatic Christian center: Reforming Christian political practice.* Nashville, TN: Abingdon Press.

Pastoral Ministry in a Fractured World: Proceedings of the 3rd International Congress on Pastoral Care and Counseling. (1987). Melbourne, Australia: International Council on Pastoral Care and Counseling.

Pattison, S. (1994). *Pastoral care and liberation theology.* Cambridge, Great Britain: Cambridge University Press.

Pattison, S. (2000). *A critique of pastoral care.* London: SCM.

Patton, J. (1983). *Pastoral counseling; A ministry of the church.* Nashville, TN: Abingdon Press.

Patton, J. (1985). A context for communication. *Journal of Pastoral Care 39*(4), 289-292.

Patton, J. (1990a). *From ministry to theology: Pastoral action and reflection.* Nashville, TN: Abingdon Press.

Patton, J. (1990b). Pastoral counseling. In R. Hunter (Ed.), *Dictionary of pastoral care and counseling* (pp. 849-854). Nashville, TN: Abingdon Press.

Patton, J. (1993). *Pastoral care in context: An introduction to pastoral care.* Louisville, KY: Westminster John Knox Press.

Patton, J. (2000). Holy complexity: Challenging the laws of spiritual life. *Journal of Supervision and Training in Ministry, 20,* 41-51.

Patton, J., & Ramsay, N. (2000). Editorial. *Journal of Pastoral Theology, 10,* vi-x.

Pellauer, M., Chester, B., & Boyajian, J. (1987). *Sexual assault and abuse: A handbook for clergy and religious professionals.* New York: HarperCollins College Division.

Placher, W. (1985). Revisionist and postliberal theology and the public character of theology. *The Thomist 49*(3), 392-416.

Poling, J. (1988) A critical appraisal of Charles Gerkin's pastoral theology. *Pastoral Psychology, 37*(2), 85-96.

Poling, J. (1991a). *The abuse of power: A theological problem*. Nashville, TN: Abingdon Press.

Poling, J. (1991b). Hearing the silenced voices: The work of justice in pastoral theology. *Journal of Pastoral Theology, 1*, 6-27.

Poling. J. (1996). *Deliver us from evil: Resisting racial and gender oppression*. Minneapolis, MN: Fortress Press.

Poling, J. (1997). Male violence against women and children. In C. Neuger & J. Poling (Eds.), *The care of men* (pp. 138-162). Nashville, TN: Abingdon Press.

Poling, J. (1998). Preaching to perpetrators of violence. In J. McClure & N. Ramsay (Eds.), *Telling the truth: Preaching about sexual and domestic violence* (pp. 71-82). Cleveland: United Church Press.

Poling, J. (2002). *Render unto God: Economic vulnerability, family violence, and pastoral theology*. St. Louis, MO: Chalice Press.

Poling, J. (2003). *Understanding male violence: Pastoral care issues*. St. Louis, MO: Chalice Press.

Poling, J., & Eugene, T. (1998). *Balm of Gilead*. Minneapolis, MN: Fortress Press.

Purves, A. (2001). *Pastoral theology in the classical tradition*. Louisville, KY: Westminster John Knox Press.

Ragsdale, K. (1996). *Boundary wars: Intimacy and distance in healing relationships*. Cleveland, OH: Pilgrim Press.

Ramsay, N. (1991). Sexual abuse and shame: The travail of recovery. In M. Glaz & J. Stevenson-Moessner (Eds.), *Women in travail and transition: A new pastoral care* (pp. 109-125). Minneapolis, MN: Fortress Press.

Ramsay, N. (1992). Feminist perspectives on pastoral care: Implications for practice and theory. *Pastoral Psychology, 40*(4), (245-253).

Ramsay, N. (1998a). Compassionate resistance: An ethic for pastoral care and counseling. *Journal of Pastoral Care, 52*(3), 217-226.

Ramsay, N. (1998b). *Pastoral diagnosis: A resource for ministries of care and counseling.* Minneapolis, MN: Fortress Press.

Ramsay, N. (1998c). Preaching to survivors of child sexual abuse. In J. McClure & N. Ramsay (Eds.), *Telling the truth: Preaching about sexual and domestic violence* (pp. 58-70). Cleveland, OH: United Church Press.

Ramsay, N. (1999). Confronting family violence and its spiritual damage. *Family Ministry, 13*(3), 46-59.

Ramsay, N. (2002). Navigating racial difference as a white pastoral theologian. *Journal of Pastoral Theology, 12*(2), 11-27.

Ramsay, N., & McClure, J. (1998). *Telling the truth: Preaching about sexual and domestic violence.* Cleveland, OH: United Church Press.

Ray, P. (1992-93). The gift and challenge: Reflections on the cross-cultural supervision of pastoral counseling trainees. *The Journal of Supervision and Training in Ministry, 14*, 181-199.

Redekop, C. (1990). Power. In R. Hunter (Ed.), *Dictionary of pastoral care and counseling* (pp. 931-934). Nashville, TN: Abingdon Press.

Redman, S. J. (2000). *Pastoral care in a market economy: A Caribbean perspective.* Barbados, Jamaica, Trinidad, and Tobago: University of the West Indies Press.

Remley, T. P., Jr. (1994). Legal issues in on-campus clinical training. In J. E. Myers (Ed.), *Developing and directing counselor education laboratories* (pp. 75-81). Alexandria, VA: American Counseling Association.

Richardson, R. (1996). *Creating a healthier church: Family systems theory, leadership, and congregational life.* Minneapolis, MN: Fortress Press.

Ridley, E. (1975). Pastoral care and the black community. *Journal of Pastoral Care, 29*(4), 271-276.

Robinson, E., & Needham, M. (1991). Race and gender myths as key factors in pastoral supervision. *Journal of Pastoral Care, 45*(4), 333-342.

Salazar-Clemena, R. M. (Ed.). (2000). *Counseling in Asia: Integrating cultural perspectives.* Cebu City, Philippines: Association of Psychological and Educational Counselors of Asia.

Sartain, G. (2000). The future of ACPE and supervision. *Journal of Supervision and Training in Ministry, 20*, 90-100.

Saussy, C. (1991). *God images and self-esteem: Empowering women in a patriarchal society.* Louisville, KY: Westminster John Knox Press.

Scalise, C. (1998). Agreeing on where we disagree: Lindbeck's postliberalism and pastoral theology. *Journal of Pastoral Theology, 8,* 43-52.

Scheib, K. (2002). Contributions of communion ecclesiology to the communal-contextual model of care. *Journal of Pastoral Theology, 12*(2), 28-50.

Schlauch, C. (1999). The need for and contours of a revised concept of faith: Implications for pastoral theology. *Journal of Pastoral Theology, 9,* 63-87.

Schneider-Harpprecht, C. (1997). Family counseling in the context of poverty: Experiences from Brazil. *Journal of Pastoral Theology, 7*(1), 129-148.

Schurmann, P. (1991). Breaking the trance: Moving beyond the straight, white, middle-class male script. *Journal of Pastoral Care, 45*(4), 365-374.

Segundo, J. L. (1976). *The liberation of theology* (J. Drury, Trans.). Maryknoll, NY: Orbis.

Seifert, H. (1990). Prophetic/pastoral tension in ministry. In R. J. Hunter (Ed.), *Dictionary of pastoral care and counseling* (pp. 962-966). Nashville, TN: Abingdon Press.

Shim, S. S. (2002). Cultural landscapes of pastoral counseling in Asia: The case of Korea with a supervisory perspective. In J. Farris (Ed.), *International perspectives on pastoral counseling* (pp. 77-97). Binghamton, NY: Haworth Pastoral Press.

Silva-Netto, B. (1985). Hidden agenda in cross-cultural pastoral counseling. *Journal of Pastoral Care, 39*(4), 342-348.

Silva-Netto, B. (1992). Pastoral counseling in a multicultural context. *Journal of Pastoral Care, 46*(2), 131-118.

Smith, A., Jr. (1982). *The relational self: Ethics and therapy from a black church perspective.* Nashville, TN: Abingdon Press.

Smith, A., Jr. (1997). *Navigating the deep river.* Cleveland, OH: United Church Press.

Snorton, T. (1996). The legacy of the African American matriarch: New perspectives for pastoral care. In J. Stevenson-Moessner (Ed.), *Through the eyes of women: Insights for pastoral care* (pp. 50-65). Nashville, TN: Abingdon Press.

Snorton, T. (2000). Self-care for the African American woman. In J. Stevenson-Moessner (Ed.), *In her own time: Women and developmental issues in pastoral care* (pp. 285-294). Nashville, TN: Abingdon Press.

Society for Intercultural Pastoral Care and Counselling. (1995). Human images and life-stories in a multicultural world. *Papers of the 9th International Seminar on Intercultural Pastoral Care and Counselling.* Mülheim/Rühr.

Sohlberg, D. H. (1994). Revising supervision. *Journal of Supervision and Training in Ministry, 15*, 42-49.

Solomon, R. (2002). The future landscape of pastoral care and counseling in the Asia Pacific region. In J. Farris (Ed.), *International perspectives on pastoral counseling* (pp. 99-118). Binghamton, NY: Haworth Pastoral Press.

Spilka, B. (1990). Psychology of religion (Theories, traditions, and issues). In R. Hunter (Ed.), *Dictionary of pastoral care and counseling* (pp.1007-1011). Nashville, TN: Abingdon Press.

Steinhoffsmith, R. H. (1999). *The mutuality of care.* St. Louis, MO: Chalice Press.

Stevens, P. (2000). Practicing within our competence: New techniques create new dilemmas. *The Family Journal: Counseling and Therapy for Couples and Families, 8*, 278-28.

Stevenson-Moessner, J. (1996). *Through the eyes of women: Insights for pastoral care.* Minneapolis, MN: Fortress Press.

Stevenson-Moessner, J. (2000). *In her own time: Women and developmental issues in pastoral care.* Minneapolis, MN: Fortress Press.

Stiglitz, J. (2002). *Globalization and its discontents.* New York/London: W.W. Norton.

Stone, A. A. (1994). Ethical and legal issues in psychotherapy supervision. In Grebe, S. E. & Ruskin, R. (Eds.), *Clinical perspectives on psychotherapy supervision* (pp. 11-40). Washington, DC: American Psychiatric Press.

Stone, H. (1996). *Theological context for pastoral caregiving: Word in deed.* New York: Haworth Pastoral Press.

Stone, H. (Ed.). (2001). *Strategies for brief pastoral counseling.* Minneapolis, MN: Fortress Press.

Stone, H. W. (1996). Sojourn in South Africa: Pastoral care as a community endeavor. *Journal of Pastoral Care, 50*(2), 207-213.

Stone, H. W. (2001). The congregational setting of pastoral counseling: A study of pastoral counseling theorists from 1949-1999. *Journal of Pastoral Care, 55*(2), 181-196.

Stone, H., & Duke, J. (1996). *How to think theologically.* Minneapolis, MN: Fortress Press.

Streck, D. R., & Schmiedt Streck, V. (2002). From social exclusion to solidarity: A Latin American perspective of pastoral practices. *International Journal of Practical Theology 6,* 138-149.

Switzer, D. (1999). *Pastoral care of gays, lesbians, and their families.* Minneapolis, MN: Fortress Press.

Switzer, D., & Switzer, S. (1980). *Parents of the homosexual.* Philadelphia: Westminster Press.

Tanis, J. (2003). *Transgendered: Theology, ministry, and communities of faith.* Cleveland, OH: Pilgrim Press.

Taylor, C. (1992). Black experience as a resource for pastoral theology. *Journal of Pastoral Theology, 2,* 38-43.

Thiemann, R. F. (1991). *Constructing a public theology: The church in a pluralistic culture.* Louisville, KY: Westminster John Knox Press.

Thiemann, R. F. (1996). *Religion in public life: A dilemma for democracy.* Washington, DC: Georgetown University Press.

Thornton, E. (1990). Clinical pastoral education. In R. Hunter (Ed.), *Dictionary of pastoral care and counseling* (pp. 177-182). Nashville, TN: Abingdon Press.

Thornton, S. (2000). Honoring rising voices: Pastoral theology as emancipatory practice. *Journal of Pastoral Theology, 10*(1), 67-70.

Thornton, S. (2002). *Broken and beloved: A pastoral theology of the cross.* St. Louis, MO: Chalice Press.

Tillich, P. (1951). *Systematic theology*, vol. 1. Chicago: University of Chicago.

Tillich, P. (1959). *Theology of culture.* London: Oxford University Press.

Tolman, A. O. (2001). Clinical training and the duty to protect. *Behavioral Sciences and the Law, 19*(3), 387-404.

Townsend, L. (2000). *Pastoral care with stepfamilies: Mapping the wilderness.* St. Louis, MO: Chalice Press.

Townsend, L. (2002). Theological reflection, pastoral counseling, and supervision. *Journal of Pastoral Theology, 12,* 63-74.

Tracy, D. (1975). *Blessed rage for order.* New York: Seabury.

Tracy, D. (1981). *The analogical imagination: Christian theology and the culture of pluralism.* New York: Crossroad.

Tracy, D. (1983). The foundations of practical theology. In D. S. Browning (Ed.), *Practical theology: The emerging field in theology, church, and world* (pp. 61-82). San Francisco: Harper & Row.

Tracy, D. (1995). Theology and the many faces of postmodernity. In R. Gill (Ed.), *Readings in modern theology: Britain and America* (pp. 225-235). Nashville, TN: Abingdon Press.

Ulanov, A. (1981). *Receiving woman: Studies in the psychology and theology of the feminine.* Louisville, KY: Westminster John Knox Press.

Van Beek, A. (1996). *Cross-cultural counseling.* Minneapolis, MN: Fortress Press.

Van den Blink, A.J. (1993). Empathy amid diversity: Problems and possibilities. *Journal of Pastoral Theology, 3,* 1-14.

Van den Blink, H. (1995). Seeking God: The way of the spirit: Some reflections on spirituality and pastoral psychotherapy. *Journal of Pastoral Theology, 5,* 12-27.

Van Leeuwen, M. S. (1988). Christian maturity in light of feminist theory. *Journal of Psychology and Theology, 16*(2), 168-182.

Van Leeuwen, M. S. (1996). Re-inventing the ties that bind: feminism and the family at the close of the twentieth century. In A. Carr & M. S. Van Leeuwen (Eds.), *Religion, Feminism, & the Family* (pp. 33-52). Louisville: Westminster John Knox.

Vandercreek, L. (1999). Professional chaplaincy: An absent profession? *Journal of Pastoral Care, 53*(4), 417-432.

Vandercreek, L., & Burton, L., (Eds). (2001). Professional chaplaincy: Its role and importance in health care. *Journal of Pastoral Care, 55*(1), 81-97. (See http://www.healthcarechaplaincy.org/publications/publications/white_paper_05.22.01/index.html).

VanKatwyk, P. L. (2002). Pastoral counseling as a spiritual practice: An exercise in a theology of spirituality. *Journal of Pastoral Care and Counseling, 56*(2), 109-119.

Walaskay, M. (1973). The liberation of women in theology and clinical pastoral education: The invisible woman. *Journal of Pastoral Care, 27*(3), 148-157.

Watkins Ali, C. A. (1999a). *Survival and liberation: Pastoral theology in African American context.* St. Louis, MO: Chalice Press.

Watkins Ali, C. A. (1999b). A womanist search for sources. In B. J. Miller-McLemore, & B. Gill-Austern (Eds.), *Feminist and womanist pastoral theology* (pp. 51-64). Nashville, TN: Abingdon Press.

Way, P. (1964). Women in the church. *Renewal, 4.*

Way, P. (1968). Community organization and pastoral care: Drum beat for dialogue. *Pastoral Psychology, 19*(4), 25-36, 66.

Way, P. (1970). An authority of possibility for women in the church. In S. Doely (Ed.), *Women's liberation and the church* (pp. 77-94). New York: Association.

Way, P. (1972). Visions of possibility: Women for theological education. *Theological Education, 8, 4.*

Way, P. (1981). Women in theological education. *Occasional Papers: #34.* Nashville, TN: The United Methodist Board for Higher Education and Ministry.

Way, P. (1990). Cultural and ethnic factors in pastoral care. In R. Hunter (Ed.), *Dictionary of pastoral care and counseling* (pp. 253-254). Nashville, TN: Abingdon Press.

Weaver, A. J., Flannelly, K. J., & Stone, H. W. (2002). Research on religion and health: The need for a balanced and constructive critique. *Journal of Pastoral Care and Counseling, 56*(3), 213-217.

White, L. (2001). Medicare passthrough update. *ACPE news* (March/April), 2-3.

Wicks, R., Parsons, R., & Capps, D. (Eds.). (1985). *Clinical handbook of pastoral counseling.* New York: Paulist Press.

Wicks, R., & Estadt, B. (Eds.). (1993). *Pastoral counseling in a global church: Voices from the field.* Maryknoll, NY: Orbis Press.

Wiley, C. (1991). A ministry of empowerment: A holistic model for pastoral counseling in the African American community. *Journal of Pastoral Care, 45*(4), 355-364.

Williams, D. D. (1968). *The spirit and the forms of love.* New York: Harper and Row.

Wilson, H. S., Poerwowidagdo, J., Mofokeng, T., Evans, R., & Evans, A. (1996). *Pastoral theology from a global perspective.* Maryknoll, NY: Orbis.

Wilson, J. M. (1988). *A coat of many colours.* London: Epworth Press.

Wilson, J. M. (Ed.). (1995). *Explorations in health and salvation: A selection of the papers of Bob Lambourne.* Birmingham: University of Birmingham Department of Theology.

Wimberly, A. S. (1994). Narrative approaches to viewing and addressing African American spirituality and sexuality: Toward a strategic pastoral theology. *Journal of Pastoral Theology, 4,* 1-18.

Wimberly, A. S. (1997). *Honoring African American elders: A ministry in the soul community.* Nashville, TN: Abingdon Press.

Wimberly, A. S. (2002). Pastoral theological reflections on congregational care as sacramental ministry. *Journal of Pastoral Theology, 12*(2), 51-62.

Wimberly, A. S. (2003). Congregational care in a wisdom-seeking age. *Journal of Pastoral Theology, 13*(1), 13-24.

Wimberly, A.S., & Parker, E. (Eds.). (2002). *In search of wisdom: Faith formation in the black church.* Nashville, TN: Abingdon Press.

Wimberly, E. P. (1979). *Pastoral care in the black church.* Nashville, TN: Abingdon Press.

Wimberly, E. P. (1982). *Pastoral counseling and spiritual values: A black point of view.* Nashville, TN: Abingdon Press.

Wimberly, E. P. (1990a). Black American pastoral care. In R. J. Hunter, (Ed.), *Dictionary of pastoral counseling and care* (pp. 92-94). Nashville, TN: Abingdon Press.

Wimberly, E. P. (1990b). *Prayer in pastoral counseling: Suffering, healing and discernment.* Louisville, KY: Westminster John Knox Press.

Wimberly, E. P. (1992). *African American pastoral care.* Nashville, TN: Abingdon Press.

Wimberly, E. P. (1994a). African American spirituality and sexuality: Perspectives on identity, intimacy and power. *Journal of Pastoral Theology, 4,* 19-31.

Wimberly, E. P. (1994b). *Using scripture in pastoral counseling.* Nashville, TN: Abingdon Press.

Wimberly, E. P. (1995). Reflections on African American pastoral care. *Journal of Pastoral Theology, 5,* 44-49.

Wimberly, E. P. (1997a). *Counseling African American marriages and families.* Louisville, KY: Westminster John Knox Press.

Wimberly, E. P. (1997b). The men's movement and pastoral care of African American men. In C. Neuger & J. Poling (Eds.), *The care of men* (pp. 104-121). Nashville, TN: Abingdon Press.

Wimberly, E. P. (1997c). *Recalling our own stories: Spiritual renewal for religious caregivers.* San Francisco: Jossey-Bass.

Wimberly, E. P. (1999). *Moving from shame to self-worth.* Nashville, TN: Abingdon Press.

Wimberly, E. P. (2000). *Relational refugees: Alienation and re-incorporation in African American churches and communities.* Nashville, TN: Abingdon Press.

Wimberly, E. P. (2003a). *Claiming God, reclaiming dignity: African American pastoral care*. Nashville, TN: Abingdon Press.

Wimberly, E. P. (2003b). Pastoral theological method and post-nihilism. *The Journal of Pastoral Theology, 13*(1), 25-35.

Wimberly, E. P., & Wimberly, A. S. (1986). *Liberation and human wholeness: The conversion experiences of black people in slavery and freedom*. Nashville, TN: Abingdon Press.

Woodward, J., & Pattison, S. (Eds.). (2000). *The Blackwell reader in pastoral and practical theology*. Oxford, England: Blackwell.

Wuthnow, R. (1996). *Christianity and civil society: The contemporary debate*. Valley Forge, PA: Trinity Press International.

Young, J. S., Cashwell, C., Wiggins-Frame, M., & Belaire, C. (2002). Spiritual and religious competencies: A national survey of CACREP accredited programs. *Counseling and Values, 47*(1), 22-33.

Zulkowsky, P. (1990). Feminist pastoral theology and pastoral care. In R. Hunter (Ed.), *Dictionary of pastoral care and counseling* (pp. 433-435). Nashville, TN: Abingdon Press.